Praise for *The Humble Economist*

'If you want to understand the origins of health economics, and the intellectual adventure of its development over the past four decades, then you must read this book.'

Bengt Jönsson, Stockholm School of Economics, Sweden

'These essays illustrate to perfection what might be called the "Culyer paradox". By minimising – or rather by closely defining – the contribution that economics should make to key social policy decisions, Tony Culyer has played a huge part in maximising its impact on them. An implacable opponent of cant, he is a passionate advocate of clarity. His work zings with wit and rigour. It can, in the nicest possible way, hurt your brain as he forces you to define your terms and understand your values before explaining where and how the dismal science can be applied to produce more illumined outcomes.'

Nicholas Timmins, Financial Times, UK

'"Had I been present at the Creation, I might have given good advice." Tony was. Tony has. On the leading edge of the modern "application of the discipline and tools of economics to the subject matter of health", Professor Culyer's work reflects a breadth of interests – in health, not just health care – and a concern for the usefulness of economic analysis. But it has also been built throughout on a careful consideration of the logical foundations of the discipline itself.'

Bob Evans, University of British Columbia, Canada

"Razor-sharp analysis with a smile".

Peter Zweifel, University of Zurich, Switzerland

'An excellent selection of academic contributions. Challenges "irrefragable taboos" with cast-iron scientific rigour and the weight of social legitimacy, against the adventures of partisan policy makers.'

Guillem López Casasnovas,
Pompeu Fabra University, Spain

'Tony Culyer may be humble, but he should not be. Many have contributed to health economics, but no one else has led the profession and systematically organized the work of so many economists and policy makers into a coherent conceptual structure the way that Tony Culyer has. *The Humble Economist* should be read for clarity and insight, but also with gratitude and respect for someone who enlarged our understanding of welfare, policy and the economics of health.'

Tom Getzen, Executive Director,
International Health Economics Association, USA

'For 30 years Tony Culyer and I co-edited the Journal of Health Economics, and we also co-edited the 2000 page Handbook of Health Economics (2000 edition). Despite differences in how we each view the world and the profound differences in our two nation's health care financing institutions and delivery systems, we had no serious disagreements in all those years about what constituted good health economics. Thus, I quibble with the Editors' characterization of Tony as a "good social scientist"; I think Tony, though certainly humble, is a great social scientist. His papers were a joy to read when first published, and they certainly repay re-reading, something this volume facilitates.'

Joe Newhouse, Harvard University, USA

'I have learned everything I know about health economics from Tony Culyer. This wonderful collection of essays will allow me – and many others – to continue to learn at the feet of the master.'

Sir Michael Rawlins, Founding Chair of NICE, UK

'Tony Culyer is that rare beast; an inspirational economist. He knows the price <u>and</u> the value of everything. A must read for those who want to discover what economics can contribute to social policy – and to general social welfare.'

Julian Le Grand, London School of Economics, UK

'A wonderful format to introduce a new generation of readers to the ideas of one of the great health economists. Culyer speaks in these essays in a unique voice – there is no one on either side of the Atlantic who writes and works with near this philosophical depth.'

Tom McGuire, Harvard University, USA

'Most academic papers end with something like "this research will help develop tools which lead to better decision making." And they stop there. Tony actually took the next step as well – he developed the tools, and implemented them for a better health care system.'

Phil Jacobs, University of Alberta, Canada

'The breadth and depth of Tony Culyer's knowledge of health economics, and the extent of his publications and achievements as an editor, are almost hard to believe. His many challenges to conventional wisdom among economists, and his never failing interest in unorthodox perspectives, are all the more impressive and enjoyable.'

Erik Nord, Norwegian Institute of Public Health, Norway

'Tony Culyer's writings were fundamental to my intellectual development as a practising health economist, and this book will enable current and new generations of health economists to benefit from his clarity and elegance of thought.'

Anne Mills, London School of Hygiene and Tropical Medicine, UK

'This book demonstrates how Tony Culyer impressively and thought provokingly bridged the gap between economics and health care decision making, eloquently advancing both in the process. His contributions to health economics are humbling for all those working in the field.'

Werner Brouwer, Erasmus University Rotterdam, Netherlands

'An insightful read for those who struggle to reconcile the two tasks of health policy – improving population health while distributing it equitably.'

Norman Daniels, Harvard University, USA

'To read Tony Culyer's penetrating analysis is to be challenged to think more carefully about economics as a discipline, about the contribution economics can make to policy analysis, and perhaps most importantly, about the role of economists as scientists and policy advisors. Culyer is a master of analytic distinctions and their importance for policy-oriented economics, distinctions between means and ends; analysts and decision-makers; reason and preferences; economic models and the real world. His analysis elucidates economics' roots (now obscure to so many) in moral philosophy and social ethics and why, no matter how sophisticated and mathematical, it cannot escape these roots. His ability to situate practical policy issues within larger intellectual ideas and frameworks illuminates the nature of both the policy issues and abstract concepts. Economists and policy-makers alike will profit from this book.'

Jerry Hurley, McMaster University, Canada

'This collection is full of Culyer classics – papers on which generations of Tony's students, including me, cut our heath economics teeth. These classics and the new (to me) papers are all full of the sharp insights that have made Tony's work essential reading for all heath economists, as well as non-economists working in the health sector. I for one am looking forward to settling down with a nice Malbec in front of an open fire and re-reading them all.'

Adam Wagstaff, World Bank, USA

'Tony Culyer is one of the world's leading health economists and has made remarkable contributions to health economics research, health policy and practice, and to building the field of health economics. Not everyone gets the opportunity to sit down with Tony to discuss health policy, ethics, and the National Health Service, but this volume is the next best thing. Enjoy the provocative and witty insights from an open minded expert.'

John Cawley, Cornell University, USA

The Humble Economist:
Tony Culyer on Health, Health Care and Social Decision Making

THE
HUMBLE
ECONOMIST

Tony Culyer
on Health, Health Care and
Social Decision Making

Edited by
Richard Cookson and Karl Claxton

© A J Culyer, R A Cookson and K P Claxton 2012

Copyright in the original versions of the essays in this book resides with the original publishers, as listed in the acknowledgements.

Published by University of York and Office of Health Economics

Edited by Richard Cookson and Karl Claxton

A CIP catalogue record for this book is available from the British Library.

ISBN 978-0-9525601-5-9

Cover design by Richard Cookson and Clare Brayshaw

Prepared and printed by:

York Publishing Services Ltd
64 Hallfield Road
Layerthorpe
York YO31 7ZQ

Tel: 01904 431213

Website: www.yps-publishing.co.uk

Contents

List of figures and tables

Figures

Tables

Notes on the editors

Richard Cookson

Reader, Centre for Health Economics, University of York, UK
richard.cookson@york.ac.uk

Richard's main research interests are in equity in health and health care, and he has served on NICE technology appraisal committee (2002-7) and public health intervention advisory committee (2007-9).

Karl Claxton

Professor, Department of Economics and Related Studies and Centre for Health Economics, University of York, UK
karl.claxton@york.ac.uk

Karl's main research interests are in methods for the economic evaluation of health technologies. He was one of the founding members of the NICE Technology Appraisal Committee in 1999 and continues to contribute to methodological development in various ways.

Both editors were fortunate enough to be taught by Tony as students, and have had the privilege to co-author a number of papers with him. We have both benefited throughout our careers from Tony's sage advice and guidance.

Acknowledgements

We – the editors of this book – would first of all like to thank Tony Culyer for his unstinting co-operation in the preparation of this book and, in particular, for revising and shortening all of the essays in this collection to suit our preferred publication format and for compiling the index. We sought Tony's input at all stages of the process, benefited considerably from his advice, and as ever had great fun working with him. However, all the final editorial decisions were our own and we take full responsibility for any errors or omissions.

We are also especially grateful to Anne Burton for her kindness, patience and good humour in sub-editing and proof reading the entire manuscript several times; to Jessica Stephens and Matthew Herring for their diligence and persistence with the seemingly endless copyright clearance work; to Clare Brayshaw from York Publishing Services (YPS) for her prompt and meticulously accurate typesetting work – and to all of the above for the painstaking care and attention they devoted to the production of this book and their fortitude in meeting tight deadlines often at short notice.

We are also grateful to Cathi Poole and her team at YPS for their excellent publication services in both preparation and printing; Kerry Sheppard, Koonal Shah and Adrian Towse at the Office for Health Economics for their warm-hearted professionalism in organising the book launch and marketing; Frances Sharp and Gill Forder from the University of York CHE Publications Office for their helpful advice and support throughout; Liz Ingham and

Kathy Crocker for their help in managing the book project finances; Bob Evans and Werner Brouwer for helpful comments on Chapter 4 ("normative rabbits") and Chapter 6 ("welfarism vs. extra-welfarism") respectively, which reproduce joint papers they both originally lead authored; Phil Jacobs and John Cullis for helpful comments on the introduction; all those who kindly agreed to read early versions of the manuscript and provide endorsement quotes; and all the many colleagues who have provided encouragement and advice at different stages of this project. We would also like to thank the following organisations and their respective leaders for their important contributions to this project: Julie Allinson and the University of York Digital Library Digitisation Programme for funding the digitisation and copyright clearance work; Andrew Jones and the University of York Department of Economics and Related Studies for underwriting the typesetting and printing work; Trevor Sheldon and the University of York Vice-Chancellor's Office for a financial contribution towards the sub-editing and proof-reading work; Adrian Towse and the Office of Health Economics for a financial contribution towards the sub-editing and proof reading work and for organising the book launch event, marketing and distribution; and Maria Goddard and the Centre for Health Economics for supporting Richard Cookson and Karl Claxton to carry out this editorial work under University of York auspices and for providing them with such a vibrant working environment while so doing.

Finally, we would like to thank and acknowledge the publishers and co-authors of all the publications listed below for their kind permission to reproduce material from those original publications, in substantially revised, shortened and in some cases amalgamated formats. We have made every effort to obtain all the appropriate authorisations from all the relevant copyright holders.

Chapter 1: Culyer, A.J., 1992, Need, greed and Mark Twain's cat, in A. Corden, E. Robertson and K Tolley (eds.) *Meeting Needs in an Affluent Society*, Aldershot: Avebury, 31-41.

Chapter 2: Culyer, A.J., 1981. Economics, social policy and social administration: the interplay between topics and disciplines. *Journal of Social Policy* 10, 311-329. (Publisher: Cambridge Journals Online).

Chapter 3: Culyer, A.J., 1984. The quest for efficiency in the public sector: Economists versus Dr. Pangloss (or why conservative economists are not nearly conservative enough), in Hanusch, H. (ed.), *Public Finance and the Quest for Efficiency*, Proceedings of the 38th Congress of the IIPF in Copenhagen, Wayne State University Press, Detroit, 39-48.

Chapter 4: Culyer, A.J., Evans, R.G., 1996. Mark Pauly on welfare economics: normative rabbits from positive hats. *Journal of Health Economics* 15, 243-25. (Publisher: Elsevier)

Chapter 5: Culyer, A.J., 1990. Commodities, characteristics of commodities, characteristics of people, utilities and the quality of life, in Baldwin, S., Godfrey, C., Propper, C. (eds.), *The Quality of Life: Perspectives and Policies*. Routledge, London, 9-27.

Chapter 6: Brouwer, W.B.F., Culyer, A.J., Job, N., van Exel, A., Rutten, F.F.H., Welfarism vs. extra-welfarism, *Journal of Health Economics*, 2008, 27: 325-338. (Publisher: Elsevier)

Chapter 7: Culyer, A.J., 1971. The nature of the commodity 'health care' and its efficient allocation. *Oxford Economic Papers* 23, 189-211 (reprinted as Ch. 2 in A. J. Culyer and M. H. Cooper (eds.), Health Economics, London: Penguin, 1973, also in A J Culyer (Ed.) *Health Economics: Critical Perspectives on the World Economy*, London: Routledge, 2006, 148-157).

Amalgamated with material from:

Culyer, A.J., 1989. The normative economics of health care finance and provision. *Oxford Review of Economic Policy* 5, 34-58 (reprinted with changes in A. McGuire, P. Fenn and K. Mayhew (eds.) *Providing Health Care: The Economics of Alternative Systems of Finance and Delivery*, Oxford: Oxford University Press, 1991, 65-98, also in A J Culyer (Ed.) *Health Economics: Critical Perspectives on the World Economy*, London: Routledge, 2006, 148-157).

Chapter 8: Culyer, A.J., 2001. Economics and ethics in health care. *Journal of Medical Ethics* 27, 217-222. (Publisher: BMJ Journals)

Chapter 9: Culyer, A.J., 1995. Need: the idea won't do but we still need it, (Editorial). *Social Science and Medicine* 40, 727-730. (Publisher: Elsevier)

Amalgamated with material from:

Culyer, A.J., Need an instrumental view. In: Ashcroft, R., Dawson, A., Draper, H., McMillan J. (eds.), *Principles of Health Care Ethics*, 2nd Edition, Chichester: Wiley, 2007, 231-238.

Chapter 10: Culyer, A.J., 2001. Equity some theory and its policy implications. *Journal of Medical Ethics* 27, 275-283. (Publisher: BMJ Journals)

Chapter 11: Culyer, A.J., 2007. Equity of what in health care? Why the traditional answers don't help policy and what to do in the future. *Healthcare Papers* 8, 12-26. (Publisher: Longwoods)

Chapter 12: Culyer, A.J., 1997. The principal objective of the NHS ought to be to maximise the aggregate improvement in the health status of the whole community, *British Medical Journal* 314, 667-669 (reprinted with changes in New, B. (ed.), *Rationing: Talk and Action*. King's Fund and BMJ, London, 95-100)

Amalgamated with material from:

Culyer, A.J., A rejoinder to John Harris. In: New, B. (ed.), *Rationing: Talk and Action*, loc. cit. 106-107. (Publisher: King's Fund and BMJ)

Chapter 13: Culyer, A.J., 1995. Supporting research and development in the National Health Service. *Journal of the Royal College of Physicians of London*, 29, 216-224.

Chapter 14: Culyer, A.J., 1990. The Internal Market: An Acceptable Means to a Desirable End. Centre for Health Economics Discussion Paper 67, University of York, York.

Chapter 15: Culyer, A.J., 1995. Chisels or screwdrivers? A critique of the NERA proposals for the reform of the NHS, in A. Towse (ed.) *Financing Health Care in the UK: A Discussion of NERA's Prototype Model to Replace the NHS*, London: Office of Health Economics, 23-37.

Chapter 16: Culyer, A.J., Lavers, R.J., Williams, A., 1971. Social indicators: health. *Social Trends* 2, 31-42. (Publisher: UK Office for National Statistics).

Amalgamated with material from:

Culyer, A.J., Lavers, R.J., Williams, A., 1972. Social indicators: health. In Shonfield, A., Shaw, S. (eds.), *Social Indicators and Social Policy*. Heinemann, London, 94-118.

Chapter 17: Culyer, A.J., 2010. Perspective and desire in comparative effectiveness research: the relative unimportance of mere preferences, the central importance of context. *Pharmacoeconomics* 28, 889-897. (Publisher: Adis Online)

Chapter 18: Rawlins, M.D., and Culyer, A.J., 2004. National Institute for Clinical Excellence and its value judgements. *British Medical Journal*, 2004, 329: 224-227. (Publisher: BMJ Journals)

Chapter 19: Culyer, A.J., Lomas, J., 2006. Deliberative processes and evidence-informed decision-making in health care – do they work and how might we know? *Evidence and Policy* 2, 357- 371. (Publisher: Portland Press)

Chapter 20: Culyer, A.J., 2006. NICE's use of cost-effectiveness as an exemplar of a deliberative process. *Health Economics, Policy and Law* 1, 299-318. (Publisher: Cambridge Journals Online)

Chapter 21: Culyer, A.J., 2012. Hic sunt dracones: the future of Health Technology Assessment – one economist's perspective, *Medical Decision Making* 32: E25-E32. (Publisher: Sage Journals)

Introduction

If economists could manage to get themselves thought of as humble, competent people, on a level with dentists, that would be splendid!

John Maynard Keynes 1932

Why read this book?

This book is a distillation of Anthony John (Tony) Culyer's most important writings on health, health care and social decision making, presented in the form of short, lucid essays accessible to a general audience. Its insights into how to improve health sector institutions and decision making processes will interest anyone working in the health field in any part of the world, whatever their disciplinary background or role. Tony Culyer is one of the founding fathers of health economics, and his work is a must read for anyone seeking to understand the health economic mind. Perhaps more importantly, it is also a must read for those trying to understand how to be an economist or indeed any type of social scientist.

Culyer is eloquent on this matter, "Whether one seeks to be a good social scientist or a good moral philosopher, a first requirement is to separate and distance the rational self from the passions that thoughts can provoke... Analysis, which must be the social scientist's forte, depends on making careful distinctions... Passion is too undifferentiating in its effects. The more social scientists seek to appear to be on the side of the angels, the more their birthright is likely to be on sale for a mess of pottage". In these essays Culyer is an exemplar of the good social scientist, more than willing to turn a dispassionate knife of reason on himself and use it mercilessly; at one point in the opening essay exploring "an incomplete list of my personal moral failures".

Culyer's humane, intelligent and pragmatic approach to social decision making – based on the values of legitimate social decision makers, rather than the commitments of academics or other "safe coteries" of like-minded individuals – is of interest well beyond the health field. His work can be read as a general set of theoretical principles and practical insights for anyone seeking to use reason and evidence to improve social decision making. The application of these principles is illustrated with reference to health sector decisions, but is potentially applicable to any type of social decision.

Culyer was closely involved in helping us select the original publications that form the basis of this book; he then painstakingly revised, shortened and in some cases amalgamated the original publications to turn them into non-technical bite-sized essays for a general audience. Our criteria for inclusion reflected the three core aims of the book – that the essays should summarise the most important, central and durable intellectual themes of Culyer's work, should be accessible to a non-specialist audience, and should be enjoyable, thought-provoking and inspirational for future generations of health and social policy students, scholars, policy makers, managers and practitioners across the world. In pursuing these three aims we decided not to restrict ourselves to sole authored publications, and so have included essays based on a small number of jointly authored publications as noted below and in the acknowledgements section. However, we have been forced to exclude many important and influential publications – most notably his early career writings on topics such as blood donation, altruism, academic tenure and drug abuse, which we felt were too technical and too old-fashioned in writing style to meet our accessibility criterion.

The essays are elegantly phrased and a pleasure to read. To say they are written in plain English would do them an injustice: the meaning is always clear but never bland. As editors, we felt it would be a shame for writing of this quality to remain inaccessible and dispersed among diverse academic journals, books and discussion papers; many of which were published in the pre-digital era. So we have brought his best work together in one place. Rather than publishing in the conventional manner through a commercial publishing house, we have opted to publish in a low-cost, easy-to-read and comfortable-to-handle paperback format that is also available on the web as an e-book, with the kind support of two institutions that, as described below, have good reason to celebrate Culyer's work – the University of York and the Office of Health Economics. We expect that Culyer's work will inspire future generations of students, scholars and decision makers, as it has our own generation, and we hope that this book will make a modest contribution towards that end.

Who is Tony Culyer?

Tony Culyer is an English economist who was born on 1 July 1942. Since the early 1970s he has played a leading role in nurturing and shaping the international health economics profession, during four formative decades of rapid growth in size and influence on health sector decision making. From 1970-1986 he helped set up and run the world's first association of health economists – the UK Health Economists Study Group – which is still going strong four decades later. In 1981, together with Joe Newhouse, he founded the world's first academic journal in the field – the *Journal of Health Economics* – which he still continues to edit, albeit now with the help of a much expanded editorial board. He has also edited several authoritative reference works, in recent years including the 2000 Elsevier Handbook of Health Economics (edited with Joe Newhouse), the 2006 Routledge four volume collection of classic readings in health economics, entitled Health Economics (Critical Perspectives on the World Economy), the 2008 Elgar Dictionary of Health Economics (2nd edition in 2010), and the Elsevier online Encyclopedia of Health Economics (forthcoming). He has also served on many editorial boards for journals of health economics, medicine, medical ethics, social science and medical law, and has published over 250 articles and more than two dozen books (a full publications list is contained on Tony's personal web page http://www-users.york.ac.uk/~ajc17/).

Culyer has also played an influential role in the UK National Health Service (NHS). Through his NHS advisory work, he has helped to develop important new institutions for generating and using research evidence to inform decision making. From 1993 to 1994 he authored the influential "Culyer Report" supporting research and development in the NHS. This report led to far-reaching changes in NHS Research and Development (R&D), ensuring both that R&D was institutionally recognised as a core priority at all levels of the NHS and that R&D funding was more transparently identified and ring-fenced. These principles paved the way for the "Cooksey Review" and the founding of the NHS National Institute for Health Research in 2006. Culyer was subsequently awarded a CBE for services to NHS R&D in 1999. From 1999 to 2003 he served as founding vice-chair of the National Institute for Health and Clinical Excellence (NICE). NICE produces guidance on the cost effective use of health care and public health interventions in the NHS, and is widely respected throughout the world for its rigorous use of evidence and its transparent and accountable processes of stakeholder engagement and deliberation. When Culyer stepped down from the NICE Board in 2003, the Chair of NICE Sir Michael Rawlins acknowledged his contribution to NICE's development: "Tony Culyer has made massive contributions to the development of the Institute. We will miss his energy, enthusiasm and commitment to the work of NICE. I will, personally, also miss his wisdom as well as the quiet advice he gave on so many occasions."

Culyer has also served as chair of the Office of Health Economics (OHE) editorial board (since 1997) and policy board (since 2001), helping to ensure the quality and independence of OHE research and publications. The OHE was set up in 1962 by the Association of the British Pharmaceutical Industry (ABPI) to commission, undertake and disseminate health economic research and data collection, and is now also funded by grant income from and consultancy services to a range of other public, commercial and charitable organisations. He is also a Founding Fellow of the Academy of Medical Sciences, a Fellow of the Royal Society of Arts, and an Honorary Fellow of the Royal College of Physicians.

Culyer started his academic career at the University of Exeter, in 1961, as an economics undergraduate and then a tutor and lecturer, before moving to York in 1969. He subsequently spent the bulk of his academic life at the University of York, where he has played leading roles in administration as well as research and teaching. He has also held various visiting research and government advisory positions in Canada since the 1970s, and still has homes in both Toronto and York. His main administrative roles at York have been as Assistant Director of the (then) Institute for Social and Economic Research (1979-82), Head of the Department of Economics and Related Studies (1986-2001), Pro-Vice-Chancellor (1991-4) and Deputy Vice-Chancellor (1994-7). He currently holds a part-time chair in economics at York and is also Ontario Chair in Health Policy and System Design at the University of Toronto, Canada.

What will you read and why does it matter?

The book is divided into five parts, reflecting different areas in which Culyer has made sustained and distinctive intellectual contributions. For ease of reading, the essays within each part follow a logical sequence rather than the chronological order in which the original versions were published. Part One presents Culyer's general views on the appropriate role of social scientists in helping to improve social decision making, which provide the intellectual underpinning for the subsequent parts of the book on health and health care. Part Two contains what many health

v

economists regard as his most distinctive intellectual contribution to the profession – the concept of "extra-welfarism" – and Part Three his contributions to clarifying the ethical concepts used by health care decision makers to formulate their objectives, with particular reference to the ubiquitous concepts of "need" and "equity". Part Four illustrates his general approach to policy analysis, with special reference to three proposals for reforming the English NHS in the 1990s. Finally, Part Five presents his contributions to the foundations of health technology assessment, including the measurement of health, the nature of social value judgements about cost effectiveness, and the role of deliberative decision making processes.

Part One: Social scientists and social science

The first two essays in this part are about social scientists in general, and the second two are about economists in particular. All four essays were originally written during the middle of Culyer's career – in 1992, 1981, 1984 and 1996 respectively – by which time he had extensive experience of engaging with social scientists and social decision makers of different stripes (and different social value judgements), as well as a distinguished track record of research and teaching in his "home" discipline of economics. By then he had also authored textbooks on the economics of social policy (1970), the political economy of social policy (1980) and economics (1985). His core theme is that the role of social scientists is not to provide passionate policy advocacy based implicitly on their own personal values, or the commitments of the particular scholarly community to which they belong, but rather to provide dispassionate policy analysis based on evidence and making explicit the values of legitimate social decision makers acting on behalf of the general population.

According to Culyer, the good social scientist should display professional humility, dispassionately exposing implied social value judgements rather than advocating particular values or, worse, allowing them to become embedded in analysis without proper recognition and critical examination. In his own words: "Their appropriate morality is a professional morality which consists, chiefly, in humility – by offering no more (but this is already quite a lot) to the process of policy making than they are professionally competent to offer: the elucidation of ends, the analysis of means, and the unpacking within explicit systems of thought of difficult and polysemic ideas, like 'need'."

These principles are deftly wielded in Chapter Two, when Culyer takes to task an eminent social policy scholar from England – Richard Titmuss – for overstepping the mark on professional humility by implicitly advocating the idiosyncratic values of his own particular scholarly community. And in Chapter Four, Culyer's eminent health economic colleague from the USA – Mark Pauly – receives a particularly severe "scolding" for committing the same kind of professional sin. This latter piece was jointly authored by another eminent colleague, the Canadian health economist, Bob Evans, who came up with the memorable title: "normative rabbits from positive hats". This essay is one of our favourites: a classic "spat" between three of the founding fathers of health economics. Alas, however, none of these essays, hugely enjoyable though they are, can give more than the faintest hint of the wit, warmth and bonhomie that Culyer exudes in person.

Part Two: Extra-welfarism

Culyer's concept of "extra-welfarism" helps to liberate health economists from the confines of the traditional "Paretian" or "welfarist" approach to evaluating alternative policies and institutions that dominated economic thinking in the nineteenth and twentieth centuries. Traditional "welfarist" economic analysis assumes that subjective individual preferences or "utilities" (understood either as the desires that motivate individual decisions or the feelings of happiness that may or may not follow those decisions) are the be all and end all of the social good when it comes to doing "economic" analysis properly. Culyer's "extra-welfarist" approach allows economists to use additional sources of information about individual wellbeing or flourishing – i.e. additional to subjective desires and feelings – for evaluating alternative policies and institutions. In keeping with his professional humility, of course, he does not endorse any specific view of what constitutes a flourishing life: "Flourishing may mean different things to different people; all I require is that it be a high goal whose accomplishment gives a deep satisfaction to the one living it, and perhaps others too, as when it is said of someone who has died 'that was a life well-lived'."

The concept of "extra-welfarism" builds upon the work of Amartya Sen, who first coined the term "welfarism" and wrote of the need to use "non-welfare" or "non-utility" information when assessing individual wellbeing. Culyer developed and refined this idea in the specific context of health care, showing in particular how non-welfare information about people's health – and not merely people's health-related preferences or desires – could be fruitfully used in the health care field. The three essays in turn set out the basic idea; develop and refine the distinction between "welfarist" and "extra-welfarist" approaches to health economics, in a multi-author essay originally lead authored by the eminent Dutch health economist, Werner Brouwer; and then explore a range of different practical applications of both "welfarist" and "extra-welfarist" approaches in the health sector, showing how both can be fruitful in different contexts.

Part Three: Ethics, need and equity

Economics is sometimes caricatured by philosophers as being merely an overgrown offshoot of moral philosophy – the modern day incarnation of Jeremy Bentham's famous eighteenth century utilitarian slogan: "the greatest happiness of the greatest number". Like most sweeping dismissals this is a gross exaggeration which misfires on a number of levels – most obviously, economic analysis need not focus on achieving the greatest happiness of the greatest number but can analyse almost any set of objectives the social decision maker chooses to set. Nevertheless, this caricature does contain a grain of truth: the disciplines of economics and moral philosophy are indeed related and can learn from one another. In particular, as Culyer argues in Part One of this book, one of the tasks of economics is to clarify the concepts used by social decision makers in formulating their objectives. Insofar as moral philosophy is also in the business of conceptual clarification, this kind of work by economists can be seen as a form of applied ethics. However, the ultimate test of conceptual clarification work by social scientists is how far it is useful to social decision makers, rather than how far it is intellectually satisfying to ethicists, economists, or any other scholarly community.

This part of the book presents Culyer's main contributions to applied ethics, focusing on two complex and contestable ethical concepts that are central to the objectives of social decision makers in the health field: need and equity. The first essay sets the scene and summarises the work of other health economists in clarifying these ethical concepts. The next three essays then show Culyer at work in this area himself, elegantly dissecting alternative conceptions of "need" and "equity" in health care, drawing out the similarities and differences between the different conceptions, and identifying the conditions under which they may or may not yield conflicting policy recommendations.

Culyer together with Adam Wagstaff published a classic conceptual analysis of need and equity – their 1993 *Journal of Health Economics* article "Equity in health and health care". The paper remains one of the health economic profession's most highly cited publications on the topic of equity, in both research publications and student reading lists. The original article is too technical for a general audience, so in this book we reproduce a non-technical distillation of its main ideas, based on two subsequent papers written for non-economists which Culyer has revised, shortened and amalgamated.

Part Four: Health policy

This part of the book illustrates Culyer's general approach to analysing health policy – i.e. clarify objectives then assess means for achieving those objectives – exemplified in relation to the National Health Service in England. The first essay provides a deliberately bold and provocative statement of the view that the principal objective of the NHS should be to maximise overall population health. It also endorses many important secondary objectives such as equality in the distribution of health, equitable processes for treating both NHS patients and employees, and the provision of non-health benefits such as information and hotel services. This essay was originally published as a debate piece in the *British Medical Journal* and is clearly labelled as a personal view, rather than a description of official NHS objectives. The next three essays are about different proposals for NHS reform – (i) a description and justification of his own 1994 "Culyer Report" proposals for reforming the NHS R&D function, (ii) an analysis of the 1989 Conservative government plans for an "internal market" in the NHS, and (iii) an unfavourable analysis of the 1993 proposals by NERA, an economic consultancy firm, for market reform to the demand side of the NHS involving (among other things) patient user charges, multiple social insurance plans, and top up insurance. The latter essay (Chapter Fifteen) also includes a simplified version of the four quadrant diagram originally developed by Culyer and Wagstaff (1993). This is the closest the book leans towards the technical, but we decided to keep this diagram in order to give readers a brief "under the bonnet" glimpse of the geometrical style of theorising that Culyer liked to employ.

In the third and fourth essays, Culyer develops and endorses the concept of "demand side socialism". The basic principle is that, for reasons of equity, the demand side of the market (health insurance) should be collectively owned and controlled as a single monopoly payer, whereas for reasons of efficiency the supply side of the market (hospitals and other health care providers) should be characterised by heterogeneous competing organisations. This concept is potentially relevant to all health systems, but has had particular traction in the English NHS: reforms along these lines have subsequently been taken forward by the Blair/Brown Labour government in the mid 2000s and currently (in the early 2010s) by the Cameron/Clegg coalition government. Culyer demolishes the NERA proposals for demand side markets by showing how they fail to specify clear social objectives or to analyse how the proposed reforms would achieve those objectives. His essay ends with the following memorable quote from the Yale political scientist, Charles Edward Lindblom, famed for his account of social decision making as a process of "muddling through": "A market is like a tool: designed to do certain jobs but unsuited for others. Not wholly familiar with what it can do, people often leave it lying in the drawer when they could use it. But then, they also use it when they should not, like an amateur craftsman who carelessly uses his chisel as a screwdriver".

Part Five: Health technology assessment

Culyer's contributions to health technology assessment lie in three main areas. First, in helping to develop an overall indicator of health suitable for comparing health gains and losses across multiple conditions. The first essay in this part is an early contribution to thinking about how such an indicator might be developed, co-authored by his colleagues Bob Lavers and Alan Williams. These ideas were subsequently taken forward in empirical work by Alan Williams and other members of the "EuroQol" group, who succeeded in developing methods for constructing the Quality Adjusted Life Year (QALY) measure of health that are now routinely used by NICE and other health technology assessment agencies across the world. Second, in clarifying the nature and meaning of social value judgements about cost effectiveness. The second essay in this part clarifies the concept of cost effectiveness in general terms, through application of Culyer's underpinning views about social decision making and professional humility, and the third essay, jointly authored with the then chair of NICE, Mike Rawlins, clarifies the concept in relation to the specific decision making context of NICE and the NHS. Third, in helping to develop appropriate deliberative processes for addressing thorny issues of scientific and social value judgement in health technology assessment. The fourth, fifth and sixth essays all develop this theme, by clarifying the nature and purpose of deliberative processes, in a piece jointly authored with Canadian health service researcher, Jonathan Lomas; setting out conjectures about the circumstances in which they might most usefully be applied; and describing how they might be used to address issues of equity that go beyond concern for cost effectiveness.

Conclusion

According to Aristotle, individual human beings can only achieve a flourishing life through "an active life ruled by reason". In developing his own "extra-welfarist" ideas about using the concept of individual wellbeing to help inform social decision making, Culyer carefully avoids endorsing Aristotle's view – referring to it as "somewhat elitist" – or indeed any other specific set of value judgements about what might constitute a flourishing life. Instead, the humble economist naturally defers to the context-specific value judgements of the legitimate social decision makers relevant to the decision in hand. As editors of this volume, however, we are happy to endorse the phrase "an active life ruled by reason" as a neat summary of Culyer himself and his work as evident in this book.

In his early career work, Culyer aimed to understand how social arrangements lead to certain results, and also how people set up social arrangements to achieve their ends. This led him into asking how social arrangements can be revised to achieve social ends – and so paved the way for the mid and late career essays in this book on how to build better institutions and how to develop and implement tools to support them. Throughout his career, Culyer has succeeded in communicating with and influencing people outside his own "safe coterie" of likeminded professional colleagues in the economics discipline. In so doing, the humble economist rose to become a grandee of all the communities he served – the University of York community, the NHS R&D community, and the international academic community of health economists and health service researchers. One of the keys to his success, we believe, lies in his love of English language and grammar and his preference – at least in his mid and late career work – for conducting theoretical argument and analysis using words and diagrams rather than algebra. This is a somewhat unfashionable preference among modern economists, for whom algebra has been the medium of choice for theorising and intra-professional communication since the middle of the twentieth century. However, Culyer's ability to scrutinise and deploy the English language in a clear and precise manner – which to us less gifted grammarians sometimes seems to verge on the pedantic – has allowed him to develop and express ideas which are not only intellectually rigorous but also clear and appealing to scholars and decision makers with no technical training in economics. As Culyer often tells his students, and occasionally his colleagues, "a good idea badly expressed is simply a bad idea".

"A good head and good heart are always a formidable combination. But when you add to that a literate tongue or pen, then you have something very special." Culyer's essays are precisely that: something very special.

Richard Cookson and Karl Claxton
York, October 2012

Part One:

Social Scientists and Social Science

1

Need, greed and Mark Twain's cat[1]

Juxtaposing 'greed' and 'need' suggests an antithesis, as though feeding one implied not being able to meet the other, or that the feeding of the one must be inherently less worthy than the meeting of the other. It takes, however, little reflection to realise that the apparent conflict between need and greed is far from self-evident. What if the greedy have needs that ought to be met? Or what if one is greedy for more for others? Questions of this sort cannot be resolved without adding some prepositions: greed for what; and, possibly, greed of whom for what; and need for what; and need of whom for what? In answering these questions it seems at least possible (indeed likely) that the apparent tension between 'need' and 'greed' will be seen as no more than a species of unhelpful rhetoric.

The unhelpfulness is particularly marked when the rhetoric of need is recruited into the social sciences in the furtherance of a political agenda (see, eg Titmuss 1968), when it actually suppresses key elements of social choice, confusing rather than clarifying the tradeoffs that have to be made and the philosophical frameworks

---

1   This article first appeared as Culyer, A.J., 1992, Need, greed and Mark Twain's cat, in A. Corden, E. Robertson and K Tolley (eds.) *Meeting Needs in an Affluent Society*, Aldershot: Avebury, 31-41. The paper was based on one given at the third conference of the Institute for Research in the Social Sciences at the University of York in 1990. It has been shortened.

in which they can be made. It is self-evidently anti-Tory. A popular conviction amongst some social scientists is that the welfare state in Britain is facing a serious threat, that the social services are seriously under-funded and that distributive concerns occupy a low priority in the thinking of our current political masters (mistresses). That is all very well in one's capacity as a citizen, but it cannot be wise to allow an academic discipline to become partisan. The danger is that the analytical and empirical strengths of the social sciences are banished to the back seat and acquire a contaminated reputation by virtue of association with a particular form of prejudicial 'commitment'. The techniques of academic social scientists then come to be seen as 'theirs' and not the 'others', let alone 'ours' collectively.

See how corrupting it is. Which academics, for example, seriously entertain the speculation that the universities are over-funded? Is it not an insidious form of self-censorship that makes them not ask the questions this way round? Yet putting the questions the other way about (i.e. are they under-funded?) surely does not change the method of analysis, nor should it change the conclusions. The answer to the question whether the universities are under-funded should not yield a substantively different answer to the question of whether they are over-funded. Either way invites bias and the possibly unconscious pretence that what is truthfully only professional greed is a need. So perhaps it is better to ask how one might set about telling whether universities were under-or over-funded, what the principles are that should determine expenditure in this field, and how one might set about making practical assessments of the reality in the light of those principles.

Whether one seeks to be a good social scientist or a good moral philosopher, a first requirement is to separate and distance the rational self from the passions that thoughts can provoke. Sharing ideas with others from different backgrounds offers one opportunity to attempt this distancing. It is often only as one writes or talks that the mind begins to engage with issues in a way that is impossible through mere silent meditation or talk with likeminded members of a safe coterie sharing the same values – safe, that is, from the threat that the consensus may be shattered, or cherished values might be shown to be merely the product of lazy (or at least cosy) thought. Social scientists must not be like Mark Twain's cat, who sat on the hot stove lid. She wouldn't sit on a hot stove lid again – but then she wouldn't sit on a cold one either. Analysis, which must be the social scientist's forte, depends on making careful distinctions; like the difference between hot and cold stove lids and the suitability of one (and only one) for sitting. Passion is too undifferentiating in its effects. The more social scientists seek to appear to be on the side of the angels, the more their birthright is likely to be on sale for a mess of pottage.

The term 'efficiency' is likely to provoke hostile responses from the 'commitment' school. Let us, however, again add some prepositions: efficiency at doing what, for whom? Can it be that efficiency in the pursuit of a moral objective is objectionable? As with need and greed, it all depends on what one is talking about. If the objective is appalling, then efficiency in its pursuit may be likewise appalling. But if the objective is good, then being inefficient at being good must imply that one is doing less good than one could or should do. In this case it is inefficiency, not efficiency, that is objectionable.

For better or worse, then, I propose to challenge what may seem to some to be irrefragable taboos.

Need

Here is a useful slogan: *Only the end can justify the means.* You will recognise at once that the slogan is consequentialist, though not necessarily utilitarian. I find theories of need cast in consequentialist terms attractive, at least in part because they lead us away from absolutism, so that needs do not have an absolute priority over other claims on resources when the resources available are simply insufficient to meet all the needs that are asserted to exist. The opening assertion does not imply that every, or even any, means can be justified by some end. There are some means that no end could possibly justify. There are some ends that justify no means. Nor indeed does it imply that there is only one end or that, if there is more than one, they cannot be in mutual conflict. Hence, it may be that a means which is conducive to one end may not be conducive to another. What, however, the slogan does uncompromisingly assert is that if a means is to be justified at all it can be justified only in terms of the ends sought.

This leads immediately to a contingent and instrumental interpretation of need. In considering the allocation or redistribution of resources, such resources are needed for the more ultimate purposes of policy. There may be more than one means available that passes this test (viz. that it serves a relevant purpose), in which case the entities said to be needed will not be uniquely determined and further criteria for choice may be required – of which one may be that of efficiency. One asks whether one acceptable means is more efficient than some other no less acceptable means. For example, if the end is the avoidance of starvation, and the need is for food, we have some choice as to what sorts of food may be most appropriate and, in this sense, most needed. Or if the end is the avoidance of the kind of circumstance out of which starvation may result, then an appropriate means may be to ensure that individuals in the relevant population are endowed with adequate 'entitlements', to use Sen's term (in Sen, 1981), though precisely which entitlements are the most appropriate would be subject to further choice according to circumstance. For example, entitlements might be those that ensure that each has sufficient tradeable wealth to enable sufficient food to be purchased, or those that ensure that each has sufficient self-dependency via own-grown food, or those that ensure sufficient price stability to guarantee the adequacy of the purchasing power of non-food forms of wealth.

It is possible, of course, to talk about the need for particular ends. For example, if one were to take 'better community health' as a possible end for whose realisation particular resources (such as food, housing and health care) may be needed, one could also push the level of discourse back (or up) a stage by talking about the need for better health (warranted, perhaps, if individuals are to flourish as full human beings, and hence still instrumental). In this way, one is likely to be driven to some ultimate good, not itself instrumental for anything. However, when one deals with needs in social policy, one is normally (invariably?) dealing at the level of resources, and at this level one is well within the stages at which instrumentality and consequentialism are dominant elements.

In this approach to need, the social scientist's contribution is twofold. The first consists in discussing the objectives or ends with policy makers, and determining whether the ends initially specified are really those they care about; in suggesting some that may have been overlooked; in finding out whether the ends are mutually inconsistent; in determining what degree of explicitness about ends is desirable (and possible); in eliciting the kind of priority attaching to each end; in working out ways in which 'success' in achieving the ends is to be assessed, and so on. The policy making customers of social scientific advice are not necessarily government ministers or opposition shadows; they may be select committees, professional or industrial pressure groups, senior managers in national public or private agencies, or local authorities of various kinds, including managers and decision takers at relatively lowly levels.

The role of social scientists in policy analysis (at whatever level) is to elicit the policy values of policy makers by trying to make explicit what is often only implicit and to clarify the policy issues at stake. It is not to insist upon their (viz. social scientists') own values. In general, there is no reason to suppose that the policy value judgements of social scientists are better than those of policy makers. Indeed there is one good reason for supposing that the policy value judgements of policy makers are better than those of social scientists – namely that they are being made by people who have been assigned the task of making them by some legitimate social and political process. Social science researchers, whatever their 'commitment', have clearly not themselves been granted such political legitimacy (unless, of course, they happen also to be legitimate policy makers themselves).

The second contribution of social scientists is as expert assessors of alternate means. The task here is to identify what is needed (and by whom) if the ends elicited by the preceding procedures are to be realised. This includes analysis of the 'in principle' consistency of alternative policy instruments with the objectives sought, and various empirical assessments of the practical (cost) effectiveness of the instruments. It is inherent in this instrumental view of need that the ends sought are not so much 'needed' as desired (perhaps on moral grounds), and that they can be traded off against other policy objectives. The need is for the means (rather than the end) and, since it is hardly sensible to talk of needs for ineffective means, the need also has to be only for effective means.

Greed

Greed is the insatiable appetite for more, usually for more wealth or food. Perhaps it is natural to think of greed as being a desire for more for oneself. But is it not possible to speak of a greed (viz. an insatiable desire for more) for others? Was not St. Francis greedy in this sense? Economists are accustomed to the proposition that more is desired. Indeed the whole edifice of their subject is erected upon this very foundation. Economists are also accustomed to dealing with the idea of externality: for example, that one may want more for others as well as, or even instead of, oneself. They even draw indifference curves for such cases!

We have, however, to be wary of assigning moral status to greed, even a noble one of the sort described, on the same grounds as I have just adduced in connection with the selection of policy objectives: namely that there is nothing in the disciplinary backgrounds of social scientists that entitles them to take on the role of moral evaluators of the worthiness or unworthiness of the desires of others. That role may legitimately belong to some, but it does not belong to those who play the role of social scientists.

The notion of greed has, however, an important role to play in the eliciting of objectives from policy makers and the assessment of alternative means. In particular, the idea of greed as a characteristic of maximising behaviour is extremely insightful in discussions of the expected outcomes of alternative means. For example, maximising behaviour by insurance agencies in a competitive environment usually results in premium setting by experience rating, which offends against a wide variety of equity objectives, especially in insurance against unemployment or ill-health. Here, assuming 'greed' enables useful predictions to be made. It is possible to make quantitative estimates of the size of behavioural responses to various institutional frameworks which may be crucial determinants in the eventual choice of policy instruments and the design of systems of finance. Almost all of economists' understanding of the workings of capitalism is based upon one or another form of maximising (the maximand is not invariably profit) as is the most widely used approach to individual behaviour (viz. utility theory).

The postulate of greed thus lies at the heart of much of positive social science (especially in economics): the basis on which we explain what has happened, what is, and predict what may be expected to happen. But greed – in the sense of an insatiable appetite for more – also underlies *normative* social science, especially, again, economics. And this brings us to the topic of efficiency.

Efficiency

Injecting the 'hard' notion of efficiency into the 'soft' notion of social policy seems offensive. I want to argue, despite this, that it is necessary if there is to be any *morally acceptable* social policy. Let us begin with some clear definitions:

- Technical efficiency means not using more resources than are necessary to achieve a particular objective.

- Cost effectiveness means not incurring a greater cost than is necessary to achieve a particular objective (or, symmetrically, maximising outcome in terms of the fullness with which an objective is achieved for a given cost).

• Full efficiency means selecting the ideal balance of achievement across a variety of objectives in a variety of programmes, each of which is fully cost effective.

These definitions are evidently clearly related to the ends/means approach described earlier and are, hence, inextricably interwoven into the business of specifying and meeting needs. The first, technical efficiency, enjoins us not to waste resources in the most obvious sense of 'waste'. This is necessarily a moral pursuit if the objective served is itself a moral objective, for to use more resources than are necessary to achieve an end means that either more of that same moral end could be achieved by some suitable redeployment of resources or that more of some other moral ends could be achieved than is being achieved. The limitation of this notion of efficiency in policy analysis is that there is usually more than one technically efficient way of delivering a policy objective. For example, it may be possible to alter the balance of institutional and community care, or that of doctors and nurses, or that of subsidies to home owners and home tenants. The question then becomes one of cost-effectiveness: which of the various technically efficient resource combinations is the least cost combination?

This really highlights the moral issue, for cost is the best of the forgone desired alternative outcomes. Using resources in one way denies their use in another. The least cost way of using them to achieve a given objective ensures that the value of what is forgone is minimised. The conclusion seems inescapable: failure to be efficient in the second sense must be immoral to the extent that it fails to maximise the degree to which other moral ends are achieved. Needs are left unmet that ought to be met, and could have been, out of the general quantity of resources at the policy maker's disposal. Failure to achieve full efficiency must likewise be judged a moral failure for, even if whatever is achieved is achieved with technical efficiency and, of the various technically efficient means available only those that are cost effective are used, then, unless we also ensure that the rate and scale of each activity are balanced correctly, it must follow that some needs are being met that, at the margin, are less urgent – or at least have a lower priority – than some which are not being met. Needs should therefore be met efficiently, for if the meeting of needs is morally right, then failure to meet them as fully as is feasible must be morally wrong. It is, indeed, not for social scientists to determine the moral ends of social policy. But once these have been identified, the evaluation of the means and the inferred identification of the need for resources must embody the moral worth of the objectives. Hence, the exercise of what may superficially appear to be 'mere' technical skills is inescapably a moral pursuit. It is neither more nor less moral than the objectives are themselves.

The social scientist as moral philosopher

The world is very unjust. A small minority of the world's population is able to (and chooses to) meet relatively trivial needs while the bulk of the human race lacks the means to satisfy the most elementary needs and, in particular, those that are fundamental to mere existence, let alone anything else that, culture for culture, might be needed for real life as a human being. I have put in the qualifying phrase 'culture for culture' because I am not as confident as Rawls (1972) that it is possible to identify a culture-free concept of justice. There is much to be said for leaving moral philosophy to the professionals. However, there are many questions of a moral kind with which social scientists cannot avoid becoming embroiled. The fairness of resource distribution ranks high amongst them. While social scientists have no legitimacy to settle such questions on behalf of society, they can often shed light on them to the benefit of those who wrestle with such matters as a practical part of their own legitimate professional life. As soon as one moves beyond slogans and broad 'commitments', the moral issues become very tough. This is true at the personal as well as the professional or collective levels.

Here, as a case in point, is an incomplete list of my personal moral failures. I do not know what is one's moral duty, mine or anyone else's, (to use the word 'duty' already assumes too much) in response to the maldistribution of the world's, or my country's resources. I do not know, starting from where we are, how far I may morally sacrifice the meeting of my children's needs for the sake of other people's children's needs, particularly if I do not know them personally, and they are far away, and there is the possibility that these others would feel no general reciprocal obligation towards my own children. I do not know what weight, if any, to attach to the fact (if it turned out to be a fact) that others, were our respective fortunes to be reversed, would be willing to sacrifice little for me or my children. I do not know what weight to put upon the merit or deserts of the needy. Are they needy because they were dissolute, or 'less eligible', or voted for the wrong government, or failed to mount the successful revolution that would have destroyed the political system that locally helped create their plight, replacing it with another that would have relieved it? I do not know what weight to place upon the difficult-to-predict second round consequences of redistributions which may be undesired. I do not know whether I am being unconscionably greedy to live by the rules of the capitalist society I inhabit, which affords me simultaneously the opportunity to be both richer than I choose to be and the opportunity to give more of that greater wealth away than I am prepared to give of that lesser wealth I actually have. Should I not maximise my wealth (in moral ways of course) in order to be able to give more away to those in need? Should not you too? But I enjoy other things too much to maximise my wealth, even in moral ways – and, further, I select priorities for the use of that wealth in which the really needy do not, in all conscience, figure particularly prominently.

I have put these questions as matters of personal morality but each has a collective and policy correspondent. For example, to what extent should the State enforce personal morality or act on our moral behalves in matters of judging need and the desired redistribution? I have also made it pretty clear that I suffer from

12

SOCIAL SCIENTISTS AND SOCIAL SCIENCE

moral turpitude. Fortunately, I do not think that this incompetence in me as a moral person is an impediment to the exercise of my professional role in policy analysis. The reason is clear. It is not the business of social scientists when giving (or selling) help to policy makers to make these kinds of moral judgements but rather to help the policy makers to make them better, that is, more consistently with that to which they truly aspire – meeting needs efficiently and fairly. In that task, the role of the social scientist is not to be on the side of the angels or to seek approval (by, of course, the right people). Their appropriate morality is a professional morality which consists, chiefly, in humility – by offering no more (but this is already quite a lot) to the process of policy making than they are professionally competent to offer: the elucidation of ends, the analysis of means, and the unpacking within explicit systems of thought of difficult and polysemic ideas, like 'need'.

2

Economics, social policy and social administration: the interplay of topics and disciplines[2]

A useful distinction has been made by Alan Williams (1979) between an 'area of study' and a 'mode of thinking'. An area of study connotes a set of phenomena to be studied, problems 'out there' to be comprehended and resolved, policies to be investigated, issues to be explored. A mode of thinking connotes the conceptual apparatus – the theory – that is brought to bear upon the phenomena, problems, policies, issues, etc. This paper follows him in using the terms 'topic' and 'discipline' as shorthand to refer to these two. Each of the nouns in the title is considered in terms of these two basic notions.

Economics as a topic and a discipline

Economics is, first of all, a topic in the sense that 'the economy' is a set of phenomena amounting to a reasonably well-defined area

2 The article originally appeared as: Culyer, A.J., 1981. Economics, social policy and social administration: the interplay between topics and disciplines. *Journal of Social Policy* 10, 311-329. It has been considerably adapted and shortened. It grew out of an invitation to present a paper at the 1981 Social Administration Association's conference on the role of economic theory in social administration. It reflects an attempt to clear some preliminary ground before tackling in greater detail the issues posed by this more specific topic. I have benefited greatly from the comments of Brian Abel-Smith, Jonathan Bradshaw, Kay Jones, Ken Judge, Alan Maynard, Albert Weale and Jack Wiseman on a draft. I did not expect them to agree with all I have said but was delighted to find there was much with which they did agree and grateful to be put right at several points. None, of course, can be held entirely responsible for the final outcome.

of study. Unemployment, inflation, the public sector borrowing requirement, the behaviour of firms, consumers, the efficiency of markets and so on, are all part of this area, which has as its basic distinguishing feature a cash nexus; a nexus that exists in markets but not only in markets, a nexus that may involve the phenomenon of price but need not; a nexus that may involve profits but need not. Invariably, what seems always to be involved is money, or monetarily valued goods and services, on at least one side of an exchange relation. The defining characteristics of economics viewed in this way as a *financial* topic are essentially conventional in nature. They are not logical. Nor are they immutable. However, the features just described seem to correspond with what it is that people usually have in mind when they talk about the topic, or area of study, called 'the economy'. 'Economics' is thus another name for the topic 'the economy'.

Economics is also a discipline, characterised not at all by what economists study but by the way they study it. In the sense of discipline, economics is a mode of analysing the allocation of scarce resources. It has, of course, positive and normative variants. The hallmark of a discipline is its theory, or theories. Most of us will agree that although there are overlaps between economics and other disciplines, the lines of analytical demarcation are sufficiently clear for us not to be in much doubt about the differences between the disciplines. For example, although both political philosophers and economists, when they are being explicitly normative, often use utilitarian theory, we do not really have much difficulty distinguishing the two disciplines. Likewise, sociologists and economists sometimes use Marxian theory, but again we do not have much difficulty distinguishing the two. In neither case is this solely due to the fact that they may be applying a shared set of fundamental precepts to different topics – though historically the evolution of political philosophers' and economists' uses of utilitarianism, and the evolution of sociologists' and economists' uses of Marxian analysis, has undoubtedly been influenced by the topics upon which they have chosen to focus. Independently of the differentiation of topic, however, it is usually possible for us to make a clear distinction between the different disciplines' uses of their common intellectual heritages. We are not really very likely to confuse a Marxist economist with a Marxist sociologist, nor a utilitarian economist with a utilitarian political philosopher, even when they are talking about the same topic. (Some political philosophers have turned themselves into rather good economists – and vice versa – and in such cases the two disciplines sometimes lose their separate identities.)

Given that theory characterises disciplines and that topics are conventional, there is an obvious corollary: the *topic* economics is not the sole topic to which the discipline economics is capable of being applied, nor is the *discipline* economics the sole discipline capable of being applied to the topic economics. It may be that most economists conventionally apply their discipline of economics to the topic of economics. That is scarcely surprising, since the discipline developed through being mostly applied to that topic. But it does not follow that economics as a discipline cannot be fruitfully applied to other topics, nor that other disciplines cannot fruitfully be applied to economics as a topic. What is true of economics is also true of other social sciences.

Social policy as a topic

In the light of the foregoing, social policy may be viewed as a topic. Like the topic economics, the topic social policy is defined conventionally. The conventions defining most topics do not have to be, and typically never are, mutually exclusive. For example, the topics 'economic policy' and 'social policy' each contain elements not shared with the other as well as some shared elements. The corporate income tax is a topic in economic policy but not social policy; treatment of young offenders is a topic in social policy but not economic policy. Unemployment, health service financing and inflation are examples of topics common to both social policy and economic policy. The conventionality of topic boundaries is emphasized because there has been a lot of misconceived effort devoted to trying to pin them down conceptually in a rigorous and mutually exclusive way. It seems wasteful of intelligence so to try, for the definitions are entirely conventional. They are subject to mutation and expansion or contraction as societies evolve new institutions for new circumstances. A good example of misconceived effort is Cahnman and Schmitt (1979), which contains a tangle of topic and discipline, together with a rather naïve view of the role of value judgements in analysis and which, not surprisingly, fails altogether in its objective of providing a definition of the 'concept' of social policy. Admittedly this is an extreme case. Other attempts at a definition founder, however, for much the same reason (that is, failure to distinguish between the conventionality of a topic and the disciplines that may be applied to it). Titmuss's (1974) attempt to distinguish social policy by means of models of social welfare fails to distinguish social from other kinds of policy. For example, his 'Residual Welfare' model need not be a model only for social policy, but may be seen to underlie the approach of some economists to, for example, anti-trust policy. Social or governmental institutions are in such a model to be brought into play only when private markets are seen (or thought) to have broken down sufficiently. Nor, moreover, is his range of possible models complete: there is, for example, the 'social choice' model of social (and economic) policy in which the choice of social institution for allocating and redistributing resources, rights and entitlements, turns on the effectiveness of alternative mechanisms, institutions and procedures in meeting conditions imposed by a pre-specified 'social welfare function'. Although Titmuss's last major work (Titmuss 1970) grew out of an attempt to distinguish the 'economic' from the 'social' in public policies, it failed signally to do that. This does not detract from the importance of the book but its importance lies in its raising issues that are common across topics and disciplines rather than in locating issues that differentiate in any fundamental sense our topics and disciplines. The postulate of caring, for example, is an idea with which all (or nearly all) the social sciences have to come to terms. It scarcely *defines* social policy or social administration.

It is also too extreme to suppose that the idea of caring pervades *all* social policy. One probably cannot give a satisfactory account of the National Health Service, nor make relevant policy recommendations about it, without acknowledging that it reflects the existence of altruism. But even if it did not and was seen, say, simply as the most efficient way of organizing health services and health insurance for selfish individuals, this would not remove the National Health Service from the realm of social policy. Conversely, there are other areas of policy, not normally regarded as social policy, where caring may be thought important: current, private and public investment affects the welfare of as yet unborn generations about whom we may care; environmental policy impinges on many about whom we may care; international relations, trade and aid affect the welfare of others about whom we may care; even defence and military policies can be seen to contain elements of caring, fellow-feeling and moral commitment to others. The key importance of the idea of caring for the well-being of others lies not in its enabling us to distinguish social topics from other topics, or one discipline from another, but in the fact that it is one of those central concepts, like the idea of welfare in utilitarianism, shared by many disciplines and which can be found applicable in many topics. It is an integrating not a differentiating concept.

Lafitte (1962) escapes most of these difficulties, but only at the cost of an empty tautological notion: 'in the main social policy is an attempt to steer the life of society along channels it would not follow if left to itself' (what, then, one might ask, does economic policy seek to do?). T. H. Marshall (1967) was much nearer the truth about the conventional nature of social policy in the preface to the second edition of his famous book: "it is taken to refer to the policy of governments with regard to action having a direct impact on the welfare of the citizens, by providing them with services or income", though this unnecessarily restricts the topic of social policy to policies actually adopted by government, rather than including also those that might be adopted but are not, and those developed by non-governmental agencies such as the voluntary social services. His definition also suffers from the introduction of a philosophical idea, viz. 'welfare', into an otherwise descriptive and pragmatic definition, as though only social policies can affect welfare.

For a thoroughly pragmatic alternative approach to the definition of social policy that is perfectly consistent with what is argued here, Donnison (1979) is exemplary. What he winds up with is a list: a list of topics that taken together constitute what he calls a research and teaching agenda in social policy. The list comes from the things concerning contemporary society in the UK that he considers important to investigate and about which people ought to be taught. It is ad hoc, contemporary and doubtless culture-bound. In short, it is conventional. Most will agree that the topics on his list together amount to the subject matter we commonly consider to add up to the subject matter of social policy. What are they? The social services, of course. The consequences for workers of various kinds of a changing industrial structure. The changing character of contracts of work. The distribution of income and wealth. The distribution of public expenditure. The consequences of changing patterns of urbanization. The consequences of changing patterns in the family. Administrative, legal, economic and political questions concerning all of these (these adjectives are used in their topical rather than their disciplinary senses). The ways in which all these elements may interact and the social institutions that evolve as society attempts – or fails – to cope with them.

Social administration as a topic and a set of disciplines

Social administration, like economics, is characterised by topic and discipline. The topic is social policy currently interpreted as the list of matters cited above. As for discipline, social administration is clearly multi-disciplinary. It centrally uses sociology, history, geography, psychology, economics, statistics, ethics and political philosophy – all viewed as disciplines rather than topics. Depending on what aspect of social policy is being studied, it may also draw on epidemiology (for health studies), organization theory (for administrative studies), accountancy (in studying financial accountability), anthropology (in comparing social customs), law (in studying the legal framework of policy) and so on. While the multi-disciplinary character of social administration is a necessary feature of teaching departments in universities it by no means follows that individual social administrators themselves need be experts in multiple disciplines. It is doubtless necessary for each to have a lively awareness of, and interest in, the complementary aspects of disciplines other than their own, and to be able to work with experts in other disciplines. There may even be a few souls with both the breadth and depth of mind to be able to become competent polymaths – or at least bimaths. But this is not necessary and for all to attempt the acquisition of multiple disciplinary skills may even be undesirable if multiple skills can be acquired by the average person only at the cost of no great expertise in any one of them. It is therefore not surprising, and not necessarily to be deplored, that most social administrators as individuals have a principal discipline in which they are expert. Of those listed, sociology is the discipline most commonly found in this principal role.

It is sometimes said that the key to an understanding of the discipline of social administration is its empiricism – a fluency, grasp and knowledge of social policies. In particular, it is argued that its empirical traditions give its practitioners special insights into the meaning of poverty, the experience of claiming social benefits, what it is like to be a nurse on a back ward of a mental hospital, what it is like to be stigmatised, and so on. It is hard to see how this could be otherwise. However, such insights into and understanding of the complexities of policy and their impact (or lack of it) upon clients, or the subtle use of qualitative research methods or grounded research, cannot be held to define a discipline of social administration, any more than economics, for example, derives its disciplinary status from the econometric skills of some of its practitioners or the fluency, grasp and insight possessed by other applied practitioners as they investigate the workings of,

21

say, industrial policy or the balance of payments. These special understandings derive from the empirical practices of disciplines – as the disciplines in question are applied to topics.

The Cinderella status of economics among the disciplines of social administration

A claimed expertise in the discipline of economics is relatively rare among social administrators and it is instructive to explore some reasons why this is so. Taking economics as a topic first, it seems that the traditional areas of application of economics have tended to exclude many of the areas we think of as falling within the topic of social administration. This is not true of unemployment nor, indeed, of much of the labour market. But it was, until relatively recently, certainly true of the social services. Since the inclusion of social policy within the scope of a discipline is merely a matter of conventions about applicability, we can now see clear indications that, whatever was not generally regarded as falling within the scope of economics fifteen or twenty years ago, today the scope is, by convention, generally regarded as much wider. There is now a greater overlap between the topics of economics and those of social administration. However, one can well imagine the frustration of those older academic social administrators who began life as economists but, through frustration at the arbitrary restrictions imposed upon them by the then conventions of economics as a topic, decided that their interests could not be pursued along the channels provided by academic economics departments. If, for this reason, some social administrators see themselves as fugitives from the topic of economics, this may help account for the Cinderella status of the discipline among the disciplines of social administration. Not everyone has the stomach for pushing out the boundaries of a discipline's conventional topic area. Those who do, run the risk of becoming suspect by their mainstream colleagues as they explore the 'fringes'; they also run the risk of earning the resentment of those in other disciplines who may feel a property in their conventional topics to be threatened. Add to this the undoubted fact that prestige in economics has invariably attached to those who contribute most to the theory of the discipline – who are, so to speak, 'disciplinarians' par excellence – and one has a powerful set of forces which jointly conspire to drive out, or make second-rate citizens of, those for whom application of economic analysis is the major interest.

There was a parallel of sorts within economics itself. For many years it was common for economics to be taught in two separate compartments, one called 'principles' and the other 'applied economics'. It was striking that the one thing that was rarely applied in the applied parts of undergraduate courses was economic *theory*. Instead, applied economics tended to be institutional and descriptive. This was particularly true for microeconomics. Applied micro-economists tended to regard themselves as practical people of affairs, impatient with theoretical constructions which they believed to be largely inapplicable to any real world problems. Micro-economic theorists, on the other hand, tended to have a philosophical detachment from the real world, with their minds set mainly on the beauty, rigour and elegance of their abstractions. Economists tended to see themselves as either the one or the other kind of economist: neither having enormous respect for the other, but the theoretical people having most of the prestige. It was the great achievement – arguably the greatest achievement – of the 'positive economics' revolution in economics that it effectively ended this artificial rift within the discipline and placed theoretical interpretation of the real world and the empirical testing of theoretical propositions about it at the centre of the stage. Positive economics was thus inevitably instrumental in the widening of economics as a topic, so making academic economics departments more comfortable places for those wishing to apply the discipline of economics to the topics of social administration.

Some of the conventional assumptions made in economics about human behaviour may have been uncongenial to social academic administrators. The idea has got around that economic analysis, and hence the discipline of economics, is predicated upon a particularly nasty reductionist conception of 'economic man': to whit, that 'he' is selfish, calculating, and completely predictable in a machine-like way. The responsibility for allowing this message to get around lies firmly on the shoulders of economists themselves, particularly those who write elementary textbooks and do often assume selfishness (quite gratuitously), calculation (quite erroneously) and predictability (on the grounds that uncertainty is a difficult subject best postponed to the third year of undergraduate studies – by which time students have forgotten that they used to worry about the monsters they were assuming in their models!).

In his fascinating exploration of the idea of welfare, Pinker (1979) notes that what he calls the collectivist bias of social administration has been more deeply influenced by socialist than by (neo)classical economic theory. The observation seems to have been based upon a misconception, namely that non-Marxian economics, particularly microeconomics, is inherently antipathetic to socialist political philosophy, or is inherently well-disposed towards laissez-faire liberalism. The mistaken belief may be seen to arise once again from a confusion of the topic with the discipline of economics. It is broadly true that the topic of economics in western society has focused upon analysis of markets. But it is also true that as many economists adopting the neoclassical view of the world have been highly critical as have been highly supportive of market structures, including notable socialists like Oskar Lange and Abba Lerner.

Commitment to welfare

Another feature of social administration corresponds neither to its characterization as a topic nor to its characterization as a set of disciplines. This has been identified by Warham (1973) as a primary commitment to the promotion of individual and social welfare through the process of social reform. It is related to what Titmuss termed 'disinterested servility' which, if correctly understood, relates to a concern for others "a concern about education rather than training; a concern about the ethics of intervention in the lives of other people; and a lack of concern with academic or professional status" (Smith 1979). In a famous remark made at the inaugural meeting of the Social Administration Association, Titmuss (1968) said "social administration as a subject is not a messy conglomeration of the technical ad hoc. Its primary areas of unifying interest are centred in those social institutions that foster integration and discourage alienation" (p. 22). The first sentence must surely be right. The second, however, cuts across the topics and disciplines of social administration by defining a special *attitude* towards them – an attitude that is richly imbued with value judgements and that is held to characterise both the topic and the discipline of social administration. These values may have arisen from the origins of social administration in the vocational and professional subject of social work. An ideological commitment to altruism, to the idea of service to the community, to universality, to the importance of understanding 'what it is like' to be poor, discriminated against, and so on, helped to provide a unifying intellectual focus that was (so it has been asserted) otherwise lacking.

If at one time this kind of idea served a useful purpose in integrating social administrators by giving them a shared vision (it is hardly a paradigm) it seems to be an idea whose day is past. For one thing, it always had the danger within it of identifying an academic subject with a particular political philosophy, liberal socialism, which tended inescapably to bring its genuine contributions into disrepute among those not sharing this political viewpoint. For another it tended to exclude from the ranks of social administration those who held different political views.

The chief objection to this injection of an idea of 'commitment to welfare' is simply that it is an encumbrance if taken as part of the *definition* of the subject of social administration. At any one time there may be a hegemony of values within any subject and if that hegemony is the hegemony of a noble and beautiful idea, so much the better. But it is wholly unnecessary to absorb that hegemony into the definition of the subject. Whatever it may at one time have needed to bind itself together, social administration does not require this encumbrance now. A commitment to the multidisciplinary exploration of the topic of social policy is an eminently worthy and rewarding commitment in itself.

There are, of course, 'commitments' within economics, too. There is no escaping the conclusion that the central idea of efficiency, which pervades the whole of neo-classical welfare economics, has a strong value content. Just ask yourself whether it matters what you are being efficient *at*. But we need to note two things that make this type of commitment different from that which has been held to be the essence of social administration. First, and most obviously, the idea of efficiency has positive uses as well as normative. Economics viewed as a behavioural science can thus use the idea of efficiency (viz. the postulated maximization of a behavioural objective function subject to constraints) in a way that is value free, that is, the test of the acceptability or otherwise of the objective function is empirical rather than ethical. It does not matter whether you 'like' it. Secondly, and more subtly, the ethical idea of efficiency, as something for which society should strive, is much less politically restrictive than the idea of 'commitment to welfare'. In inviting an answer to the question 'efficient at what?' the scope of economics is widened. Dissenting from the answer 'maximising subjective utility' does not destroy the subject (though it certainly changes it). Dissenting from 'commitment to welfare' must destroy your identity as a social administrator – if that commitment is indeed its essence.

Economics as a discipline of social administration

With all this as background, we may now turn to the contribution of economics (the discipline) to social policy. The contribution of the discipline of economics to the topic of social administration and the contribution of the discipline of economics to the other disciplines of social administration are considered first. I shall argue that there are some topics in social administration that are almost exclusively proper fields of application of the discipline of economics, that there are some topics in social administration where the discipline of economics is a necessary but by no means sufficient contributing discipline, and that in the purely intellectual realm there is a contribution of the discipline of economics that can enrich the contributions of the other disciplines of social administration. Those topics of social administration where the discipline of economics has no, or little, contribution to make will not be considered.

As a preliminary, it should be emphasized that the three distinctions just made should not be seen as hard and fast independent categories: there is a shading-off between them. The broad distinctions are none the less useful as an organising principle for discussion. It is also worth noting that the relationships between the discipline of economics and the topics and other disciplines of social administration is a reciprocal one. Here I shall focus on the contribution of economics to the topics of social administration but there can be no doubt there is a reciprocal contribution from the disciplines of social administration to the topics of economics. Moreover, each discipline may also grow through its interactions with the others.

Exclusively proper topics of social administration to the discipline of economics

The general character of the topics falling under this head consists of problems arising in the topics of social administration that involve the efficient allocation of scarce resources and/or the modelling of human behaviour individually or in groups, where considerations making the application of other disciplines relevant are not immediately present. Since nearly all problems of social policy ultimately involve the making of ethical judgements, it follows that topics falling under this head are usually ones whose full consideration will eventually involve the other disciplines of social administration: for example ethics and political philosophy. That accounts for the use of the qualifying adjective 'immediately' above. This, of course, is merely to say that there is no ultimate sense in which economics as a discipline is ever really sufficient to resolve a policy problem. The kind of issue that none the less falls fairly unambiguously into this set is illustrated by the following:

- the effects on the supply of labour time of changing marginal rates of income tax

- reducing the impact of moral hazard on health care consumption and the demand for pensions

- the impact of changing retirement dates on pension costs

- adjusting hospital budgets to promote medical education and medical research

- making comparisons of the efficiency of universities

- the value of preventing deaths through road accidents or chronic diseases

- determining the distribution of health care expenditures by socio-economic class

- the effect of minimum wages on wages and employment

- the relative costs of renovating or rebuilding public housing.

The whole answer is never provided only by economics. Its contributions – sometimes quantitative, sometimes qualitative – are only partial. They provide necessary pieces of information to inform intelligent social policy-making; they do not provide any final solution – the least cost hospital is not necessarily the one that should be built, lives saved do not have to be equally valued, some efficiency may always be worth sacrificing for greater distributive justice.

Topics of social administration where the discipline of economics complements and is complemented by other disciplines

Common (though not necessary) features of topics under this heading are that they concern the measurement and evaluation of outcomes of policies and that they involve non-market transactions. In the following illustrations, some of the other disciplines that may be usefully involved are in parentheses:

- the effects on the rate of particular types of criminal activity following changes in the probability of its being detected and/or the severity of punishment (economics, psychology, sociology/criminology)

- measuring health status (economics, sociology, epidemiology, psychology, clinical subjects)

- the effects on population growth of more effective birth control methods (economics, demography, sociology)

- the provision of education free of charge (economics, sociology, educational psychology, political philosophy, ethics)

- measurement of inequality (economics, political philosophy, statistics)

- choosing a profession (economics, psychology, sociology)

- defining poverty (economics, sociology, political philosophy).

We need not prolong the list. As can be seen, topics of this sort contain many of the great questions of social policy. It is scarcely surprising that so many of the disciplines of social administration have something to contribute to these issues. The contributions of economics as a discipline alongside the other disciplines are, first, a behavioural model that has proved remarkably robust in prediction; second, a quantitative technique (econometrics) that enables one to incorporate non-economic variables (in the topical sense) in observational studies; third a clear conceptual organizing framework enabling one to make elementary but often elusive distinctions between fact and value, input and outcome, means and ends, and the like; fourth a normative basis for the partial appraisal of means and ends, namely that of efficiency. It is, of course, partial in the sense that efficiency is not the only value held by individuals in society, nor does it commit one to any specific notion of what one ought to be efficient *at*.

Intellectual enrichment of other disciplines

The central disciplines of social administration (economics, sociology and political philosophy, including ethics) have each evolved analyses of the burning issues of social policy. It is mainly for this reason that each discipline can, at the purely intellectual level, contribute much to the others. Insularity, disciplinary amours propres, and academic institutional structures often militate against the kind of interplay here in mind. There are some intellectual topics where the evidence is overwhelming that such interplay is very productive. They are relatively few, but immensely important. Two illustrative cases of fruitful interplay between disciplines in the realm of ideas concern the idea of 'need' and the idea of 'social justice' (or 'distributive justice').

The concept of need has had a hard time from economists. It is, nonetheless, clearly a central idea in the intellectual framework associated with the disciplines of social administration. At one time the idea of need was typically used by academic social administrators in an ill-defined way that opened analyses employing it to the charge of special pleading. Of late, however, things have improved enormously. The work of Barry (1965), Culyer, Lavers and Williams (1971), Bradshaw (1972) and Bebbington and Davies (1980) from their various disciplinary viewpoints (respectively, political philosophy, economics, multidisciplinary social administration and, again, economics) has created something of a revolution in the thinking of social administrators (of whatever principal discipline or multiple expertise). There is now a genuine dialogue over substantive issues and some meeting of minds, so that we can now all see more clearly the relationship between need and demand (Williams 1978), need and equality (Weale 1978), the interplay of fact and value in the idea of need (Culyer 1978) and one can now handle the idea with some confidence that one will neither be misunderstood nor have suspicion cast upon one's motives for using it.

The idea of social justice as a question of political philosophy has always been fairly penetrated by economics as a discipline by virtue of the common intellectual heritage of utilitarianism. The dialogue between political philosophers and economists on, for example, the social desirability of equality is as old as the discipline of economics and new contributions from the economics wing show no sign of drying up (eg Sen 1969). Alongside the utilitarian approach to questions of social justice that has been centre stage for decades, two new theories have emerged: Rawls' (1972) development of social contract theory and Nozick's (1974) development of the Lockean idea of natural rights. The important roles played by economic theories of choice and welfare in the former and economic theories of entitlement in the latter are well known. The theories, indeed, are unimaginable without them. The enormous excitement generated by these new ideas and their rapid incorporation into the intellectual streams of all the disciplines of social administration are evidence enough of the fruitfulness of interdisciplinary penetration.

Conclusions

I have tried to argue that social administration is both a set of topics and a set of disciplines; that economics as a discipline has an important role to play in the exploration of the topic of social administration; and that economics as a discipline deserves greater prominence among the disciplines comprising the set used in social administration. In summary, I have tried to show that there are important topics within social administration with which economics as a discipline is uniquely equipped to deal; that there are other topics in which economics has an important complementary role to play; and finally that economics has an important role to play at the purely intellectual level at which the disciplines of social administration interact.

Who knows, but this multidisciplinary endeavour may, in the fullness of time, lead to the emergence of a new discipline of social administration, sui generis. Only time, of course, will tell. Meanwhile there is plenty of work for everyone to be getting on with. Social administration is likely to focus most particularly on those topics and ideas where the various disciplines are most frequently complementary. There are two reasons for this. One lies in the paramount practical and philosophical importance of those topics. But the other is that academic departments of social administration provide one of the few examples of an institutionalised commitment to multidisciplinary research and teaching. One can be highly optimistic about the future of social administration – provided that it can hold on to its strengths and eschew its peripheral, mostly ethical, weaknesses. Economics has a contribution as a discipline in this future of social administration, a contribution whose fruitfulness has been indicated. But it is only one discipline of several. Moreover, it is only one of several equals.

3

Economists versus Dr. Pangloss
(or why conservative economists are not nearly conservative enough)[3]

Economists all – or nearly all – subscribe to the fundamental postulate that humans are (expected) utility maximisers. This, coupled with the harmless further assumption that individual tastes vary and the obscurer assumption that compensated demand curves have negative price elasticities, leads to nearly all the important propositions that economists make about the world, whether they are being normative or positive, or simply fudging the difference between the two. For example, the positive theory of exchange uses the assumptions just mentioned to predict that there will be only one price for each economic good. Any variance in prices is explained by the presence of transaction, transport costs, etc. Since these are real social costs, we do not consider such a situation as a market failure, just as a fluttering falling leaf as breezes toss it about does not refute the law of gravity. The market is doing just the job it should. How does this happen? It happens because prior

---

3   A longer version of this article appeared originally as Culyer, A.J., 1984. The quest for efficiency in the public sector: Economists versus Dr. Pangloss (or why conservative economists are not nearly conservative enough), in Hanusch, H. (ed.), *Public Finance and the Quest for Efficiency*, Proceedings of the 38th Congress of the IIPF in Copenhagen, Wayne State University Press, Detroit, 39-48.

decisions have been taken about the institutions that enable trade to take place: the definition and enforcement of private property entitlements, the law of contract, conventional ideas of trustworthy behaviour, and so on. These institutional arrangements are also the product of individual maximisation and bargaining. Private property rights, for example, will be established only when the expectation is that enforcement costs, etc will not exceed the gains from trade and the orderly conduct of affairs. Individuals will not change existing arrangements unless those seeing a benefit from the change can compensate those who anticipate a loss. It is not just our theory of processes within markets that depends on utility maximising subject to constraints; it is our theories of political action, family behaviour, public or private bureaucracy, and our theories of the choice of allocative institution (market or state) that also depend on the same behaviour-generating postulate.

Economic efficiency (Pareto-efficiency – the two are synonymous), is an allocation to which no change can be made that does not impose uncompensated harms on someone. This does not imply consumer sovereignty, as is sometimes crudely supposed, but the sovereignty of all individuals. It therefore follows that, since at any point in time our theory of exchange tells us that all genuine gains from trade will have been exhausted, then at every point in time there will be an efficient allocation of resources. Were it not so, and unexploited net social gains existed, then it cannot be the case that individuals were expected utility maximisers. They may, of course, regret consequences they did not foresee. But, at the time, what was, was efficient. This will be true of gains from market transactions within a constitutional and institutional context and also of the chosen (or existing) constitutional and institutional context itself. It is true of market activities. It is true of non-market activities. One may regard the constitutional context as unfair, unfree or unjust, so that, for example, the powerless and poor have no means to bribe the powerful and rich. But that is a question of distribution, not efficiency. Logical consistency, then, requires that, at any moment in time, all is for the best (efficiency-wise) otherwise it would have paid someone to incur costs persuading others to agree to change it, to incur costs identifying and compensating those who lose, and to incur costs of enforcing any contracts thus made. Turning specifically to a topic of abiding concern to conservative economists, it follows therefore, that *the public sector too is always efficient*. The quest for greater efficiency in the public sector is an empty quest, not because the public sector can never, inherently, be efficient (as some economists argue), but because it is *always* efficient. The size, scope and composition of the public sector in all countries must always represent a locally economically efficient allocation. And that has to be as true of North Korea as it is of the United States.

Not all, or even most, institutional changes that take place are Pareto-efficient moves. Change is invariably costly and nearly always involves uncompensated harms and so may even result in a less efficient consequential state of affairs, with uncompensated changes. Putting the change into reverse will not necessarily improve things either, for the reverse change is itself costly and may also involve uncompensated changes. There is an asymmetry here: absence of change implies that all is for the best; the presence of change may, but only "may", imply that things are going to be for the better. One can't be sure. Cautious conservatism seems the wisest way.

Recall Dr. Pangloss: "Il est démontré, disait – il, que les choses ne peuvent être autrement; car tout étant fait pour une fin, tout est nécessairement pour la meilleure fin. Remarquez bien que les nez ont eté faits pour porter des lunettes; aussi avons – nous des lunettes. Les jambes sont visiblement instituées pour être chaussé, et nous avons des chausses... par consequent, ceux qui ont avancé que tout est bien ont dit une sottise; il fallait dire que tout est au mieux."

(*"It's obvious, he said, that things can't be other than they are, for everything has been created for an end and everything is therefore necessarily for the best end. Observe how well the nose is fitted to carry spectacles, so we have spectacles. Legs plainly exist for breeches, so we have breeches... consequently those who claim that all is well are hopelessly confused; one should say that all is for the best.")*

Also sprach Dr. Pangloss.

As economists, what should *we* say? Were Pangloss not right, things would have been changed: gainers would have bribed losers from any change in the composition, scale or organisation of the public (or private) sector, or in the balance between public and private, and Pareto-efficient moves to Pareto-efficient states would be made. If they were not, then all must have been for the best (really one should, of course, say a best), for the costs of making the change, of overcoming inertias, bribing bureaucrats, or meeting whatever other transaction costs might exist, must have been – as evidenced by behaviour – too large or too uncertain relative to benefits (which may themselves also of course be uncertain).

You might object that the means available to a society for effecting change are needlessly cumbersome, costly and imperfect and that they lead to extremely poor revelations of people's preferences. But the same Panglossian argument applies here too: constitutional and institutional change is costly; to ignore such costs is therefore to encourage Pareto-inefficient constitutions and institutions. Absence of constitutional or institutional change, or of any change in the procedures by which decisions are reached, is behavioural evidence for their efficiency, whether the society in question is feudal, capitalist, socialist, or anything else. Optimal institutional structures and optimal preference revelation are not going to be perfect structures nor perfect revelations, for an efficient constitutional and institutional arrangement will normally entail the presence of residual costs of decision making, bargaining and transacting in the everyday world. These are opportunity costs like any other. Most conservative economists are not nearly conservative enough:

their presumption that merely the market is efficient is not enough. The public sector is efficient too. The political system is efficient. Everything is efficient. Everything is wonderful!

One may be unhappy with these inescapable tautological truths. Candide too had his doubts. Yet Panglossianism does have one signal virtue: in trying to account for social phenomena it compels us to ask the question: why does something happen or why does a particular arrangement exist – it has to be efficient for *something* or *someone*? The question has led to remarkable, Nobel Prize-winning, developments in the economics of politics, bureaucracy and the family. But, suppose one was to escape the good doctor's entrapment. How might one set about it?

Escaping Dr. Pangloss' clutches – the unpersuasive case for persuasion

One escape from Panglossian enchantments is to retain (conservatively) the individualistic postulates as both the underpinnings of behavioural models and the ideological basis for identifying welfare and changes in it, and to seek to promote change (perhaps radically) through persuasion. This escape is founded on the proposition that economists know some things better than others. In particular, that economists have a relative advantage in identifying Pareto-efficient states and Pareto-efficient moves. The possibility is thereby opened up that absence of change is not itself evidence of the efficiency of the current state of things; it is merely the result of failure of gainers (and losers) either to perceive the net advantages of change or to have devised appropriate means of ensuring the acceptability of change. But the claim is disturbingly weak. How many cost-benefit analyses of public sector activity, for example, press beyond the computation of net benefits to the detailed identification of losers from the change, the size of their losses, and the means by which they may be compensated sufficiently to accept the change? And who takes any notice, anyway?

Into this category of persuasion falls an immense range of economic policy advice: marginal cost pricing for nationalised industry; vouchers for education; redistribution in cash rather than kind; removal of price controls; reliance on markets for resource allocation. Intellectual activity here consists in the invention, reinvention, or resurrection of policy means that are alleged to lead to improved efficiency in the public (or private) sector, where the means proposed may be rules, mechanisms or behavioural constraints. Yet, while economists may succeed in persuading one another of the value of such things they often fail dismally to persuade anyone else. One set of reasons for this may simply be that efficiency is but one of the moral objectives that societies seek and that its pursuit may conflict with other objectives. But, even in the quest for efficiency itself, it may be that economists are giving unpersuasive advice. Efficient pricing rules, for example, are not only subject to the problems of second best, there are a set of even more fundamental issues relating to the very notion of opportunity cost. In particular, there is its evanescent and subjective nature as a decision maker's perception of the most highly valued alternative course of action at the point of decision in a highly uncertain world, a perception not available to planners and regulators – nor to economists. So maybe economists fail to persuade because it isn't true that they know better.

Escaping Dr. Pangloss' clutches – pruning the roots

Another manner of escape for those still wanting to be normative is to be radical both about the basic postulates as well as about the promotion of social change. For example, one may reject the essentially static concept of Pareto-efficiency and advance instead competition as an agent of efficiency via the process of discovery and invention. This 'Austrian' way of looking at things emphasizes process (and progress) so that efficiency is, as it were, a process of becoming, rather than a state that can be usefully described in terms of the familiar marginal conditions, even if they include uncertainty, externality and inter-temporal trading.

It is not clear, however, that competition is so easily measured that one can say that it is more here and less there (is a race between 500 more competitive than one between two?), nor is it clear that the types of competition observed in the public sector are systematically more or less conducive to dynamic efficiency than those observed in, say, the tomato market. In any case, whatever promotes dynamism is bound to be subject to Panglossian inevitability, so growth and change can never be too slow, or too fast. They are always just right.

Escaping Dr. Pangloss' clutches – rebuilding the foundations

A third escape route is to question the maximand. The traditional individualistic framework provides both the basis for the utility maximising analysis of behaviour (whether in groups or individually) and also the basis for the social welfare function: the rockets of both positive and normative economics are fired from the same launching pad. It is unsurprising that Dr. Pangloss poses a problem for economists who use neoclassical individualism as their modus operandi. But for those who adopt more proximate maximands, say, a target for steel output, or who view the business of health services as increasing the health of populations, or the business of schools as keeping teachers in employment, the problem disappears. Similarly, those enamoured of a 'merit want' approach to many of the activities in the public sector cut the Panglossian knot with a single bold sweep of a sword. Economists who adopt this strategy attract the contempt of the methodological individualists. But they do have the virtue of using a method that gets them decisively out of Dr. Pangloss' clutches and that enables them to relate much more easily to policy customers unencumbered with one awkward (and hard to communicate) part of the utilitarian baggage of neoclassicism.

Should we take Dr. Pangloss seriously?

We should. It is common to label prima facie departures from Pareto-efficiency in the market as market failures. Setting aside adverse distributional affects, (which are important, but are not directly relevant to questions of efficiency) the usual sources of failure that are adduced include phenomena like monopoly (natural or otherwise), externalities, and failure to establish and enforce exchangeable property rights. Sources of government failure can be similarly categorised. The standard microeconomic approach to such issues is to identify potential efficiency gains. We do not assert that the optimal degree of pollution is necessarily zero, but that it is determined by equality between the marginal benefit of reduced pollution and the marginal cost of effecting a reduction. We do not assert that all monopoly must be prohibited, but contrast, say, the loss of scale economies that may be incurred by breaking monopolies with the net gains in consumer and producer surpluses that may result. We do not assert that all entitlements and contracts should be clearly defined in law, be legally binding and coercively enforced, but balance expected gains against prospective costs of enforcement, etc. But we do not go far enough: market, or government, failure, according to Dr. Pangloss (seriously taken), is apparent not real: it is the product of imperfectly specified optimality conditions, in particular, conditions that omit some relevant marginal (or total) social costs of deciding, organising and trading.

Conservative economists display a bias. Market allocations are presumptively efficient and public sector allocations presumptively inefficient. This leads to an asymmetry in the locations of burdens of proof: economists advocating, for example, a transfer of activity from the private to the public sector are required to demonstrate the a priori and empirical reasons for so doing (there being no general presumption that such a transfer of activity will yield a Pareto-improvement). By contrast, economists advocating a transfer of activity from the public sector to the private are rarely required to do other than rehearse some general a priori arguments, for in this case there is a shared presumption about the Pareto-efficiency of such a transfer of activity. Neither side wins Pangloss's approval. The Panglossian burden of proof lies on those who advocate *any* change; the general presumption is that whatever is, is Pareto-efficient; and the quest for efficiency in the public sector is neither more nor less problematic than the quest for efficiency in the private sector.

Escape routes

There remain two other escape routes. A fourth is to argue that most of what economists deplore in the public sector is the result of mistakes: collective policies were originally adopted in high expectation of success and were even, perhaps, Pareto-efficient in terms of expected utility. But hopes are dashed and economists pursuing the quest for public sector efficiency are there to document the failure, explain why it occurred and show how to avoid it in the future. The trouble with this view is that the so-called mistakes seem to persist beyond any reasonable learning period. For example, what public regulatory policy has been more consistently decried by economists for a century than rent controls. There are dozens of articles allegedly demonstrating their inefficiency. They are a classic case study in nearly every textbook. Moreover they have also been demonstrated to have regressive distributive consequences. I cannot think of a single economic voice in their support. Yet rent controls persist and they persist in nearly every developed country in the world. Yet if they were really inefficient, their removal would have enabled a net gain to accrue to everyone, landlords and tenants. But they persist! There seems little mileage in this way out.

The final escape route is simply to ignore the basic problem of inconsistency to which Pangloss is really drawing our attention. After all, we have got along for many years with the inconsistencies between, say, macroeconomics and microeconomics. One could simply sweep the problem under the carpet. However, I don't think this is a route many of you would choose, for even if an ultimately completely consistent economic theory of human action can never be attained, we are surely bound to seek it; whether it be the inconsistency of accounting for some opportunity costs but not all;

or the inconsistency of assuming that individuals simultaneously realise all achievable mutual gains from trade while leaving some unexploited; or the inconsistency of assuming that individuals choose rationally within institutional contexts but choose their institutions irrationally; or the inconsistency of having differential presumptions about the degree of efficiency in the public sector relative to the private. Inconsistency is a great enemy.

As for me, my own escape route is number three.

4

Mark Pauly on welfare economics:
normative rabbits from positive hats[4]

Mark Pauly (1994) dismisses as irrelevant an approach to the evaluation of social arrangements in health care that many economists consider to be useful. His seemingly innocuous statement: "The approach that is special to economics, however, is one based on welfare economics, which does (given the acceptance of the assumptions) permit normative conclusions to be drawn." (quotation 1, p. 370) is followed later by a remarkable claim: "Using economic welfare, as it is customarily understood, rather than health status, allows us to avoid the murky area of 'societal decision-making'... Those whose benefits, though positive, fall short of the costs, are the services that ought not to be provided; no recourse to 'societal values and objectives' is required to make this judgement" (quotation 2, p. 371). Here is a puzzle. If the first statement is taken to include value judgements amongst those assumptions (as it must), the second seems to deny that it is necessary to make such judgements. Pauly is making a firm

---

4   The original version of this article was jointly written with Robert G. Evans. It has been abridged and edited. It appeared originally as: Culyer, A.J., Evans, R.G., 1996. Mark Pauly on welfare economics: normative rabbits from positive hats. *Journal of Health Economics* 15, 243-251. The authors acknowledge the assistance of Morris Barer, Bill Gerrard, Robert Will and particularly David Donaldson, without implication.

declaration of independence from Hume, the classic source for the argument that one cannot derive 'ought' from 'is', morals from facts, normative conclusions from positive propositions (eg Hudson, 1969). For Pauly, health outcomes resulting from particular interventions are of relevance only insofar as they are reflected in individual consumer preferences. But since preferences, in conjunction with cost information, provide in themselves a complete basis for making normative judgements as to what ought and ought not to be done, no additional information is gained from the explicit consideration of health status. QED.

We are here dealing with the broad issue of the characterization of welfare economics as a source of normative propositions. There is indeed much 'murkiness' that needs to be clarified, of which a major source is the qualifying phrase "as it is customarily understood" attached to "economic welfare" in quotation 2 and, we infer, to "welfare economics". Pauly is plainly appealing here to a cultural convention among economists. One needs to distinguish between agreement amongst economists as to the positive assumptions necessary to generate an analytic result, and agreement as to either the empirical relevance of that result, or the normative judgements necessary to evaluate it. There is general agreement among economists as to the structural and behavioural conditions under which the theorems of welfare economics hold as a theoretical result (distinction 1) but there is profound disagreement among economists in general, and health economists in particular, as to the extent to which these conditions are, or could conceivably be, approximated in the arrangements for health services delivery and finance in any real-world society (distinction 2). There is equally profound disagreement as to what sorts of normative principles should be annexed to these theoretical propositions in making evaluative judgements among alternative social arrangements for health care (distinction 3).

That the disagreements exist and have long persisted among health economists is clear. But the divisions go beyond health economics.

Theoretical welfare economists have been particularly critical, on technical as well as ethical grounds, of precisely the evaluative procedure (adding up of consumers' surpluses) recommended by Pauly. For example, Blackorby and Donaldson (1990) conclude, in a review of the use of compensating variations in cost-benefit analysis, that: "the arguments presented above present an overwhelming case against the use of consumers' surpluses in cost-benefit and general applied welfare analysis. Although these arguments are not new, many economists continue to use consumers' surpluses. How can such behaviour be justified?" (p. 491). The "customary understanding" to which Pauly appeals is one that is particular to some economists but not all.

Quotation 1 is consistent with (at least) two quite different interpretations of what constitutes 'welfare'. One is conventional, based on the classic individualistic assumptions and (minimalist) value judgements of Paretian welfare economics. These do, in principle, yield some normative conclusions, but without augmentation by explicit interpersonal comparisons of utilities, not very many. The other, labelled 'the decision-making approach' by Sugden and Williams (1978, p. 181) assigns the economist a more humble advisory role in policy analysis. The 'relevant' sources of value judgements are people who are responsible for policy. They can be held to account for their decisions, directly or indirectly, by those affected. The ethical values of the irresponsible (i.e. unaccountable) economist, whether or not shared by other professional colleagues, are irrelevant. This second approach has been pursued by Sen (1979) and Sen (1980), developing the idea of 'basic abilities' as the appropriate metric of welfare economics. One of us introduced the concept of 'extra-welfarism', i.e. the basing of policy evaluation on values (drawn from those responsible for policy) attached to the characteristics of individuals – such as their health (Culyer, 1991). Quotation 2, however, seems to place Pauly in opposition to both of these approaches. Not only that: he claims to be able to make normative statements based on welfare economics while apparently denying the logical necessity of any normative priors at all. This must (we hope!) be a minority view, even among economists.

The fundamental theorems of welfare economics refer to the linkage between the initial resource endowments of transactors in an economy, with given preferences and technology, and the potential outcomes – through transformation, exchange, and consumption – in multi-dimensional utility space. If utility-maximizing consumers and profit-maximizing firms interact in a perfectly competitive environment, with all the stringent structural and behavioural assumptions that underlie the price theory of the textbooks, then the economy will reach its utility possibility frontier. Those assumptions, however, include not only full information, no externalities, no public goods, but also, if there is uncertainty, a complete set of contingent claims markets, undistorted by such informational problems as adverse selection or moral hazard. Many health economists, ourselves included, have difficulty recognizing the fit between this list and the health services sector in any country in the real world.

At this frontier – the potentially infinite set of Pareto-optimal points – no transactor's utility can be increased through reallocation of factors in production or commodities in consumption without reducing that of another. What the theorems demonstrate is that an allocation process equating all the relevant marginal relationships will map any given pattern of resource endowments into some point on the utility – possibility frontier, and that any given point on that frontier can be reached from some initial pattern of factor endowments. None of this tells us anything about the goodness or badness of different points on that frontier, relative to each other or even to some points off it. Hence, one can draw no conclusions from these theorems about more or less desirable ways of ordering social arrangements.

Terms like 'efficiency' or 'optimality', sound normative, whether or not modified by 'Pareto'. When used in conversations with the laity (and all too often among economists themselves) they tend to be given the normative weight that they have in ordinary language. This is at best confusing, and at worst deliberately misleading. "Although... economists have endowed the term 'efficiency' with impeccably precise technical meaning, in practical applications that term seems to be widely misunderstood and misused, even by economists, who should know better.., greater 'efficiency' may mean an increase in 'social welfare', or it may not. It is a point every economist has clearly grasped once in his or her graduate-school career, but one many of them seem to forget in the course of their professional careers" (Reinhardt, 1992, p. 315). One might add, if greater efficiency does mean an increase in social welfare, then the normative content of 'efficiency' becomes manifest and that content is plainly contingent on what one means by social welfare (welfarist or extra-welfarist?). If, on the other hand, 'greater efficiency' is merely describing a condition predicted to be preferred by decision-makers (consumers or producers) then the normative content vanishes. The distinction matters!

Any normative statement as to what *ought* to happen embodies a judgement that state A, where it does, is better (ceteris paribus) than state B, where it does not. Such a ranking process, explicit or implicit, may be referred to as a social welfare function (SWF). But it makes no difference whether or not we use such a term; values are necessarily involved in the process of ranking, or evaluation. These need not be 'societal values or objectives' but they have to come from somewhere and if they do not correspond to some broader political consensus it is hard to see why the resulting ranking should be of any interest to, let alone binding upon, those responsible for public policy.

Without interpersonal comparisons, we cannot rank any Pareto optimal point on the welfare (or health) frontier with respect to any other. To do so is an undergraduate blunder. Any point on the frontier will be preferable to those in a generalised south-westerly direction from it, but that is all we can say. When just a little ethics is put in, just a few rankings come out. Since it is difficult to find any modification of social arrangements that does not leave someone worse off, a welfare economist who really refuses to make interpersonal comparisons will have little to say about the world around him/her. Hypothetical compensation tests are attempts to get around this problem, but why the possibility of compensation that does not in fact take place should influence the ranking of different states has never been clear. It would certainly not be clear to the losers! Reinhardt (1992) skewers the hypothetical compensation criterion, with brutal ridicule, as the "Unrequited-Punch-in-the-Nose Test" (pp. 312 -313). But the more fundamental point is that it does not matter two pins whether or not economists agree on such a criterion. Even if every economist in the world were solemnly to declare that the hypothetical compensation test was a valid basis for social decision-making, that statement would be irrelevant unless most of the other members of their societies agreed. The *personal* values of economists have no more general significance than those of anyone else. We can enlist Pauly's teacher, James Buchanan, in support of this view: "propositions in political economy find empirical support or refutation in the observable behaviour of individuals *in their capacities as collective decision-makers* – in other words, in politics" (emphasis in original; Buchanan, 1987, p. 7).

It seems to be common in clinical circles, and amongst senior policy makers, to judge states of the world as better (ceteris paribus) when people are healthier than when they are not. Consequently, effective health care is better than ineffective, where 'effectiveness' is defined in terms of the impact of resources on health. In Britain, such an objective has been repeatedly articulated, by a series of Conservative governments, for the National Health Service; it forms part of the preamble to the Canada Health Act, passed unanimously by the Canadian Parliament; and in one form or another it has been declared by governments in legislation and people in surveys and polls in a number of other countries (Taylor and Reinhardt, 1991; Wagstaff and van Doorslaer, 1993). It therefore seems appropriate for economists adopting the decision-making approach to policy, to give it particular significance in their analyses.

A natural corollary of the extra-welfarist perspective is to use it to analyse the influence of policy on the distribution of health. But of course policy also has implications for the distribution of wealth and of the goods and services that are inputs in the health production function (Daedalus, 1994; Evans et al, 1994). There are few societies in which (explicit or implicit) debates over such distributions do not lie close to the top of the political agenda. In particular, the provision of health care in all modern societies involves massive redistributions, transfers of wealth and well-being, because most people pay for much more care than they use, while a few use much more than they pay for. These redistributions are not merely ex post, as in any insurance system, but ex ante – we know quite a lot in advance about who the higher users are going to be, and in every modern society we deliberately choose to subsidise them. Any change in the arrangements for delivery or payment of health care will modify this extensive system of redistribution, with (more or less) empirically predictable patterns of gainers and losers among users, payers, and providers. Thus any recommendation for change – or even for no change – has to embody powerful notions of greater or lesser deservingness for identifiable groups of people. These may not be explicit (or consistent) but they are always present.

Or almost always. There is, in fact, a way around the problem of inter-personal comparisons, a way that permits one to draw normative conclusions with the bare minimum of ethical input. But it is not very attractive. It was used by Arrow (1973) in exploring the welfare implications of varying coinsurance rates for health insurance: "Only efficiency aspects are studied;... I ignore distributional considerations and assume a *single person* in the economy (our emphasis)." The only value judgement one then need make, is that whatever is good for that single person is good for the economy/society of which he/she is the only member. (In fact, Arrow made a slightly different assumption: that the economy consisted of a number of clones, identical in income, tastes, risk status with respect to illness and health care needs, and extent of participation in the supply of health care.) However, normative conclusions derived for this economy have no implications whatever for any economy composed of many and highly differentiated transactors. The remarkable aspect of Arrow's analysis is that he made explicit, highlighted on the first page of his paper and then repeated on the next, the absurd assumptions necessary if one wishes to make normative claims about welfare while avoiding distributional issues. Yet economists, including some of the most prominent names in the field, continue to derive normative conclusions from similar theoretical analyses, making assertions about the welfare-improving or welfare-reducing implications of particular health care policies. Never is the reader warned that the conclusions either depend on an implicit set of value judgements – which may not be widely shared – regarding the relative deservingness of the various gainers or losers, or are applicable only to economies consisting of single (or multiple identical) individuals.

Pauly is right that the process of making such social judgements is typically murky and in many respects unsatisfactory. But the measurement and aggregation of consumers' surpluses, even when the consumers are as well-informed as one may imagine they could be, and the reliance on subjective willingness to pay, do not avoid this murky business. It is, in fact, just another process for making and aggregating value judgements – but one that pushes the values behind a screen, making it more difficult to see exactly where the ethical assumptions are smuggled in.

In particular, basing normative statements on aggregate willingness to pay implies that only aggregate income, not its distribution, matters in ranking social states. As Blackorby and Donaldson (1990) note, this ethical postulate has a long history. Harberger (1971, p. 785) explicitly states that because economists have no special professional competence in making interpersonal comparisons, and because there is no clear agreement among the members of any social group as to the relative deservingness of its members, "costs and benefits.., should normally be added without regard to the individual(s) to whom they accrue." In other words, having (correctly, it would seem) noted that economists have no professional qualifications to make comparisons, he then recommends that they do exactly that by giving each person the same weight.

A ranking that is insensitive to income distribution is also insensitive to the distribution of utilities. Pauly would thus appear to be indifferent as to where different states lie in utility space, or how their position might change in response to different arrangements of, for example, factor endowments. Any Pareto-optimal point, being on the utility possibility frontier, is then as good as any other, and better than any point inside the frontier. This is of course precisely what the classic Paretian framework does *not* say: it bids us hold our peace.

Most economists (and non-economists) think that for a number of reasons the health consequences of health care matter quite a lot, and that their welfare implications are by no means all subsumed under the preferences even of the most perfectly informed consumer, let alone the consumers of reality. We also have some interest in distributional questions, and find analyses that suppress them a priori to be (at best) unhelpful. But whatever one thinks of Pauly's ethical predispositions, or ours, they are not part of the corpus of welfare economics, and are not entitled to any extra credit from being associated with it. The normative conclusions that Pauly claims to derive from welfare economics are generated from the values put in before the analysis starts. Hume may be dead, but his principle lives on!

Part Two:

Extra-Welfarism

Part Two

Lizzie Wellington

5

Commodities, characteristics of commodities, characteristics of people, utilities and the quality of life[5]

I want to begin by making some distinctions based on ideas developed by Sen (1982). The key idea is to distinguish between descriptions of things and their characteristics on the one hand, and descriptions of people and theirs on the other.

Relationships between commodities, characteristics and utilities

On the left hand side of Figure 5.1 is the universe of things. This consists of commodities, that is, goods and services in the everyday sense, whose demand and supply, and whose growth, have been a traditional focus of economists' attention and whose interpersonal distribution has been a traditional focus of all social scientists who have an interest in distributive justice. These commodities

5 This article has been amended and shortened but originally appeared as: Culyer, A.J., 1990. Commodities, characteristics of commodities, characteristics of people, utilities and the quality of life, in Baldwin, S., Godfrey, C., Propper, C. (eds.), *The Quality of Life: Perspectives and Policies*. Routledge, London, 9-27. I have benefited from correspondence with Amitai Etzioni, Michael Mulkay, Amartya Sen, Alwyn Smith, and Peter Townsend, from discussions at the conference, and I am also grateful for the comments of the editors.

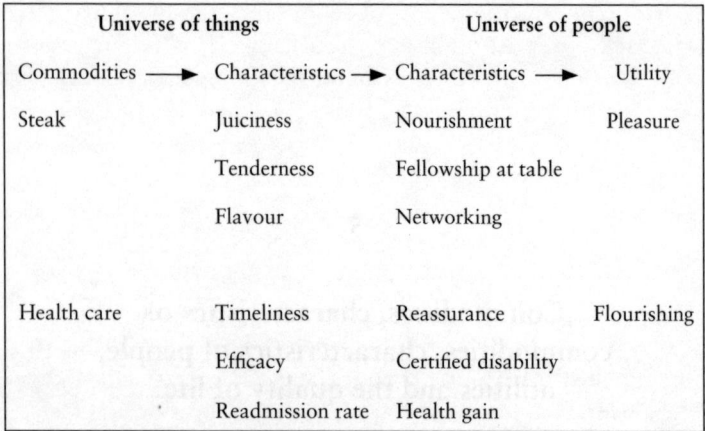

Universe of things		Universe of people	
Commodities ⟶	Characteristics ⟶	Characteristics ⟶	Utility
Steak	Juiciness	Nourishment	Pleasure
	Tenderness	Fellowship at table	
	Flavour	Networking	
Health care	Timeliness	Reassurance	Flourishing
	Efficacy	Certified disability	
	Readmission rate	Health gain	

Figure 5.1

have characteristics, which are a way in which we often describe the quality of commodities. It is self-evident that the quality of commodities is not at all the same thing as the quality of life. Nor are the characteristics of things (like their juiciness in the case of steaks) the same as the characteristics of people eating steaks. In explaining aspects of consumer behaviour some economists (notably Lancaster 1976) have reinterpreted traditional demand theory (for commodities) as a demand for characteristics (of commodities). This has been done by supposing that rational utility-maximisers derive utility not so much from goods and services per se, as in the traditional approach, as from the characteristics of goods. In terms of the first row in Figure 5.1, the demand for steaks is to be explored in terms of the demand for the characteristics of steaks (juiciness, etc). Similarly, the welfare (or quality of life) of individuals is to be explored in terms of the utility of characteristics such as these, if the third column is leap-frogged, though their welfare might also be interpreted as actually dependent on their characteristics and how these are enhanced by the consumption of commodities – characteristics such as being nourished.

Both traditional welfare economics and the 'characteristics' approach proceed to utility (provisionally taken as synonymous with happiness or pleasure) directly without the intervening category 'characteristics of people' (we had better avoid the seemingly eugenic term 'quality of people'). It is in this way that quality of life is usually defined: either directly in terms of the welfare that is got from goods, or indirectly in terms of the welfare that is got from the characteristics of goods. The intervening category in the third column consists of *non-utility* information about people. This may relate back (in a causal way) to the consumption of either commodities or the characteristics of commodities. It may also simply relate to inherent characteristics of people – for example, their genetic endowment of health, their relative deprivation independent of the absolute consumption of commodities or the characteristics of commodities, their sociability. It may, further, relate to the character of relationships between people such as the quality of friendships, community support for the individual when in need, social isolation, or changes in them, such as becoming (as distinct from being) divorced. These non-utility bits of information about people do not usually form a part of the conventional approach to demand theory or to measurement of standards of living (at least in the work of economists). This may not matter very much in the case of some commodities, like steaks, but it may omit something of critical importance in others, such as health care. So one can move from steak to its characteristics to the utility steak gives or, more conventionally in economics, from steak directly to utility. With health care, however, one might want to move from care, to its characteristics (such as timeliness and efficacy) to the characteristics of people (being reassured, healthier, etc) and, ultimately, to something of possibly even greater significance than 'utility' – a state of flourishing as a human. The conventional approach was welfarist (Sen 1979). Welfarism, as conventionally practised in economics, holds that the standard of living, quality of life, efficiency of social arrangements, even the justice of distributions and redistributions, are all to be judged or evaluated in terms of the utilities of the individuals concerned and, furthermore, that the utilities are ascribed either directly or indirectly (via characteristics of commodities) to consumption of commodities, where utility is merely a synonym for 'pleasure' or 'satisfaction'.

The explicit introduction of characteristics of people opens up an alternative or supplementary, non-utility, view of the quality of life, defined in terms of these characteristics. As in the first example in Figure 5.1, the characteristics may be related to levels of nourishment, fellowship at meal times, and the like. This approach seems to be characteristic of, for example, Townsend's (1979) concept of poverty (though that is still rather heavily commodities-focused). It is also characteristic of the health measurement movement (QALYs, health indices, etc). The categorization in Figure 5.1 is also one into which at least one tradition in the discussion of need fits (eg Culyer 1976). If the characteristics of people are a way of describing deprivation, desired states, or significant changes in people's characteristics, then commodities and characteristics of commodities are what are often needed to remove the deprivation or to move towards the desired state, or to help people cope with change. They are the necessary means (i.e. they are needed) for a desired end. To compare the ill-health of different individuals or groups is not the same as to compare the health care they have received (they could receive the same amounts and still be unhealthy, or different amounts and be equally healthy). Nor is it the same as their pleasure (a sick optimist may have far more pleasure from life than a well grumbler). In short, a focus on characteristics of people is not the same as a focus on commodities, characteristics of commodities, or utilities.

Which approach offers the best insights is a matter for judgement. My suggestion is that the choice will usually be context dependent. Not all commodities are equal. In particular, treating health care as though column three is without interest seems to fly in face of a lot that we believe to be important about health and health care.

Why characteristics of people, not utilities?

One set of reasons for paying more attention to characteristics of people than utilities has been given by Williams: "The characteristic approach of economists to the valuation of social goods is to try to find some private good which is systematically related to it, and by measuring the values people place on the latter, make some inferences about the implicit (upper or lower bounds of) values they place on the former... On occasions, however, social policy confronts problems where the community has explicitly rejected one or another of the basic assumptions on which this approach rests. Among these basic assumptions, two are especially important: people are the best (or even sometimes the sole) judges of their own welfare, and the preferences of different individuals are to be weighted according to the prevailing distribution of income and wealth. In some areas of social policy (eg mental illness and physical handicap), the first assumption is challenged, and over a much wider range of social concerns the second one is considered ethically unacceptable as the basis for public policy valuations." (Williams 1977: 282).

There is, however, a more general argument for the 'characteristics of people' approach: more general in the sense that it will encompass both efficiency and distributional types of concern and more general also in the sense that it transcends traditional utilitarianism. The odd idea has grown up (even amongst non-economists) that welfarism is the economist's only way of approaching these questions. For example, in discussing Williams (1985) on QALYs, Smith (1987) stated: "A cost-effectiveness approach to the allocation of health resources presupposes a simple utilitarian or Benthamite concept of justice" (p.1,135). Fortunately, that is not so. It is just not true that the QALY/CEA approach commits us to "simple" welfarist concepts (for example, less "simple" are maximin notions or a specially weighted sum of utilities). More important is that the QALY/CEA approach need not be welfarist at all. For, although the QALY/CEA approach *can* focus on the fourth column in Figure 5.1 (utility), it can also focus on the third column: characteristics of people, and evaluate these either in terms of their contribution to utility or in terms of their contribution to flourishing.

Suppose that there were two individuals whose claims on resources were being assessed. One is a perfect pleasure machine who gets ten times more pleasure out of a given income than the other, a chronic arthritic. "Simple" utilitarianism will take no cognisance of this fact, focusing on the marginal utility of each. If the arthritic had a lower marginal utility of income than the pleasure machine, simple utilitarianism would have us take income from him or her and transfer it to the pleasure machine, because the utility loss to the low marginal utility person will be smaller than the utility gain to the high marginal utility person, and the arthritis is an irrelevance – unless suffering from it affects the utility of income (at the margin). Utilitarianism may even have us do that if the pleasure machine were already richer (in income) than the arthritic, provided of course that the machine's utility gain still exceeded the poor and arthritic person's utility loss. Now that seems out of tune with what we intuit to be the right thing to do. Suppose, then, one focused on total utilities instead of the marginal. Suppose one wanted to equalise each person's utility as much as possible given their initial combined incomes. If the arthritic had lower utility than the pleasure machine all would be well, or at least the redistribution would go in the right direction (just as it would had the arthritic had a higher marginal utility of income under simple utilitarianism). But now suppose that is not the case. The arthritic, despite the pain and incapacity, has an invariably sunny disposition while the pleasure machine, though efficient at manufacturing pleasure out of income, is of a melancholic cast, a Calvinist, say, convinced of not being among the chosen. Now, even if the arthritic has the higher marginal utility of income, we shall no longer even judge that state to be deprived (in terms of total utility or pleasure). Once again, something seems to have gone wrong. Intuition tells us that the arthritic is in some sort of need, does need help, is deserving of our sympathy. What may be going wrong is that the utilitarian approach, like all welfarist approaches, rejects all non-utility information about people as being irrelevant in judgements about efficiency and justice. This is why the QALY/CEA approach to decision-making is not dependent on welfarist concepts. It is its ability to exploit other descriptive characteristics of people (like whether they are crippled from arthritis) that makes it decisively non-welfarist.

Sen (1980) developed the notion of 'basic capabilities'. These refer to one's capability of functioning: what one can do – getting around, looking after oneself (and others), earning a living, having discussions about the quality of life, and so on. If you think of 'standard of living' or 'quality of life' in terms of capabilities of functioning then you can immediately see that one may be rich (have lots of commodities) but have a low standard of living. One may be deliriously happy (have lots of utility) but have a low standard of living. Sen's notion of capabilities shares with my characteristics of people the idea that utility focuses too much on mental and emotional responses to commodities and characteristics of commodities and not enough on what they enable you to do. The notion of basic capabilities has lots of attractions. One is that it seems to provide what is missing in welfarism. Another is its evident culture-contingency. Yet another is the (again evident) way in which the notion encourages practical people to think explicitly about the capabilities that are to be reckoned relevant, how they are to be weighted, and so on.

Yet we should be cautious before committing ourselves to the basic capabilities approach. For one thing, we need to give a lot more thought to the meaning and significance of 'basic'. Indeed, it may be prudent to use the more general notion 'characteristics of people', precisely because it does not involve the prior exclusion of some characteristics (whatever they may be) that the criterion of 'basic' (whatever it may be) clearly does. Another reason for caution is that it does not seem that only capabilities enter the notions of standard of living or quality of life. There are other attributes that we may want to add in that are not commodities, characteristics of commodities, or utility, yet are not capabilities. If our arthritic is, for example, in pain, that is a factor to take into account in assessing the quality of life. If the arthritic is bereft of friends, that too should be taken into account. So is whether or not a person is stigmatised (even if the stigma does/does not deprive a person of commodities) and freeing someone from stigma is more than just a capability. So is the freeing of a captive, or the enabling of a previously sick person to flourish. 'Characteristics' is altogether a more open category and one capable of exciting the imagination out of conventional and tram-lined ways of thinking about quality of life.

Utility without utilitarianism

Etzioni (1986) identified three main variations in economists' use of the concept of utility. First is the original concept, that of the pleasure of the self. This concept provides the human psychology of neo-classical economics and underlies the ethics of welfarism. The second is an expanded version of the first, encompassing the satisfactions a person gains both from his own consumption of goods (or characteristics of goods) and from that of others. This is utility interdependence, a species of externality, that is increasingly used (though still not widely) by economists working on topics in social policy, and that has given rise to economic interpretations of altruism and caring (eg Culyer 1983). The third is the use of the term 'utility' as a formal attribute, having no substantive attributes: merely a means of ranking preferences or choices. As Alchian put it: "For analytical convenience it is customary to postulate that an individual seeks to maximise something subject to some constraints". The thing – or numerical measure of the 'thing' – which he seeks to maximise is called 'utility'. Whether or not utility is some kind of glow or warmth, or happiness, is here irrelevant; all that counts is that we can assign numbers to entities or conditions which a person can strive to realise. Then we say the individual seeks to maximise some function of those numbers. Unfortunately, the term 'utility' has by now acquired so many connotations, that it is difficult to realise that for the present purposes, "utility *has no more meaning than this*" (Alchian 1953:73; italics added). Etzioni condemns all three forms of what he calls the 'mono-utility paradigm' on the grounds that they omit too much that is relevant (echoes on the behavioural front of Sen on the ethical) and in particular he heaps scorn on the poverty of the third use as a motivational basis for behaviour (animal or human).

This condemnation, no matter how right on the grounds of making a satisfactory theory of human behaviour, seems too total. In particular, the third usage of the concept of utility is important in measuring the quality of life. Its importance is twofold: in the first place, by its extensive exploration of the idea of measurement the literature has clarified important meanings (eg ordinal, interval, and ratio scales), identified false interpretations (eg the non-uniqueness of elasticity measures of dependent variables measured on linear scales), and yielded experimental techniques like the rating scale, the standard gamble, and the time trade-off method for the empirical study of the values that people have (and the differences that exist between them) (Torrance 1986). In the second place, this genre of the literature very precisely pinpoints the need for value-judgements, not merely about the selection of the characteristics to be included in an assessment of the quality of life, but also about the selection of the selectors; not only about the scaling of characteristics as better or worse, but also about the ways in which characteristics should be traded-off; not only about overall weighted measures of the quality of life of one kind (for example, health) but how that compares and interacts with other aspects of the quality of life (for example, education).

The key to what is happening here is the realization that 'utility' has lost its association with 'pleasure' or 'satisfaction'. In behavioural economics, it becomes simply an index of 'preference', stipulating what will be chosen over what else. In welfare economics (or 'extra-welfare' economics), it can become a measure of the characteristics of people (such as health) and acquire ethical significance not necessarily through its contribution to preference satisfaction but through the contribution made to people leading flourishing lives.

Systematic consideration of these aspects of the inherent value-content of quality of life measurement is often wholly absent from discussions of quality of life that are not informed by utility theory (eg Townsend 1979). These advantages of utility theory are most to the fore when one is dealing with multi-attribute notions of poverty, quality of life, health, and so on. As a practical matter, it frequently happens that one is comparing individuals (or the same individual over time) for whom some attributes worsen and others improve. This is a good example of the way in which an aggregation process, instead of destroying information, can actually create it: specifically creating information about the severity (etc) with which various attributes (whether they be commodities or characteristics) are regarded and the degree to which improvement in one (or more) may be regarded as compensating for worsening in others. Unless the researcher is prepared with a method for dealing with these issues, there will be little alternative than to have recourse to arbitrary (usually personal) value judgements which may be proper for parents, or even social workers, but are scarcely appropriate for social scientists.

Quality of life: relative or absolute

People's characteristics include their relationships and social positions. Sen has used the distinctions of Figure 5.1 in order to comment on the literature on relative deprivation (a literature whose contribution to the discussion of poverty he regards as valuable). In particular, he argues the subtle point that absolute deprivation in capabilities relates to relative deprivation in terms of commodities. This adds a useful insight into the meaning of poverty. The argument is that poverty is an absolute notion to do with the characteristics of people rather than a purely relative one (in the sense of a ratio rather than context-dependent), though it remains relative (again in the ratio sense) in the universe of commodities. For example, the absolute element in poverty relates, let us suppose, to a further notion of being a member of the community. Being relatively deprived of particular commodities denies one this full membership. The absolute element is not fixed. It takes different things in different times and different places to enable each person to be identified as a member of the group. You can even conceive of degrees of membership (eg first -and second-class citizenship). But, for all that, the basic notion is an absolute one and is to do with characteristics of people. The relativist notion depends upon your access, possession, ownership, entitlement, and so on, to and of commodities relative to others. That is why poverty in Britain is different, and seen differently, from poverty in Bangladesh. That is why, in today's Britain, it is important (following Townsend 1979) not to be deprived of holidays, TV sets, and Christmas presents. But, if you are relatively deprived of these things, in Britain today, you are absolutely poor.

The distinction may seem elusive. For a good example of how it can elude some subtle minds, see Sen (1983), Townsend (1985) and Sen's reply (1985). It is rather like the notion of positional goods discussed by Hirsch (1977). If you want to enjoy the absolute advantage of sunbathing on an uncrowded beach, your ability to do so may well depend on your relative knowledge of the various available beaches compared with the knowledge of others. A differential advantage in information gives you an absolute advantage in enjoying the beach. Sen (1983) gives an example from Adam Smith: "the Greeks and Romans lived... very comfortably though they had no linen, [but] in the present time, through the greater part of Europe, a creditable day labourer would be ashamed to appear in public without a linen shirt" (p. 161). To avoid shame in different contexts and times may require different bundles of commodities. The bundles required (and the resources to acquire them) will often be defined relative to the bundles (and resources) of other people. But the avoidance of the shame is absolute not relative. It is not a question of being more or less ashamed, or even of having equal shame, but of avoiding shame altogether: absolutely.

If one were to take another negative aspect of the quality of life, unemployment, cannot a similar argument be mounted? For example, even if the benefits in cash and kind available to the unemployed were sufficient to protect them from poverty, unemployment remains an evil (and not merely a waste of resources). This is because unemployment is doubly stigmatising: one is stigmatised in one's own eyes as a failure and one is stigmatised publicly in the eyes of others. To avoid stigma it is necessary in our culture for people of particular ages, sexes, and physical and mental abilities to have employment. Stigma is absolute; the avoidance of stigma is absolute. This is perfectly consistent with the possibility of stigma being scalable (viz. measurable) in terms of more or less, worse or better. Stigma, of whatever degree, is the state you are in – but whether you are in it depends on your employment status relative to others. That status is positional. If no one works, no one is stigmatised.

Is the instrumental role of commodities, or characteristics of commodities, relative or absolute? In part it is clearly relative: keeping up with the Joneses. But it is also no less clearly absolute: the quality of my life rises when I have more of particular commodities independently of whether I have relatively more. It is not the same to me whether I have £1,000 worth more of commodities per year or everyone else each has £1,000 worth less.

End-piece – extra-welfarism

I hope to have given some prima facie grounds for questioning some of the common approaches to the quality of life, especially those dubbed welfarist, and some prima facie good reasons for pursuing an 'extra -welfarist' alternative, based on characteristics of people. I have argued that quantification of some sort is inescapable and that utility theory has some cautionary as well as practical lessons to teach in this regard (especially for those who fear or are sceptical about quantification and/or utilitarianism).

6

Welfarism vs. extra-welfarism[6]

Welfarism and welfare economics

Welfarism is not a synonym for welfare economics, though it is an important element in it. The central objective of the study of welfare economics is to provide a coherent ethical framework for making meaningful statements about whether some states of the world are socially preferable to others (Boadway and Bruce, 1984). Neo-classical welfare economists have developed a dominant framework for assessing particular states of the world as better than others. The framework is built on four key tenets (eg Hurley, 2000):

1. the utility principle (i.e. individuals rationally maximise their welfare by ordering options and choosing the preferred option)

2. individual sovereignty (i.e. individuals are themselves the best, and some might say 'the only' judges of what contributes most to their utility and the size of that contribution)

---

6   The original of this article was W B F Brouwer, A J Culyer, N Job, A van Exel, F F H Rutten. "Welfarism vs. extra-welfarism", *Journal of Health Economics*, 2008, 27: 325-338. It has been abridged and edited. We are grateful to Richard Cookson and two anonymous reviewers for their useful comments on an earlier draft of this paper. The usual disclaimer applies.

3.   consequentialism (i.e. utility is derived only from the outcomes of behaviour and processes rather than the processes themselves or intentions that led to the outcomes)

4.   welfarism (i.e. "the proposition that the 'goodness' of any situation... be judged solely on the basis of the utility levels attained by individuals in that situation" (Hurley, 1998, p. 377) or, as Sen puts it (1986, p. 111): "judging the goodness of states of affairs only by utility information".

The predominant welfare economics stream that is built on these four tenets is what, following Sen (eg 1977), we shall call 'welfarist economics' from here on. Modern welfarist economics has two broad subdivisions. In one, the Paretian tradition, utility is usually ordinally measured, interpersonal comparisons are held to be 'impossible' or 'meaningless' or 'unscientific', and an overall social judgement is reached by using the Pareto principle: any increase of utility for one individual that involves no utility loss for another is an improvement, and an optimum is where no reallocation of resources can be made without reducing at least one person's utility. There might be many such 'optima', where the choice is impossible using only the Pareto criterion. In the other tradition, interpersonal comparisons are made by using a Bergson-Samuelson social welfare function (Bergson, 1938; Samuelson, 1947). This enables analysts to select preferred distributions of welfare on a welfare frontier, provided some explicit normative choice is made regarding distributional concerns (the matter on which the Pareto criterion was silent). In all variants of welfarist economics, however, non-utility information is irrelevant in the making of social orderings. Welfarism, narrowly interpreted, is only the fourth of the four main tenets of the dominant welfarist economics framework. Conventional welfarist practice, however, entails all four. Taken together, "...these four tenets require that any policy be judged solely in terms of resulting utilities achieved by individuals, as assessed by the individuals themselves"(Hurley, 1998, p. 377).

The concept of utility

'Utility' has a long and varied ancestry. 'Utility' is commonly treated in a fairly cavalier fashion, for example, by being considered synonymous with 'welfare', 'satisfaction', 'happiness' or 'preference', as though each of these were the same thing and carried the same ethical weight, and as though 'utility' must necessarily have a normative use. This is distinct, for example, from a merely predictive or descriptive use as an index of choice. We shall take it that utility numbers are a representation of an individual's preference ordering over bundles of goods or states of the world and, in welfarist economics, an individual moving to a preferred state of the world is an equivalent statement to an individual having a higher level of utility. We shall not assume welfarism to require that these preferences have any particular grounding, for example, that preferences need to be only self-regarding, or a reflection of the pleasure to be had from anticipated consumption. We do not caricature welfarism as assuming hedonism or selfishness. However, welfarists do not usually enquire as to how these preferences may have come about nor do they judge them on grounds of decency, ethics, aesthetics or anything else. Some economists have slipped into solipsistic treatments of social welfare, holding, for example, that all choice, social as well as individual, can be reduced to preferences by the simple device of allowing people to have preferences about anything at all, including preferences themselves. Such reasoning merely adds new dimensions to what Robinson (1962, p. 47) called the "impregnable circularity" of the concept of utility.

In economics, welfare or positive, the idea of utility is, at root, simple: it is a number signifying preference assigned to entities according to an explicit choice-related rule (Alchian, 1953). Likewise, one can also assign numbers to verbal descriptions of specific human characteristics and circumstances, like 'literacy', 'cognitive ability', 'personal security', or 'health', so as to enable states to be identified in which there was 'more' or 'less' of the relevant attribute, any one of which might also, of course, be the object of government policies.

These numbers provide a rationale for choice, but, depending on how they are elicited, do not necessarily have a direct bearing on anyone's 'satisfaction' or 'happiness', nor are they necessarily based on the preferences of those affected by the choices they might inform. This divorce from preferences is particularly apposite when the numbers are used to make interpersonal comparisons (Brouwer and Koopmanschap, 2000).

We use the term 'welfare' from this point onward to indicate the utility of people in a narrow, welfarist, sense. When we refer to a broader indicator, which may include more than only individual utility, we will use the term 'wellbeing', which allows something extra-welfarist to be considered. It seems also better (at least from an extrawelfarist perspective) not to call such numbers 'utilities', though this is precisely what is done in 'cost-utility analysis', where the denominator of incremental cost-utility ratios is a measure of health, like the (extra-welfarist?) EQ-5D.

Sources of utility in welfarist economics

I took a narrow view of welfarist economics by locating the source of utility only in goods and services consumed by the individual (Culyer 1991, p. 67). Others (including me in Culyer 1971a, b), while remaining broadly welfarist, extended the sources of welfare to others' consumption of goods and services, or others' characteristics (such as their health), or even more generally to others' utility (but still individually and subjectively defined). Thus, Hochman and Rodgers' (1969) pioneering analysis of Paretian income distribution extended welfarist economics' scope in one direction, to incorporate utility interdependence as a kind of externality.

A similar inclusivity might be claimed by welfarist economists regarding consequentialism. Sometimes this tenet has been criticised for excluding the welfare consequences of processes and procedures, or even freedoms, though some welfarists have allowed that individual utility can be derived from processes, procedures and freedoms. A growing body of literature, both in the general economics literature as well as in the health economics literature, uses procedural or process utility (Hahn, 1982; Benz and Stutzer, 2003; Frey et al, 2004; Birch et al, 2003; Brouwer et al, 2005; Tsuchiya et al, 2005). So narrowly defined consequentialism is not intrinsic to welfarist economics, though welfarist economics considers only procedures and consequences that have utility consequences rooted in the preferences of individuals.

From individual to social welfare

Classical utilitarianism, in which the maximisation of total utility was also the sole objective, was less nervous of making interpersonal comparisons than the 'new' welfarist economics: "Utilitarianism is a species of welfarist consequentialism – that particular form of it which requires simply adding up individual welfares or utilities..." (Sen and Williams, 1982, p. 4). Sen (1986) judged that no approach to welfare economics has received as much support over the years as classical utilitarianism. According each an equal weight has superficial democratic (egalitarian) appeal, though it begs questions concerning, for example, the justice of a loss of 10 utilities for a poor person being given the same weight as the same loss to a rich one. But if differential weights are used (eg Roemer, 1996), it is not clear what such weights represent. They are not utility information (see eg Dolan, 1998, 1999a; Johannesson, 1999), yet it is plainly possible to speak of distributions that are themselves more or less 'preferred'. The question is 'by whom?' The extra-welfarist would claim that an independent (extra) source of values needs to be imported from 'outside' to determine the weights to be attached to individual utilities.

The central characteristic of welfarist economics remains that it confines the evaluative space to individual utilities only. This can be severely limiting, especially when any comparability of utilities between individuals is deemed impossible as a *matter of principle*.

71

Extra-welfarism

The extra-welfarist approach differs from the welfarist in four general ways:

1. it permits the use of outcomes other than utility

2. it permits the use of sources of valuation other than the affected individuals

3. it permits the weighting of outcomes (whether utility or other) according to principles that need not be preference-based

4. it permits interpersonal comparisons of wellbeing in a variety of dimensions, thus enabling movement beyond Paretian economics.

In this section we highlight these points, but first we indicate, without claiming the intellectual history to be complete, that extra-welfarism has had a number of roots in the literature over the years (Culyer, 2007b).

Roots of extra-welfarism

An early root appeared in public finance in the shape of 'merit goods' (Musgrave, 1959): goods that need not be public goods but that are deemed so 'meritorious' that they ought to be subsidised by the state. What qualified such goods as 'meritorious' was never quite clear. Nor was it fully clear how these goods differed from goods whose consumption generated externalities (Culyer, 1971c).

A second root is due to Tobin (1970). He argued that the desire for equality is specific rather than general (specific egalitarianism) and that some basic goods and services (like health care) are, as a matter of fact, commonly thought to be more properly allocated in egalitarian ways than others. Similar ideas abound in other disciplines, such as the notion of 'basic goods' used by the philosopher John Rawls (1971), though he explicitly excluded both health and health care from the list of 'primary goods'.

A third especially influential root was grown by Sen (1980) in arguing that a focus on mere individual utility was too narrow and ought to be replaced by a broader perspective that took account of the quality of utility and of people's capabilities, rather than exclusively of the emotional reaction (i.e. utility) of individuals to the possession of goods or capabilities. Sen directly attacked the tenet of welfarism on the grounds of its being too narrow and too focused on mental reactions to goods and states rather than on what goods and states enabled people to do and be. He also warned against the strict application of the Pareto principle. The sublime Paretian indifference to alternative distributions of income and wealth has produced some of Sen's most caustic comments: an economy can be Pareto optimal, yet still "perfectly disgusting" by any standards (Sen, 1970, p. 22) and "A state can be Pareto optimal with some people in extreme misery and others rolling in luxury, so long as the miserable cannot be made better off without cutting into the luxury of the rich. Pareto can, like 'Caesar's spirit', 'come hot from hell'" (Sen, 1987, p. 32).

A fourth root might be regarded as the explicit rejection of strict welfarist economics by governments. Some governments are very explicit about the proper role of willingness and ability to pay in allocating goods and services, particularly in the 'welfare state sector'. In the UK, for example, the 1944 white paper on health 'A National Health Service' stated that "The government wants to ensure that in the future every man, woman and child can rely on getting the best medical and other facilities available; that their getting them shall not depend on whether they can pay for them or any other factor irrelevant to real need" (as quoted in van Doorslaer et al, 1993). In the face of such explicit statements from politically authoritative sources, it seems curmudgeonly to insist on not going further than Pareto will allow. Moreover, the emphasis in the health care sector is clearly on improving health, which contrasts with the evaluative space under welfarist economics.

A fifth significant root was the 'decision-making' approach to cost-benefit analysis proposed by Sugden and Williams (1978), through which they contrasted the welfarist approach with its embodiment of 'individual sovereignty' with one in which 'decision-makers' were the source of values (and weights) in public decision-making. The focus on the relevant decision-maker identifies a potential solution to the 'who?' question above. An accountable officer (whether private or public), might determine what weights are used and, even more fundamentally, the scope of the 'effects' (costs or benefits) to be taken into account.

The term 'extra-welfarism' has been particularly used by health economists (for example, Hurley, 1998, 2000; Williams, 1993). My own use of this term was based on the idea that 'capabilities' might be broadened to embrace a wider range of human characteristics associated with what is commonly thought of as 'well-being' and that judgements might appropriately be made on behalf of, rather than by, affected individuals. This seems especially relevant for judgements concerning the production and distribution of public and socalled 'merit' goods. Extra-welfarism, therefore, has been described as introducing "...an important class of 'extra' welfare sources... the non-goods characteristics of individuals (whether they are happy, out of pain, free to choose, physically mobile, honest...). Extra-welfarism thus transcends traditional welfare: it does not exclude individual welfares from the judgements about the social state, but it does supplement them with other aspects of individuals (including even the quality of the relationships between individuals, groups and social classes)" (Culyer, 1991, p. 67). This form of extra-welfarism thus rejects the exclusive focus on individual utility. There is a clear parallel with the capabilities approach advocated by Sen: "the capability approach is concerned primarily with the identification of value objects, and sees the evaluative space in terms of functionings and capabilities to function" (Sen, 1993, p. 32). This rejection of individual utility as the sole outcome of interest in an evaluation marks a clear separation between welfarist economics and extra-welfarism.

Other outcomes than utility

While extra-welfarism does not focus solely on individual utilities, neither does it completely eschew them. It complements utility information with other 'non-utility information', of which the quality of utility, use of equity weights, measurement of characteristics and capabilities, and changes in them, are some examples. Such a shift of focus allows the consideration of something extra. Sen, for instance, stated that "because of the nature of the evaluative space, the capability approach differs from utilitarian evaluation (more generally 'welfarist' evaluation) in making room for a variety of human acts and states in themselves (not just because they may produce utility, nor just to the extent that they yield utility)" (Sen, 1993, p. 33). Kaplow and Shavell (2001), by contrast, sought to represent extra-welfarism (which they called 'non-welfarism') as involving no more than inserting an additional non-utility argument into the social welfare function. There may, indeed, be additional arguments in the function but that is not the sum of extra-welfarism. There may also be a shift of focus away from individual welfare, the use of non-individualistic sources of value, differential weights attached to arguments of the welfare function and types of value that are not preference-based. In health economics, this seems a broad match for what many economists appear to have done in treating 'health' (rather than the utility derived from health) as both a maximand and a distribuendum of a health care system.

A more fruitful way of characterizing the evaluative space of extra-welfarism, therefore, is not in terms of any weighted sum of individual utilities, but as an assembly of other characteristics of individuals, of which health is but one, some of which might be, but need not be, measured, as in 'cost-utility analysis', by utility-like scalings but which are neither determined a priori nor combined by following a priori rules. It is therefore possible for an optimal state under welfarism to be classed as sub-optimal under extra-welfarist criteria if there is judged to be a maldistribution of any one such characteristic or capability or if individualistic preferences are taken as the basis of all valuation. The use of quality-adjusted lifeyears (QALYs) demonstrates, however, that it is not necessary to reject preference measurement completely within extra-welfarism. Brouwer and Koopmanschap (2000) claim that in an extra-welfarist framework there still can be a role for preference measurement in, for example, ranking health gains, though it is a characteristic of the literature in this genre that the values tend to be collective averages.

Under extra-welfarism, public policy makers become one important potential source of value judgements, with clear links to the decision-making approach advocated in Sugden and Williams (1978).

Sources of valuation

It seems a short hop from these considerations to the conclusion that amongst the decisions to be taken is one concerning the values to be used to underpin utility and other preference- or value-based estimates of benefit and costs. Whereas in welfarist economics, the affected group of individuals is the primary source of valuation, in extra-welfarist economics any number of stakeholders might be regarded as appropriate sources of different values for different entities and how they ought to be traded off against one another and compared interpersonally (Culyer and Lomas, 2006). This choice might vary according to the level of aggregation of decision-making and the size and character of the jurisdiction in which the decisions are being made. Moreover, in acting as agents for their clients, the public, we do not have to assume that decision-makers are acting as they think the principals whom they represent would act, but rather as they think they ought to act.

Extra-welfarism may thus be inherently paternalistic. If it is wished to weight utilities, to define the outcome parameters of interest and to allow changes not sanctioned by the Pareto criterion, an authority (decision-makers, wise women, the general public, an elected or appointed committee, a citizens' jury, or some other organ) is plainly required. Economists are not, of course, equipped to make value judgements regarding the evaluative space, but they can help those who are charged to make such judgements and who need to understand the options and their consequences. Economists may also be able to derive values from experimental groups or samples of relevant populations through modern methods for eliciting preferences. Choices about which groups to sample are not normally for the analyst to make but for the ultimate decision-maker advised by the analyst.

Weights

Williams (eg 1997) argued cogently for the 'fair innings': society ought to attach more weight to health gained by the young (or, rather, those who have not yet had their fair innings) than the elderly (or, rather, those who have already had their fair innings). In contrast, the WHO's age weights (eg Murray, 1996) reflect the productive contribution to society of persons at different ages, something which is normally reflected in the calculation of indirect costs (see eg Sculpher, 2001). Others (eg Nord, 1995; Stolk et al, 2004) have suggested that health gains for persons with poor levels of initial health or those who stand to lose a large proportion of remaining health should receive more weight compared to gains in persons with a higher initial health level or standing to lose a smaller proportion of remaining health.

Rather than applying such relative weights on a presumption of generalised diminishing marginal utility of health, it is applied for reasons of equity. Although a consensus amongst extra-welfarists on why and how health ought to be weighted does not exist, it is apparent that such weights need neither be utilities themselves nor information about utilities (see for a discussion Dolan, 1999a); they do not, as a rule, even relate to the utility, as distinct from the health, of individuals. They are 'extra' to welfarism. In extra-welfarism, concern about distribution may reflect concern for fairness that is not rooted in individual preferences but derives from another universe of value, rather like an individual's struggle with

'I would *prefer* to do X but I *ought* to do Y' and his or her decision to do Y. The weights now reflect a view about what is 'right'. They may reflect perceptions of need, desert, just compensation, or other criteria that are 'extra' to welfarism and welfarist economics.

Closing remarks

The main difference between welfarism and extra-welfarism relates to the delineation of the relevant evaluative space. Under welfarist economics, this is individual utility. Whereas extra-welfarism broadens the evaluative space to include other relevant outcomes in addition to utility, for instance capabilities or characteristics such as health. The other differences between the two schools to a large extent follow from this first difference. For example, extra-welfarism requires other sources both to identify the other relevant outcomes, to value them and, ultimately, to combine them with preference-based outcomes. Extra-welfarism explicitly makes interpersonal comparisons, and does so via individual characteristics and capabilities. Extra-welfarism is pragmatic (Brouwer and Koopmanschap, 2000) focusing on relevant outcomes contingent on the policy problem at hand.

Despite these differences, extra-welfarism remains a species of normative welfare economics (Boadway and Bruce, 1984). It is not welfarist, but welfarism is contained within it.

7

The welfarist and extra-welfarist economics of health care finance and provision[7]

Introduction

There have been several reviews of the empirical literature on health economics and health service 'reform' (eg Culyer et al 1988). This chapter is a review of the main contributions of a more conceptual kind. I shall compare 'welfarism', by which I mean the received doctrines of standard welfare economics, with 'extra-welfarism', an approach that allows more explicit consideration of the factors that affect people's well-being. A key concept is efficiency. But it is far from being an unambiguous notion and, because it is also so central a concept, it is the one that preoccupies me here. The

7   This article is an amalgam of Culyer, A.J., 1971. The nature of the commodity 'health care' and its efficient allocation. *Oxford Economic Papers* 23, 189-211 (reprinted as Ch. 2 in A. J. Culyer and M. H. Cooper (eds.), *Health Economics*, London: Penguin, 1973, also in A J Culyer (Ed.) *Health Economics: Critical Perspectives on the World Economy*, London: Routledge, 2006, 148-157) and Culyer, A.J., 1989. The normative economics of health care finance and provision. *Oxford Review of Economic Policy* 5, 34-58 (reprinted with changes in A. McGuire, P. Fenn and K. Mayhew (eds.) *Providing Health Care: The Economics of Alternative Systems of Finance and Delivery*, Oxford: Oxford University Press, 1991, 65-98, also in A J Culyer (Ed.) *Health Economics: Critical Perspectives on the World Economy*, London: Routledge, 2006, 148-157). I am grateful for the helpful comments of Richard Arnould, Gwyn Bevan, Paul Fenn, Alistair McGuire, Gavin Mooney, John Posnett, and Alan Williams. The usual disclaimer applies.

practical context in which the concept can illuminate is, evidently, scarcely less important. For the purposes of this chapter, the practical context relates to broad policy questions about the efficiency (somehow defined) of ways of financing health care (eg through private, competitive insurance or via compulsory public insurance), and of the user-prices that it should carry (eg whether 'free', partially subsidised, not at all subsidised, differentially subsidised according to particular categories of user). These are the principal 'demand side' contextual questions whose discussion forms the bulk of the chapter. There is, of course, a host of related questions that arises in specific policy formulation and a whole raft of supply-side efficiency questions.

The conventional ways in which economists use the term 'efficiency' are the following:

* technical efficiency: obtaining when for a given output the amount of inputs used is minimised or (what is the same thing) when for a given combination of inputs, the output is maximised. This is a supply side concept that is a necessary condition embodied in the subsequent concepts of efficiency. In economic jargon it means 'being on an isoquant'. Since there is usually more (many more) than one way of producing an output that meets this condition, the implied balance of resource use even for a given target output is not unique

* cost-effectiveness: this exists when for a given output, the cost is minimised or (what is the same thing) when for a given cost, the output is maximised. This is also a supply-side concept. It embodies technical efficiency (clearly if one were using more inputs than were technically necessary to produce an output that cannot be cost-effective) and the cost-effectiveness version of efficiency is also embodied in the next concept of efficiency. Being cost-effective necessarily eliminates as 'inefficient' some technically efficient combinations of inputs but it leaves unsettled the

question of the efficient rate of production. In economic jargon, cost-effectiveness means 'being where an isocost line is tangential to an isoquant'

- ideal output: obtaining when cost-effective outputs are produced at a rate that is 'socially' optimal and allocated to individual members of society in a socially optimal fashion. This is 'top-level' efficiency and arises from combining supply-side and the demand-side considerations. In a society with limited resources, it entails establishing rates and allocations of outputs that are such that no better alternative rates of reallocations can be perceived. In economic jargon it entails setting marginal rates of transformation on the production-side equal to marginal rates of substitution in consumption.

While this trio is a useful sorting device in discussions of efficiency, the main focus in this paper is on the third, though ambiguities about the concept of 'output' will also force us also to look to some extent at the other two notions of efficiency. Of the various tricky things embodied in 'ideal output' as a concept of efficiency, one that has come to the fore in health economics in a distinctive way concerns the meaning of 'socially' and 'better' (or 'optimal').

Welfarism and extra-welfarism

One approach in health economics, which is also the traditional one in economics as a whole, is what Sen (1977) calls 'welfarist'. This is very much in accord with liberal political opinion and asserts that social welfare, in which any increase is better than none, is a function only of individual welfare (or utility) and judgements about the superiority of one state of the world (defined by reference to these utilities) over another are made irrespective of the non-utility aspects of each state. The other approach, which might be termed 'extra-welfarist', relaxes what its adherents see as an undue information restriction in welfarism so that other aspects of each social state are also embodied in the judgement.

Since, in the conventional welfarist approach, the basis of social welfare (or dis-welfare) is only the utility obtained from goods and services (including labour services), an important class of 'extra' welfare sources is the non-goods characteristics of individuals (like whether they are happy, out of pain, free to choose, physically mobile, honest) and the ways in which goods and non-goods are distributed across the population. Extra-welfarism thus transcends traditional welfare: it does not exclude individual welfare from the judgement about the social state, but it does supplement them with other aspects of individuals (including even the quality of the relationships between individuals, groups, and social classes).

This distinction is actually quite old in the history of (the so-called 'new') welfare economics. In Bergson's (1938) classic theoretical article, for example, his social welfare function included unspecified terms that could be interpreted as extra-welfarist elements of the sort just described. But he dropped them after a page, in favour of an explicit partial analysis! Another famous extra-welfarist strand in the wider literature is the notion of merit goods (Musgrave 1959) – goods whose consumption is considered so meritorious (by government) that they are made available on terms that are more generous than in the market place. Despite (unsuccessful) attempts to bring merit goods into the welfarist scheme of things (eg Culyer 1971), it seems altogether more preferable to adjust the scheme of things so as to incorporate such considerations fully, rather than leaving them as a kind of ad hoc escape clause (Margolis, 1982) lying outside traditional theory – not fitting into it but necessary in order to prevent theoretical emasculation (inability to explain why some common phenomena are observed, inability to discuss in a consistent normative framework some matters that are of evident normative importance). This plainly involves the possibility of overruling individual judgements of value and raises the question not only of the weights to be attached to individual utilities in a social welfare function but of who should be assigning those weights. Should the values of some members of society count for more than those of others?

More recently an explicit departure from welfarism was advocated by Williams (1972) and discussed further by Sugden and Williams (1978) in the context of cost-benefit analysis. This is the decision-making approach which they contrasted with the Paretian approach. The Paretian is one example of welfarist analysis where welfare is a function only of the utilities to individuals of goods and services. The former allows that governments (and other decision-makers) may have other objectives than the making of (actual or potential) Pareto improvements. This may involve not only imposing their own values on the consumption of individuals as with merit goods, and their own view of the appropriate inter-temporal discount rate, but also taking into account some extra-welfarist elements of choices that pure welfarism excludes. In this context the answer to the question 'who decides what entities with what weights go into the social welfare function?' is 'decision-makers'.

Economists are apt to slide between the normative and positive, and not always in negligent ways. Some of the literature on the NHS (eg Lindsay 1969; Culyer 1976) was ostensibly explanatory: the authors sought to provide empirically falsifiable accounts of some of the institutional features of the NHS by postulating the presence of particular arguments in individual utility functions. Under welfarism, it is quite easy to re-interpret these theories as claims for the Pareto-efficiency of the NHS, a normative idea. In the positive interpretation, the institutional features are phenomena shown (or so it is claimed) to be the predicted results of utility-maximising individuals' behaviour in particular environments; in the normative interpretation, the institutional features are seen as desirable attributes rather than merely explained phenomena: the theory justifies what is or implies what ought to be, prescribing rather than predicting.

The welfarist approach to health care finance and provision

It was (and is) common for these issues to be addressed by considering a set of factors that make health care different from other goods or services and which may constitute a reason for wanting to allocate it differently from these 'other' goods or services and to evaluate the efficiency of differing allocations in a different way (Klarman 1963, Culyer 1971). Implicit in this approach, is the presumption that goods and services are in principle best allocated by market mechanisms and that departures from that mechanism require special warrants. This somewhat arbitrary allocation of the burden of proof is the product of a particular bit of cultural conditioning to which many economists are prone but, since it is my purpose more to outline an approach than to make sociological comments on its culture-contingency, I shall say no more on that here. The following sections embrace the usual 'list' of factors that make health care 'different' and I shall indicate the kind of welfare reasoning that relates to each.

(i)   The competence of the consumer

The welfarist approach requires that choices made by or for consumers be rational in the particular sense of that term used by economists. Should choices not be founded on axioms that include, for example, an ability to compare alternatives and to rank them consistently (transitively, if weakly) in order of preference, the entire edifice tumbles because it no longer becomes possible to infer from actual behaviour that the choices made were (subject to resource constraints) those most preferred. Even if consumers were better informed than they typically are about the pros and cons of alternative actions (for example, choices between alternative strategies of personal medical treatment) there are occasions when even mentally healthy people prove incapable of choosing (especially between alternatives that involve horrid consequences). Mentally ill and mentally handicapped people may more frequently be found to be irrational in this sense. There are also occasions, of course, in which they are incapable of making any choices at all (for example, when they are the traumatic and unconscious victims of accidents).

It is common for the consumer, who is almost invariably incompetent in some degree, to defer some of the judgements involved in clinical choices to professionals, especially medical doctors, who act as agents on his or her behalf: ideally, choosing in the way the individual would, had he or she been possessed of the same informational advantages as the professional, in a system characterised by what Evans (1981) has termed 'incomplete vertical integration' between consumers and producers. The particular technical skill possessed by the professional that is relevant here is a better knowledge of the effect that health care will have on health. If one supposes that it is health that generates utility for individuals, both directly via a sense of well-being and indirectly in the sources of welfare of which better health enables one to take advantage, then health care is itself only instrumental: a means to an end. Even if the consumer is able rationally to value health, he or she will usually have much less information about the process of medicine and the risks that different processes imply. Contrary to the usual welfarist assumption, the buyer is not the best judge of his or her interests, but must rely on the seller's advice. It is quite easy to imagine circumstances in which the selfish interest of the professional can conflict with the best interests of the patient. Health itself is not a traded commodity, yet that is what the rational consumer may be expected to seek. The traded commodities are information and health care, which the consumer unaided cannot normally be expected to evaluate, and neither of which are valued for themselves. The technical expert is thus required to be more than 'merely' a technical expert. In acting as agent, the expert enters, as it were, the skin of the patient. This is what seems to endow a professional relationship with its most important, but also most elusive and delicate, characteristic (Trebilcock et al, 1979). Being delicate, it is vulnerable. It is vulnerable to cultural assumptions not shared by agent and client (the male-dominated specialty of obstetrics is often charged with sexist disregard of the interests of its wholly female clientele). It is vulnerable to misplaced technological zeal, in which the expert subjects the patient to painful diagnostic testing that yields little usable additional information, or makes presumptions about a patient's trade-offs between short-term risks and long-term benefits. It is vulnerable to class bias, in which the professional, as a member of a higher class than at least some patients, is incapable of entering their skins. It is also vulnerable to financial distortions, whereby some systems of medical remuneration encourage the supply of services whose principal justification is the income they bring to the expert rather than the benefit they bring to the patient. This is supplier-induced demand (Evans, 1974, 1976). These vulnerabilities are forms of market failure and are widely regarded as justifications for regulatory measures to protect both consumers and doctors; the former from quacks and the exploitation of a professional monopoly, the latter also from quacks (unfair competition) and the unreasonable demands of dissatisfied (and possibly litigious) customers. They also provide the basis for universally observed systems by which medical education is determined and entry to the profession regulated, and for subsidised in-service training systems and other professional activities. The existence of such market failures means that there are inevitably nice balances to be struck between, for example, the self-regulating monopoly awarded to doctors in medical practice and its possible abuse by inhibiting innovation (eg alleged but not actual quackery, inefficiency in doing whatever is done, and the earning of monopoly rents). While economics is helpful in identifying the risks, and in predicting the consequences of policies designed to mitigate them, its role is mainly qualitative: much judgement is required in making assessments of alternative possible arrangements, with their pros and cons, and respective strengths.

(ii) Supplier – induced demand (SID)

Evans' idea that physicians have a target income and adjust workload (under a fee-for-service system of paying doctors) in response to changes in the environment, seems to have grown out of the empirical observation that regional utilisation of health care is positively associated with the regional stock of doctors, holding price and other variables constant (Fuchs, 1978; Cromwell and Mitchell, 1986; Phelps, 1986). The thesis is that physicians will induce patients to use more services in order to maintain income. A positive association has sometimes been found between physician stock and prices, though this result is even more disputed than the fundamental utilization effect (Sloan and Feldman, 1978; Auster and Oaxaca, 1981; Green, 1978). There are, of course, huge econometric and empirical problems in testing for SID: only one study for example (Pauly, 1980) controlled (approximately) for patient health status. But Rice's claim (Rice, 1983, 1987) that experimental rather than routine data strongly support an inverse relationship between reimbursement rates and use of services seems persuasive.

SID is an area in health economics where we suffer an embarras de richesses. The target-income hypothesis is one possible explanation. But there are others that have never been rigorously compared and tested: increasing the numbers of doctors increases their availability (less distance to travel, less time to wait) and hence reduces the time price to patients; there may be 'excess' demands on the existing stock and a non-market-clearing price, so that increasing utilisation following increases in stock is simply the meeting of previously unmet 'excess' demand. Doctors may be less vulnerable to the effects of consumer detection of SID in communities with a high doctor/population ratio since, given extensive consumer ignorance, new patients can always be found to replace any who leave because of the SID they detect. This being the case, cross-sectional analysis will produce the observed correlation between physician stock and utilisation. It is unfortunate that this unsatisfactory state persists, and is compounded by empirical uncertainty about the very existence of SID at all, given the huge potential threat that SID constitutes to the welfarist approach and especially to the pro-market camp within the welfarist school. If demand curves really do reflect the health-irrelevant preference of suppliers, then, depending on the depth of this contamination, the use of willingness-to-pay as an indicator of consumer welfare is more or less illegitimate. Hence the considerable amount of passion found in the literature on this subject.

(iii) Where does this get us?

The chief lesson for health care finance to be drawn from this catalogue is *not* that the 'market' is inherently more flawed than the 'state' in the way in which medical care is financed (or vice versa) but that there are no simple lessons to be drawn. Market systems and their (usual) fee-for-service methods of paying doctors are prone to violate the underpinnings of welfarism in one way. State systems and their (usual) salary or capitation systems are prone to violate the underpinnings in another. If fee-for-service may encourage an excess of interventionist zeal then salaries and capitation fees may do the opposite. Under either system it is common to see a lot of inter-regional variation (McPherson et al 1981, Vayda et al 1982).

The agency relationship must inherently be incomplete. The professional may know best about the instrumentality of health care and, if he or she is working in a system that encourages a concern for the whole patient, may also come to know a good deal of relevant information about the patient's values, financial circumstances, working life, and family context. In such circumstances the agency relationship is likely to be as perfect as it probably can be. But even in this situation, the agent too has his or her own values, financial interests, working relationships, and family and social characteristics, which need not be congruent to those of the patient (Evans 1984). In both market and non-market systems of health care finance and provision, the medical monopoly is strong. This seems to produce higher monopoly rents in the more market-orientated systems (but see Lindsay 1973).

As regards the terms of access for consumers, much of this discussion casts doubt on the usefulness of marginal willingness to pay as an adequate representation of the marginal benefit to consumers, but it is not clear what the notion of welfarism requires to be put in its place, nor is it clear whether 'free' care under the NHS or under first-pound zero deductible health insurance encourages inefficient rates of use relative to the 'true' optimum. On this issue the extra-welfarists are able to be more forthright.

(iv)   Caring and sharing

In the early days of the welfarist literature, there was little recognition of the possibility that health care was different because the medical care consumption of others, or the health of others, could be a direct influence on one's own welfare. There was early recognition (eg Weisbrod, 1961) that a direct physical externality might exist in cases of communicable disease (via infection or contagion). In choosing or rejecting vaccination, an individual may fail to take account of the benefits accruing externally (viz. to others) in the form of a reduced probability of the others contracting a disease. This was conceded to provide a case (abstracting from the problems arising from consumer incompetence) for subsidised prices for such services and, in some cases, for making them compulsory (eg for immigrants). But the scope for interference with the market on this ground alone was evidently highly limited, and the marginal externality probably falls quite fast as the proportion of immunised individuals rises.

The subtler kind of externality, direct interdependence of the form that makes one person's welfare directly dependent on the consumption of others, was not taken very seriously (eg Lees 1960, 1962; Jewkes 1963; Klarman 1963, 1965; Buchanan 1965). The view is well encapsulated by Lees (1967):

> "It is argued that there is another relevant externality, namely, the disutility felt by an individual at the thought that others are not getting adequate medical care. This is no doubt so and is the basis of philanthropic support for health services, but the important point here is that there is nothing special about health services in this regard. Similar disutility is felt at the thought of others not getting adequate food, clothing, housing, and other goods commonly regarded as necessities. Apart from philanthropy, the community approach to this problem has typically been public subsidies to those in need. Externalities of this kind do not establish even a *prime facie* [sic] case for the abolition of markets

and the substitution of collective arrangements. Even where externalities exist, recent studies have shown that the scope for government spending to correct market imperfections and raise the general level of economic efficiency is less than conventional analysis had led us to believe. The implications of these studies may be summarised thus:

1.   many externalities are irrelevant to human action and the achievement of optimal solutions

2.   many relevant externalities can be, and are, dealt with voluntarily

3.   the costs of governmental intervention, even when it is 'perfect', may outweigh the benefits

4.   the imperfections of government as a decision-making and choice-making process may make an 'imperfect' market situation more imperfect."

Such was the dominant idea at that time in the 1960s: the 'nothing special' about health argument; the distinction between philanthropy approved at one level of collectivity (private charity) but not at a higher (governmental) level; the reference to studies showing the scope for corrective government action to be limited; the mention of things which 'may be' (but which are not) measured to find out what actually is. One of the ironies of the period was that these remarks and others in the same genre were being made in societies that had substantially altered the terms of financial access to health care, possibly for reasons (in part) of externality. At least, such a view would imply the possibility that the subsidy arrangements were a rational response to a real situation rather than the irrational constructions of ideologues unversed in the eternal truths of neoclassical economics. It might be thought that the reasons for this intervention were like those for similar interventions in education and housing. Since even crude policies might have gone sufficiently far to eliminate most Pareto-relevant marginal externalities, casual observation could not have revealed massive failures to internalise at efficient rates of utilisation: one needed both observation of what was *and what otherwise would probably have been* to make an assessment of the significance of externalities; at the very least, one needed the imagination to envisage what a counterfactual uninternalised world might look like.

What sort of evidence might settle this issue of the existence and size of what some have called 'caring' externalities (eg Culyer 1980)? One is introspective. Are sufficient numbers of introspectors prepared to sacrifice some of their own consumption so that others may have more? If so, they care in the externality sense. In particular, invite introspectors to try to imagine a society in which health care was supplied entirely by commercial organizations without public subsidy or by private charities. Ask each, given that they had imagined themselves in such a society, whether they would be willing to sacrifice some of what each has so that others would receive more. If each would (and they may want to add the side condition that each would sacrifice only if others similarly placed also made sacrifices) then they would be providing evidence for the existence of caring externalities of this sort.

One of the issues that arises in this context is the question of whether subsidies should be specific (eg in-kind or directly tied to purchases of specific goods and services as with voucher schemes) or general (essentially income support). The basic line of argument has tended to be that it seems that generalised support may be appropriate for goods and services that are highly income elastic at low levels of household income, where there will be a strong presumption that income supplements will be spent by most families on basic necessities like food (so there is no need for a 'National Food Service'!), but that where this is not the case, or where people are held to be poor judges of their own welfare, specific subsidies are a more cost-effective means of promoting consumption of particular goods since they utilise substitution effects as well as income effects. It should be clear that the potential superiority of specific subsidies arises from the welfare gain to the subsidy-provider: in any comparison of alternatives, provided that the subsidy-receiver is not worse off under one than the other, then the one yielding the largest benefit to the subsidy-provider is Pareto-preferred.

There has been some speculation about the way in which inequality in health care consumption enters welfarist utility functions. From the late 1960s into the early 1970s, focus continued to be upon the consumption of health services as the principal source of external 'concern' (rather than, say, the effect of such consumption on health). For some, the focus was on absolute rates of consumption while for others it was relative. Pauly (1971) argued that the (negatively sloped) external demand (marginal valuation) for a person's care was invariate with respect to the identity of the person of concern and that the demand for health care was, in general, income elastic. Detailed micro empirical studies (all North American) on this latter question yield little unambiguous evidence about direct income elasticities (though they seem to be positive) because of income-related upper limits on out-of-pocket expenses under health care insurance (see, eg, Manning et al 1987), although aggregate studies show income elasticities of between 1.18 and 1.36, so that a 10 per cent increase in (aggregate) income can be expected to lead on average to a roughly 12.5 per cent increase in health care spending (for a review see Culyer et al 1988 and, for a critique, Parkin et al 1987).

There seems little doubt about the overall negative slope of demand curves. The econometric evidence is not easily interpreted, partly because in those systems which have been most studied (North American), fee-for-service and the possibility of supplier-induced demand can cause supply-side contamination of the pure substitution effects of changing user-prices. Beck (1974) estimated that the reduction in use following the introduction of charges of $1.50 per surgery visit and $2.00 per house call in Saskatchewan in 1968 was about 7 per cent for the whole population but 18 per cent for the poor. Early studies of price-elasticity found values in the range -0.4 to -1.0. Subsequent work by Phelps and Newhouse (1974), Newhouse and Phelps (1976), and, most recently and most authoritatively, the Rand study reported in Manning et al (1987), found price-elasticities for all health care in the -0.2 to -0.1 range (i.e. a 10 per cent increase in user price causes demand to fall by one to two per cent). The effects in the Rand study were, however, much stronger for the poor, for children's demands, and especially for the children of the poor (see Lohr et al 1986). These results have tremendous significance: the handicapping effects of, say, untreated otitis media in children far outweigh the short-term functional impairment, as further socializing and educational handicaps will almost inevitably become added for children already disadvantaged from birth.

The implications of the Pauly model are quite explicit: given a similar cost of care per person in a particular diagnostic group, efficient internalising of the external effect requires a variable subsidy: varying from 100 per cent in the case of the lowest income group to 0 per cent at a sufficiently high level. This is archetypical selectivity in social policy.

In contrast to these absolutist externality models of caring, Lindsay (1969; see also Cullis and West 1979) offered a relativist model of sharing in which equal treatment for equal (medical) need was implied. He showed that the most cost-effective method of achieving a given level of equality is by a combination of standard subsidy (but not in general to reduce price to zero) and enforced denial of access via non-price rationing ('abstention' in his terminology) to the better off.

One set of problems arising from this set of externality models is that, while each provides an account of some of the features of health care subsidy (eg some selectivity, some 'free' care, some degree of reduced inequality in access), their practical implementation means that the apparently sharp distinctions between their implications at the theoretical level become blurred in practice. On empirical grounds, it is consequently hard to discriminate between them. There are also more deep-seated difficulties. One arises from the characteristic that the externality is in each case public, so that its internalisation is of benefit to all, whether or not one contributes. It is in everyone's interest to free ride. While the 'club' view of government as a mechanism by which individuals voluntarily agree to be coerced to provide more optimal levels of public goods can be seen as a collective solution to the free-rider problem, it is quite clear that there are several types of activity (most notably private charitable giving) that are not collectivised and that are fully exposed to the problem of free-riding. Strictly, the free-rider problem implies that no-one (save one whose marginal value of the external benefit most exceeds its marginal cost) has an incentive to contribute. Consequently, charities will have either no supporters at all or only one. Since this is plainly not so, there seems to be something wrong with the theory. And if each is therefore a wrong theory, none can be used to justify the kinds of public subsidy often seen in health care. The free-rider theorem is an example of over-kill: its implications are too strong.

One solution to this sort of problem has been offered by Collard (1978) among others, which appeals to the rationality rather than the public spiritedness of individuals. This is the Kantian principle: "if the interest of the action can, without self-contradiction, be universalised it is morally possible" (Kant 1930). A non-Kantian altruist will consider only his own (usually) negligible contribution to the financing of public good and free ride. If all are non-Kantian, all free-ride and the classic prisoners' dilemma result ensues. The Kantian altruist, per contra, reckons with the behaviour of others: if all do as he does and he free-rides he knows (rationally) that the worst outcome will result, so he (and all other Kantians) behave morally and pay up. While it is in many ways attractive to suppose that rules of morality actually may affect behaviour, it is plain that this approach is, in the welfarist context, ad hoc. It is also, in fact, extra-welfarist.

Another attempt to find a solution is to posit that individuals attach utility not only (possibly not at all) to changing the consumption of goods and services by others, but to the act of contributing itself: utility is derived from what one gives away rather than what it is used for. This would get one quite neatly out of the free-rider problem, for the source of utility is no longer public: if B gives to the charity rather than A, A derives no utility. However, this seems to lead nowhere if one wishes to build a welfarist model of collective health care subsidies, for it is the very publicness of the external effect that generates the public subsidy argument. Perhaps a mixture of what Margolis (1982) calls 'goods altruism' and 'participation altruism' might be developed that would help to account for the simultaneous existence of collective and private acts of altruism.

Another problem has been pinpointed by Sugden (1980, 1982), again attacking the roots of the theory of welfarist altruism. Reverting once more to the private charity case, suppose you have decided to donate £100 to a charity. Under welfarism, you have selected this as your best choice given your income, what you know about the charity, etc. You are on the point of writing out your cheque when you discover that your neighbour has just posted a cheque for £100 to the same charity. Since the charity is now as well off as you thought it would be with your own contribution, but you can now be £100 better off, your welfare is undoubtedly higher if you no longer write the cheque. In fact, since you are a bit richer than before, and charitable giving has a positive income elasticity, you may want to revise your initial view about how much to give slightly upwards, but even if you gave £10 instead of nothing, 10 per cent is a very large proportion of extra income (£100 in this case) for anyone to give away (see Collard 1978 for a survey). Even more dramatically, suppose the charity's annual income is £10,000 and you are contributing £100 each year out of personal disposable income of £1,000 (you are, by the way, unusually generous). Now suppose, entirely by coincidence, that your income falls by £1 at the same time as everyone else's contributions rise from £9,900 to

£9,901. With your preferences and the terms of trade constant, your initially preferred combination (£10,000 for the charity and £900 for yourself) is still available and will therefore still be preferred so you give £99: a fall in an altruist's income that is exactly matched by an increase in everyone else's contributions means that an altruist, as welfarists see it, will choose to reduce their contribution by the full amount by which personal income has fallen!

A theory that has such counter-intuitive (and counter-factual) empirical implications has to be regarded as an unusually weak foundation upon which to build normative propositions. Yet this is the same theory that underpins all these externality arguments for public subsidy (of one form or another, depending on which of the rival externality theories one is using). Sugden suggests that it is preferable to invoke another (extra-welfarist) theory (specifically, of 'duty'). It was precisely in the language of duty (as well as altruism and reciprocity) that Titmuss couched his defence of the NHS (Titmuss 1970). This may not be the welfarist way – but it may be the right way!

Thus we reach a rather destructive end of a chain of welfarist attempts to build rationales based on altruism or philanthropy. One interesting possibility that may yet rescue welfarism has been developed by Margolis (1982). He postulates that individuals have a split preference system in which one set of preferences relates to group-interests and another relates to selfish ones. This develops hints dropped by, for example, Harsanyi (1955), Pattanaik (1968), Meade (1973), and Rawls (1972), in which the ancient distinction of Plato between man as citizen and man as individual is developed in various ways, but each having the characteristic that one (higher) set of 'preferences', or morals, constrains or interacts with another (lower) set.

As a model of altruistic behaviour, this has several attractive welfarist features. Since it does not appeal to externality arguments, it is not flawed by free-rider problems, nor does it have any of the Sugden anomalies. It does not require that the individual be indifferent to the uses to which group-oriented spending is put. It does not elevate group-oriented preferences to a higher status than self-oriented ones (they are both preferences; one is not a set of moral rules) so it is amenable to the usual welfarist interpretations.

(v) ... and where does this get us?

Since the literature on externalities and caring is largely a priori in nature, its value is primarily as an aid to introspection and judgement. One needs first to form a view about the existence of the general events that may fall into this class by imagining a state of the world devoid of attempts to optimise via subsidy and regulation, and to determine whether externalities are Pareto-relevant in total or at the margin (Buchanan and Stubblebine 1962) or whether group-orientation is likely to be pervasive. Beyond this there are questions as to whether group concerns are better conceived as relating to absolute or relative levels of consumption and whether they are better seen as questions of preference (arguments of utility functions) or of morals (constraints on selfish welfare maximisation). These rather useful sorting devices are further supplemented by the enrichment the literature affords of the concepts of 'altruism', 'selfishness', and 'caring'. As an aid to clarity of thought, the welfarist literature is valuable; although it cannot be claimed that it has yielded settled conclusions on those issues that require judgement. The view that the externality or group concern derives not from health care consumption but from health itself is not directly addressed in this literature but occurs under extra-welfarism.

(vi) Uncertainty

The stochastic nature of disease and ill-health has been held to be another respect in which health care is different from at least some other goods and services. The standard welfarist economics of health insurance (eg Arrow 1963; Culyer 1979; Evans 1983, 1984) is based on the expected utility maximising model of risk-aversion (for a survey see Schoemaker, 1982). The financial cost only of medical care (loss of employment income is not considered here) is the aspect of health-affecting events that is insured against. In this analysis, the welfare gain to the insured risk-averse individual arises from the implication that the welfare loss from paying a *certain* premium is less than the welfare loss of the *expected* financial loss of income if sickness strikes and health care has to be purchased (with a probability of p) plus the prospect of having one's income entire if sickness does not strike. This analysis assumes that the more the marginal utility of income falls the more one has, that insurance premiums are actuarially 'fair', and that the only welfare effects occur through the impact of health care costs on net income (for example, loss of employment or the disutility of illness itself are not a part of the basic analysis) and that there is no direct link between health and income (Shavell 1978). The basic lesson of the expected utility model is that fair insurance increases welfare. The important question for health care financing is, of course, whether a voluntary competitive health insurance market is better able to maximise these welfare gains than a compulsory system of social insurance or tax finance.

(vii) Loading

The analysis so far assumes that there is a competitive insurance market in which many insurers compete for trade (or potential entrance deters oligopoly premium-setting) and premiums are set at actuarially fair rates: the product of the probability and the estimated expense. In practice the genuine opportunity costs of insurance provision, together with any X-inefficiency and monopoly rent, will also be 'loaded' on to premiums, which consequently rise above their actuarially fair level. In large group plans in the USA the loading is about 10 per cent (Pauly 1986). This implies that the welfare gains for consumers of insurance are reduced, so some risk-averse individuals will no longer insure. To the extent that the loading represents costs in excess of opportunity costs, this will thus cause deadweight welfare losses. To the extent that opportunity costs themselves can be lowered by scale economies and other measures that might be taken to reduce costs, the competitive insurance system itself may cause unnecessary welfare losses.

Loading also leads to a preference for deductibles (Arrow 1963). Suppose that the loading is not simply proportional to the size of the premium but is a relatively high proportion of small claims (say, checking for fraud, etc, is equally costly for probable and less probable events). Then the probability of the loading charge exceeding the welfare gain rises: very probable events (eg routine dental care) will be more self-insured via deductibles; very expensive events (eg cancer care treatment) will be more likely to be fully insured (no deductibles).

(viii) Adverse Selection

Another problem that arises has its roots in another kind of informational asymmetry. This time, however, the informational advantage lies with the consumer rather than the supplier of the service (financial in this case). Suppose that premiums are set according to the calculated risks for groups in the community. In the simplest case, the premium is set according to the population-wide probability of consuming health care. The typical consumer will, however, usually be more aware of his or her own probability. Those whose 'probability x expected expenses' is greater than the premium will gain welfare in excess of that expected and may gain even if they are not risk averse. Those whose 'true probability x expected expenses' is less than the premium will tend (depending on their risk aversion) to self-insure. This phenomenon is known as adverse selection. It leads to a progressive upward pressure on premiums (as low potential users are driven out), with insurance cover increasingly restricted to the very worst risks. The upshot is a pool of uninsured people, many of whom are risk averse, in addition to those who are uninsurable by virtue of chronic disease or other disqualifying features, with a heavy financial burden on the sickest uninsured members of society. In the United States, estimates vary of the numbers who are uninsured or inadequately insured, but seem to indicate a total of around 50 million (Farley 1985; Mundinger 1985). In any event, adverse selection, unless checked, is likely to cause massive externalities of the sort described earlier and become a major affront to most principles of equity. Left to itself, adverse selection would destroy the market entirely. In practice this does not happen, partly because insurance plans are often based on employee groups in which a condition of employment may be that each joins the company plan; opting out is not possible unless the gains from doing so would outweigh the losses from changing one's employment. Partly, it does not happen because the presence of adverse selection itself affords gains from trade between self-insurers and profit-seeking insurance agencies (and non-profit seeking, too).

It pays insurers to offer policies with premiums that better approximate the true expected expenses of those driven out by adverse selection, even though the acquisition of this information is not costless. This erodes the principle of community-rating which becomes replaced by experience-rating and by packages of cover that fall short of fully comprehensive (eg 'major medical' only). In this fashion, good risks are creamed off. While there will remain some inefficiency, in that some very low risk groups may still fail to find a suitable package at an actuarially appropriate premium, experience-rating is more efficient than community-rating. It differs also from community-rating in that, whereas under community-rating wealth is redistributed from low to high risk individuals and families in advance of any health care consumption, experience rating has the effect of redistribution ex post from those (insured) who are well to those who are sick.

Though more efficient from a welfarist perspective (Arrow 1963), experience-rating is likely to violate the usual distributional criteria of equity: those with a history of sickness will face the highest premiums, have the less comprehensive cover, be most likely to pay deductibles (both of these latter options have the effect of reducing premiums as they reduce probable pay-outs by the insurer) and, since ill-health and income are correlated, will on average be the poorer members of the community. Many, moreover, can be expected to find their risk aversion insufficient to warrant insurance of any kind.

(ix) Moral hazard

Another difficulty with insurance systems is moral hazard. One form of this has already been met in the shape of supplier-induced demand – a kind of producer's moral hazard, whereby producers on a fee for service system of reimbursement have an incentive to adjust the client's demand in pursuit of their personal income objectives. This is easier done if the cost of supplier-induced demand can be passed on to the insurer.

More commonly discussed, however, is consumer's moral hazard. Here, the fact of being insured encourages the individual to take less care in ensuring that the undesired state (illness) does not occur (ex ante moral hazard) and, when sickness occurs, encourages the consumer to maximise the consumption of services beyond the point at which marginal cost (assuming that services are priced at marginal cost) equals marginal value (ex post moral hazard). In health insurance, ex post moral hazard seems to be the principal problem on the consumer-side. Two caveats are worth noting. One is that consumer demand is, as we have already seen, mostly interpreted by an agent, so the distinction between consumer's and producer's moral hazard is at best fuzzy. The other is that if hospital and other services are priced at above marginal cost, second-best considerations would dictate that the usual welfarist efficiency conditions may no longer apply. Consumers may be receiving false signals about marginal cost from market prices and should probably be encouraged to consume at higher rates than those determined by current prices, quite apart from any externality considerations, even if this implies yet bigger rents for monopoly suppliers of health care via the insurers.

The effect on the insurance market is predictable. With moral hazard, consumption exceeds the rate on which premiums have been (historically) set, the (retrospective) reimbursement of suppliers rises to levels higher than predicted, and premiums rise. Higher premiums will drive out some risk-averse individuals from the insurance market but may also cause an inefficiently large rate of consumption. To retain their market, insurers offer packages that do not include 'first pound coverage' and the consumer has to pay deductibles (eg the first £x of any expense) or coinsurance (eg x per cent of the total bill).

While the likely offence to equity principles is plain, the efficiency implications are less obvious in a welfarist context. With full 'first-pound' cover, and zero marginal (money) user price, the individual may be expected to consume a more than optimal amount of health care when sick. This generates inefficiency, since the cost of provision exceeds the value of the care to the consumer, making the welfarist assumption that consumer marginal willingness to pay is adequately reflected in the demand curve and that price truly reflects marginal social cost. This so-called 'excess burden' can be reduced by co-insurance. If the consumer pays a proportion of the daily cost, the price to the consumer rises, consumption falls, the excess burden falls (more than proportionately) and total expenditure falls, implying a lower (future) premium.

In one of the few thorough empirical attempts to measure welfare effects in the literature, Feldstein (1973) estimated that the maximum reduction in the excess burden of health insurance in the US, by raising co-insurance from an average of 0.33 to 0.5, would have been $10 billion in 1969 prices after allowing for the loss of welfare to those who would no longer choose insurance. However, the implications of this analysis hinge crucially on the adequacy of prices as measures of marginal cost and on the absence of externalities. They also depend on the welfarist assumption that demand adequately represents the consumer's true estimate of the worth of medical care.

(j) ... and where does this get us?

Insurance, under welfarist assumptions, has welfare-increasing properties, but optimal insurance is less than complete insurance. The analysis does not typically take account of contrary indications suggested by externality or equity considerations, and is entirely dependent on the strong assumption that consumer choices adequately reveal consumer preferences (viz. that the agency relationship is perfect).

Provided that it is not accompanied by compensating X-inefficiencies, welfarist reasoning may suggest that a system of compulsory universal public insurance operated through the general tax system may have substantial cost advantages over competitive insurance. Compulsion avoids adverse selection and enables scale economies to be gained (if they exist), reducing loading and increasing the welfare gains from comprehensive insurance cover. Universality and tax finance avoid the necessity of risk assessment and premium setting, billing, reimbursement, checking for fraud, and so on. These costs appear to vary substantially across different systems, being less than three per cent of total expenditure in countries with a tax-based social insurance system, like the UK and Canada, and in excess of 10 per cent in private insurance systems, or in systems with public finance but with complex systems of billing and reimbursement, like the USA and France (OECD, 1977). It may be technically possible for a large country to operate a competitive system that would avoid monopoly exploitation and that would also realise scale economies but might not be plausible in smaller countries. Moral hazard may be controlled in public or private insurance systems by the adoption of (private or public) regulatory schemes defining the appropriateness of packages of care, and by prospective reimbursement according to an agreed charge per case-type rather than retrospectively, according to whatever the suppliers happen to have charged. Given a non-competitive health care industry (whether public or private), such regulation is commonly observed, and it is a question of judgement whether the regulation is better done by a publicly accountable agency or by the (insurance) industry itself.

(k) The welfarist approach: an overview

The welfarist techniques of analysis have been the traditional way in which issues of health service finance have been addressed in the economics literature. Granted the acceptability of welfarism's value assumptions, its implications for policy hinge on judgements about the empirical significance of consumer rationality, the purity of the agency relationship, the nature of any externalities (physical or utility interdependence or group-concern), the extent of adverse selection, moral hazard, supplier induced demand, unnecessary premium loading under insurance and the empirical validity of the neoclassical behavioural model that, in its normative form, is welfarism's centrepiece. Each will draw his or her own conclusions based on the (patchy) evidence and more casual experience.

The extra-welfarist approach

Whereas welfarism holds that standards of living, the efficiency of social arrangements and the justice of distributions and redistributions are all to be evaluated in terms of the individual's utility (or welfare), an extra-welfarist approach (Sen, 1979) admits non-utility information about individuals into the process of comparing social states. Using an illustration from Sen, consider three social states x, y, and z, with the following (cardinal and even interpersonally comparable) utility numbers for persons 1 and 2.

	x	y	z
Person 1's utility	4	7	7
Person 2's utility	10	8	8

In x, person 1 is hungry while 2 eats amply. In y, 2 has been forced to surrender some food to 1 and 2's utility loss is less than 1's utility gain. Under welfarism, the fact of coercion is an irrelevance: the sum total of utility is higher in y than x so y is socially preferred. This is an example of the way in which non-utility information is excluded in the making of social comparisons under welfarism.

In z, person 1 is as hungry as in x and 2 is as amply fed but 1, who happens to be a sadist, is allowed to torture 2 (who is no masochist). It so happens that 1's utility gain and 2's utility loss are the same as under the food transfer programme. Under welfarism, y is socially preferred to x but z is the same, utility-wise, as y, therefore z too, is socially preferred to x. Again, the relevance of non-utility information (in this case the fact of torture) is denied.

Sen (1980) argues that a particularly important class of non-utility information about individuals is 'basic capabilities': a person being able to do particular things. It is, he suggests, because a cripple is unable to perform particular activities that he or she is seen as having special needs that are independent of his or her total or marginal utility. Culyer (1989) advocated the more general notion of 'characteristics of people' – for example, their genetic endowment of health, their relative deprivation independently of the absolute consumption of commodities or the characteristics of commodities, their moral worth and deservingness, whether they are in pain, or stigmatised by society. Characteristics may also relate to the character of relationships between people such as the quality of friendships, community support for the individual when in need, social isolation, or changes in characteristics, such as becoming (as distinct from being) crippled.

Only some of the characteristics of people (which will include some of their capabilities) will be deemed relevant and the list of such relevant characteristics is likely to vary between cultures, climates, historical periods, and so on. It is, in short, contingent. It is related to a concept of need. If the characteristics of people are a way of describing deprivation, desired states, or significant changes in people's characteristics, then commodities and characteristics of commodities are what is often needed to remove the deprivation or to move towards the desired state, or to help people cope with change. They are the necessary means to a desired end. To compare the ill-health of different individuals or groups is not the same as to compare the health care they have received (they could receive the same amounts and still be unhealthy, or different amounts and be equally healthy).

(i) Need and extra-welfarism

Whereas the notion of 'need' has received a bad press from many welfarist economists, extra-welfarists have been able to use the term with some precision and confidence. In its most rudimentary form, a need for health care would seem to imply that someone is better off with the needed treatment than without it (Williams 1974) and that the 'better offness' has to do with the person's health (Culyer, Lavers, Williams 1971). Thus, health services are needed (viz. are a necessary condition for achieving a particular outcome) only if the outcome is desired and there is no alternative (or more cost-effective) way of realizing it. Since inputs are nearly always substitutable, it will not normally make sense to say that a specific resource in a specific quantity is needed, and since there is no effective treatment for some conditions, it is nonsensical to say that persons suffering from such conditions need health services. (They may need the fruits of research and they may need love and comfort, but they cannot need ineffective care, even though they may demand it.) Since health services are needed only for what they enable to be accomplished, in a world of scarcity, judgements must be made about the value of what might be accomplished. Some services are bound not to be supplied in the light of such judgements and so it does not make much sense to require that all needs should be met. One of the first lessons of the theory of need is the ethical acceptability of unmet need (Wiggins et al 1987) which parallels the welfarist efficiency argument that optimal insurance is less than full insurance.

Since health services can be needed only if their outcomes are desired, the important question arises as to whose judgement ought to be decisive in assessing desirability of outcome. While the judgement of technicians (such as doctors) may be appropriate in evaluations of effectiveness, technical experts have no particular authority for making value judgements, so it does not make much ethical sense to pretend that these essentially political decisions can be desanitised by being left to the experts. At the centre of this problem lies the issue of how one person's needs are to be weighed against those of another.

In health economics, the extra-welfarist approach has taken 'health' as the proximate maximand. This does not imply the complete ousting of welfare, with its usual normative connotations, but the use of both sets of data to evaluate alternatives. 'Health' is itself a descriptive characteristic of people, but in practice has been interpreted in the literature as a composite bundle of other characteristics, such as freedom from pain and restriction of activity (Culyer, Lavers and Williams 1971). The implications of the extra-welfarist approach for the finance of health care seem partly to take negative forms. Insurance arrangements, user prices (money, time, etc) should not act so as to discourage use of care that contributes to the objective of maximising health. There are also implications for rationing care (equalizing marginal products in terms of health per unit of resource), selecting patients from waiting lists, and conducting cost-benefit analyses in the health service.

At the core of the extra-welfarist approach is the issue of how the maximand is to be measured. This has proved to be an issue involving much cross-disciplinary collaboration between (for example) economists, physicians, psychologists, and political scientists, which has exposed the complexities involved in defining and measuring health and which has also developed a battery of experimental techniques designed to test theories and quantify the hitherto unquantified.

(ii) Measuring health

Extra-welfarists identify health as the principal output of health services and its efficient production (technical efficiency, cost-effectiveness) as an issue upon which its insights can be particularly valuable. This is in contrast to welfarism, under which it is natural to take goods and services as the units of output. Much of the cost-effectiveness literature in health economics is implicitly extra-welfarist, in seeking to identify the least-cost method of delivering a given health improvement (or prevention of deterioration) for a given patient group (or across patient groups). In many cases, extra-welfarist economists have joined hands with non-economists in the search for better measures of health and, of necessity, in identifying the production functions that underlie cost functions and cost-benefit relationships.

One approach to health measurement has been to use ad hoc numerical scales to quantify the bundle of characteristics (usually in the context of planning exercises or studies of the effectiveness of medical procedures). This approach involves the individual being assessed in several dimensions, with numbers being associated with each assessment and the resultant scores (sometimes weighted) being added up (eg Harris et al, 1971; Grogono and Woodgate, 1971). The arbitrariness of such procedures has been spelled out several times (eg by Culyer, 1978a and b):

1.   criteria for selecting characteristics were usually unspecified

2.   the scaling systems often implied only order but were subsequently used to construct a cardinal index

3.   the possibility that combinations of characteristics might have higher or lower numbers than the sum of the separate scores was often excluded

4.   increasing marginal severity was rarely allowed

5.   criteria for selecting those making these (value) judgements were usually unspecified.

The approach that has most frequently been adopted by economists has become known as the Quality-Adjusted Life-Year, or QALY, and has been mainly developed by Torrance in Canada (see Torrance 1986 for a survey, and Drummond 1991, for an extended discussion) and Williams in the UK (eg Williams 1985, 1986). The QALY has two dimensions: life-expectancy (as a measure of the extra life-years that may be procured) and a quality adjustment (as weights indicating the healthiness of the expected life-years). In the context of the measurement of output of health services, productivity is thus to be seen as the difference over a period of time between expected QALYs with a particular procedure and without it (or with an alternative). The ways in which the quality weights have been developed and interpersonal comparisons made are of particular analytical interest. A historical review of the health index literature (of which these quality weights form a part) is Rosser (1983) and a review of the techniques for measuring health indices is Torrance (1982).

There are three commonly-used methods of measuring scales of health (on this and other important distinctions see Culyer 1986): the rating scale; the standard gamble; and the time trade-off (see Drummond et al 1987). These are defined in detail in Drummond (1991). However, such measures present a potential problem. The literature frequently characterises measures of health as utility measures (eg Torrance, 1986). Here it is important to distinguish between the welfarist notion of utility as welfare and the extra-welfarist notion. Under Paretianism, for example, the notion of welfare relates to goods and services and is the utility of the individual affected by their consumption. Under extra-welfarism, while this notion of utility may still apply, there is the further idea that uses utility theory in order to derive measures of characteristics of individuals that are not goods, not services, nor necessarily having a value content corresponding to the Paretian notion that the individual is the best judge of his/her own welfare. Confusingly, however, these too are called utility measures, making it important to appreciate the possibility that one can have utility measures that are not welfarist.

One of the normative issues that the extra-welfarist approach identifies (but does not resolve) concerns who shall decide the weights to be applied to different health states and to the components of health states. Who shall decide the categories of functioning, etc, to be considered? Who shall decide who shall decide? The answers may well depend upon the nature of the problem under consideration. Politicians, civil servants, managers, representatives of the public, persons at risk of particular disease, patients, doctors, nurses – all may have some claims by virtue of identity, skill, or position of trust. It does not necessarily follow that those judged best able to exercise a judgement about, say, the effectiveness of a medical procedure are those best qualified to exercise a judgement about how pain and disability are to be traded off.

(iii) Extra-welfarism and distributional weights

The extra-welfarist literature clearly sees information like cost-per-QALY as a means of guiding resource allocation decisions in health care, whether on equity or efficiency grounds, and the literature is quite explicit in its departure from consumer-based willingness-to-pay as the basis for benefit valuation (Williams 1988). The next question that naturally arises relates to whose willingness-to-pay is to be substituted for that of the consumer. The most recent work has addressed this issue in the following way: "… is a particular improvement in health to be regarded as of equal value no matter who gets it; and, if not, what precisely is its relative value in accruing to one kind of person as opposed to another?" (Williams 1988). This research began by seeking to identify the views on the matter that were actually held by surveyed individuals. It would seem from the early results that there is a consensus that particular phases of the life-cycle are regarded as times when health is of greatest value. Of the ten phases used in Williams' survey, two stood out: 'as infants' and 'when bringing up children'. Other questions concerned the relative value of good health at different points in the life cycle, and whether it is useful to unscramble life-cycle phases into elements that are age-, role-, and sex-related.

If ethical authority is to be accorded these (or similar) results, a departure is implied from the distributive value-judgement normally (if only provisionally) embodied in measures of health, such as QALYs: a unit of health is of equal value no matter who gets it. It thus seems possible that distributive judgements will be able to be built into outcome measures and, via cost-effectiveness analyses, into efficiency analysis (eg Culyer, 1988b). Indeed, if all of the features of distributional equity that are of (legitimate) concern could be built into outcome data in this way, then a full integration of equity and efficiency will have been achieved in health policy: given routine information about population characteristics (disease incidence, etc), medical technology (the possibilities for changing health states for the better), and cost information, it will be possible to make informed routine judgements about resource allocations made to providers of health care.

(iv) Objections to QALYs

One type of objection is represented by Smith (1987) who argues that the use of a quantitative algorithm obscures a process by which essentially arbitrary assessments of the values of people's lives are being made. To this Williams' (1987) retort seems compelling: that far from obscuring the need for value judgement the procedure highlights the value-judgemental elements and offers techniques by which they could be made more explicitly; that far from imposing essentially arbitrary values, the process of quantification is, by virtue of its explicitness, open to criticism and change at every stage.

Rather deeper is an objection of Broome (1985) that the measures ignore population: the outcome of health services may include not only the extra health for people who may also be having extra time, but also more people if an additional outcome includes children being born who would not otherwise have existed. In the welfarist tradition this poses a problem because although it might be possible to find out how extra QALYs are valued, it is not possible to determine the value that unborn place on being born. But this also poses a problem for extra-welfarists, in so far as they too wish to ascribe a value to unborn lives as well as the lives of the children of the unborn, and so on ad infinitum. Unfortunately, we have no basis at present for valuing population changes, therefore (says Broome) we have no basis for valuing life or QALYs.

Earlier, Broome (1978) argued that the only appropriate value for a statistical life was infinity on the grounds that, eventually, statistical probabilities of death (or of opportunities for life extensions not taken) translate into deaths of actual individuals who might reasonably be expected to exercise a veto. A welfarist may find something of a defence in the reflection that he might himself agree to an option offering some benefit but with a very small prospect of its entailing his own death, so why should not a society of like-minded folk feel similarly? An extra-welfarist might take the view that he/she would be guided by the majority view on the value of (or differential values of) life.

There is nothing to be gained in the context of resource allocation decision-making from taking an ontological view of QALYs, or life, or lives. One is not concerned with the inherent cherishable worth of people but rather with the value of resources that we might spend in order to gain better health or prevent (or postpone) death or change the prospects of either for the better. If we spend £2,000 per person to protect them from the consequences of some risk that is fatal for say one in five hundred, it is merely arithmetic that we shall spend, on average, £1 million per life saved: only in this sense is a life 'worth' £1 million.

Loomes (1988) mounts a far more powerful assault on both welfarist and non-welfarist traditions by attacking the usual behavioural axioms that are shared by both. He focuses on the systematic differences in measure that have been observed as between rating scales, standard gambles, and time trade-offs (eg Torrance, 1976, Bombardier et al, 1982). His analysis hinges on a distinction between the utility gained as the result of one's own choice and 'choiceless' utility: viz. the utility experienced as the consequence of a happening generated in any other way. The importance of the distinction lies in the fact that only in the former is there the possibility that, in an uncertain world, you may come to regret or rejoice over a decision you have made. The rating method does not involve choice; it requires the subject only to locate a state on a utility scale. The standard gamble, by contrast, does involve choice and so does the time trade-off method.

Regret theory is recommended as a prima facie better foundation for future work in the QALY territory. It seems clear that research should be expanded to incorporate regret theory into health status and QALY measurement experiments in order to compare results systematically with the other techniques. The potential from exploiting other substitutes for expected utility theory (such as prospect theory) remains to be explored.

(v)   Where does extra-welfarism get us?

As far as the demand side is concerned, extra-welfarism in health economics may be seen to take health as the maximand. The emphasis, in principle, is not exclusive, for extra-welfarism is not exclusive, and it seems unlikely that any extra-welfarist would assign zero weights to such factors as consumer choice, privacy, speed of service, hospital hotel-services, and other factors that may be only remotely causally linked to health.

Extra-welfarism thus immediately implies another notion of efficiency, in which explicit (non-welfarist) value judgements are incorporated into the maximand, which is, in turn, a cardinal utility index of health. This index is extremely useful in supply-side efficiency studies. It is not uniquely applicable under socialised systems of care and may, for example, be used in market systems where insurance companies seek to control producer moral hazard by reimbursing providers only for procedures that are demonstrably relatively cost-effective in restoring health, and in any clinical research with a similar objective. In this territory, extra-welfarists have been more active empirically than welfarists typically have been.

As a matter of necessity, the literature has focused on the difficult issues of measuring health itself (or changes in it) in order to improve the ability of the system to produce health cost-effectively. It is quite possible for these efforts also to serve the cause of welfarism: after all, better information on outcomes can enhance the physician's ability to act as a good agent for the patient. But it is quite clear that other causes are served as well, and that the implications of extra-welfarist health maximisation are not the same as welfarist analysis.

Extra-welfarism resembles the welfarist externality arguments in implying free or subsidised terms of access to healthcare. Under welfarism, however, the reason for the subsidy lies in the optimal internalisation of externalities. In extra-welfarism, the reason lies in more engineering sorts of concern: optimal resource use is determined by equality of marginal health output per unit of resource in various activities and across various client groups. Willingness-to-pay is an irrelevance and may be directly counter to this objective if willingness-to-pay is positively associated with ability to pay, but ability to pay is inversely associated with potential for health improvement. The extra-welfarist approach, therefore, attaches great importance to the identification of potential for benefit. Indeed, it is possible to see some traditional policy arguments cast in equity terms as possibly extra-welfarist health-maximisation arguments. Assume, for example, that a (satisfactorily measured) QALY is judged to be equally valuable socially to whomsoever it may accrue. Now allow that the sickest in society are by and large those for whom the marginal product of health care in terms of QALYs is highest, that these are also the poorest, and that when (ceteris paribus) health service per capita rises, the marginal product in terms of health falls. It evidently follows that efforts to equalise the geographical distribution of resources, to channel more of them to the sick and more of them to the poor, might be seen not as distributional policies to be justified by equity arguments, but efficient policies justified by heath maximisation.

There is a danger in extra-welfarism of becoming too fixed on the bottom line. The great advantage the approach can claim in issues like outcome measurement is rather like the claim made earlier on behalf of welfarism: it provides a conceptual framework for handling extremely complex issues in a systematic fashion, clearly exposing each aspect of an argument. The cost-per-QALY is less important than the fact that individuals with responsibility for resource allocation in health care have a means of working through the issues so that they can come to their own informed view about the pros and cons of different resource allocations. The method is intended (in an archetypical decision-makers approach) as an aid to, rather than a substitute for, thought.

Conclusions

It will be clear that there is a paradigm clash in the normative economics of health, though it would be wrong to overdraw the differences. The extra-welfarist approach is, after all, inclusive of welfarism. There can be no question that the extra-welfarist approach is more tolerant of what may be seen as paternalism and can be readily enlisted on behalf of the sorts of access terms and distributional issues that have lain at the heart of the ideology of the British NHS, and increasingly of policy towards it. Extra-welfarism is also providing a theoretical basis upon which usable output measures can be derived.

Ultimately, however, neither approach can yield final answers. Each provides an economic framework on which to build empirical studies answering questions set by those with policy responsibility. It seems to me that health policy raises questions arising from the character of health, health care, and the feelings people have about both, that extra-welfarism, by not being bound by the traditional restrictions of Paretianism, can better address.

Part Three:

Ethics, Need and Equity

8

Economics, economists and ethics in health care[8]

Introduction

It is timely to have a snapshot of what economists have (and have had) to say about some key ethical and value-judgemental issues that arise in financing and providing health care subject to resource constraints. The picture should convey what economists think about their approaches to these questions as well as the substantive things they have to say about them. While the questions are timeless, the timeliness is particular, in that economics has now come of age as one of the key disciplines that underpin a good deal of policy– at least in the UK. The recent white paper, *The NHS Plan: a Plan for Investment, a Plan for Reform* (Department of Health, 2000) devoted a whole chapter (3) to a discussion of the pros and cons of alternative means of funding health care in the UK, in which the ethics of both efficiency and equity were reviewed for the first time in such a document. Moreover, the National Institute for Health and Clinical Excellence (NICE) is a key element in the UK government's reforms of the National Health Service (NHS) in England and Wales, and it employs economics explicitly in its appraisal of technologies for possible use in the NHS and in its clinical guideline development programme.

---

8   This article appeared first as Culyer, A.J., 2001. Economics and ethics in health care. *Journal of Medical Ethics* 27, 217-222. It has been adapted and shortened.

It therefore seems appropriate to review how it is that economists set about the ethical issues that arise, partly to encourage wider professional participation and partly to support the increasing lay participation in health care decision making at all levels in the UK by making explicit and accessible what may otherwise be hidden within arcane processes and be too technical to enable wider dialogue. Another reason is that economists (or, come to that, other professional groups) are not qualified to make the value judgements that are embodied in public policy decisions. They are good at identifying the necessity for making value judgements and at spelling out the nature of the value judgements that are needed. They are often forced to make value judgements in the absence of any other more appropriate mechanism for making them, but value judgements made in this way must be seen as provisional, or as cockshies to focus the attention of others better qualified to engage with the issues. Such value judgements cannot be regarded as authoritative or as having been arrived at through an authoritative process. A third reason for a contemporary review is that economists, along with many others, have recently devoted much thought to the question of equity, both in general theorising about it and in the context of national and international programmes which have increasingly come to be seen as needing to address issues of equity through explicit analysis.

The kinds of value judgement with which economists have been mostly concerned relate to the objectives of health care systems, to distributive justice, and to ways of resolving clashes between efficiency (maximising something subject to resource constraints) and equity (distributive fairness). A good example of the first of these is the question of what health services are *for*. The usual approach adopted by economists is to assume that the objective is a specific but weak form of utilitarianism, so that the test of an improvement in social welfare becomes the Paretian one of whether any change can be made that (after compensation via market and other transactions) increases an individual's welfare without reducing anyone else's. If so, the change ought to be made (it would increase efficiency); if not, the change ought or ought not to be made – the test cannot tell since it does not allow interpersonal welfare comparisons. It is silent, hence the aforementioned "weakness" of this brand of utilitarianism. Many health economists, however, adopt a different approach to the social maximand. Instead of postulating a Pareto-style utilitarian objective, they are more empirical, drawing on evidence about what it seems that those with "legitimate" authority (such as government ministers?) seem to think the objective ought to be. They are also much less squeamish about making interpersonal comparisons. Using this approach, health economists have tended to take, as an approximation to the objective, the maximisation of "health" or "health gain", which are oft-stated ministerial objectives. There are two ethical issues that immediately arise (and about which most health economists have been very explicit): one is the question of what indeed the objective ought to be (and the related question of what or who is to be regarded as an "authoritative" source) but the other is the question of what "health" or "health gain" is to be taken as meaning.

In the case of the latter question, the typical approach is reductionist and the following "ought" questions arise (I make no claims to exhaustiveness here). Ought it to be about human physical and mental functioning? Which aspects of functioning ought to be taken into account? How ought they to be scaled in terms of "better" or "worse"? How "strong" ought the scaling measurement to be (ordinal or cardinal)? How ought different ratings of different aspects be combined or traded off? What score ought to be attached to combinations of ratings? Ought the resultant scored combinations to be discounted when they relate to future health states and, if so, at what discount rate? Ought they to be further discounted for uncertainty and, if so, how? How ought any aggregations across individuals be done? More specifically, what weight ought to be attached to rated health states accruing to the relatively healthy compared to the relatively sick, young relative to old, rich relative to poor, chronic sufferers compared to acute, and so on? As the list makes clear, questions of distributive fairness lurk even within a question that began as one about efficiency.

Long history of normative health economics

The ethical questions of how best to finance health care and regulate its production and distribution have a long history in health economics and, indeed, may be said to have been the questions that set the subject going (eg Arrow, 1963). Economists have been divided on the "right" answers to these questions, broadly falling into "libertarian" and "collectivist" camps (these are very loose terms) – that is, when they go beyond mere economics and engage in advocacy. See Towse (1995) for an example of such a division, Culyer, Maynard and Williams, 1982, for relative objectivity and Culyer and Evans, 1996 (chapter 5 here), for a scolding.

In contrast to this "high level" sort of ethical debate, it is easy to see that the increasing explicitness of health care decision making (albeit still at quite a high level, organisationally speaking) will inevitably focus attention on difficult ethical posers that were formerly fudged. Explicitness is largely taken for granted by economists as a desideratum. How some of these 'ought' issues can be explicitly addressed is well illustrated by NICE. NICE is required to make recommendations to the NHS as to the medical technologies that ought to be used to maximise health gain, and it develops authoritative clinical guidelines for medical and other practitioners. Cost-effectiveness is a major consideration in both these required activities. The most widely used measure of health gain is the Quality Adjusted Life-Year (QALY), which has the advantage of enabling inter-technology comparisons to be made. As a first approximation, maximising health gain entails setting the marginal cost per QALY as near as possible to equality across all technologies.

Thus, technologies with a "low" marginal cost per QALY are to be preferred to those with a "high" marginal cost per QALY. The logic is straightforward: if resources were to be transferred from a high to a low cost per QALY technology, with a given budget for the NHS, overall health gain would rise and would continue to rise until (at the margin) the cost per QALY for each conceivable technology was brought into equality. If health maximisation is an ethical objective, then the use of such a method is also ethical (provided, of course, it is done in a way that does not violate other ethical desiderata). Over time (and it may be only a very short time), it is apparent that there will emerge a marginal cost per QALY that becomes a kind of threshold. A technology lying above it (at the margin) will not be recommended. Expectations about what can be expected from increased spending will become much more focused and policy too will become much more focused as confidence in any estimated threshold rises. The UK experiment with clinical governance is essentially concerned with just such a focus: clinical governance is a procedural means of assuring central budget-holders that additional expenditures will generate real improvements in health, rather than simply create rents for those who provide care while perpetuating inefficient and probably inequitable resource allocations.

Creation of the NICE Citizens Council

NICE also confronts explicitly the question of which values are to be adopted in QALY (or any other) outcome measures. In the UK, the setting up of a Citizens' Council was motivated by just such a consideration. The idea here is that important matters of ethical judgement (of which the ethics embodied in QALYs must surely count as amongst the most important) ought to be tackled by a representative sample of the general population. This form of "citizens' jury" is thus seen as one answer to the question of the "authoritative" source of value judgements.

Dearth of evidence

NICE's decision making will also inevitably cause it to confront possible clashes between efficiency and distributive fairness. Whereas ethicists, like economists, are likely to have considered such conflicts mainly in the abstract, or at least in imaginary circumstances, NICE decision makers have to consider them in concrete circumstances. NICE's inheritance has included a dearth of evidence on cost-effectiveness and only patchy evidence of inequity. Dearth of evidence itself generates ethical dilemmas.

Consider a scenario in which a particular treatment for a chronic condition has had an unknown cost-effectiveness and, as a consequence, is available in some localities but not in others because different local decision makers have reached their own conclusions as to whether to fund it. Suppose NICE determines that the cost-effectiveness of the treatment lies well above any threshold cost per QALY. The recommendation on efficiency grounds is clear: do not use. Suppose, now, that a prime principle of distributive fairness is a form of horizontal equity: persons in like need ought to be treated in the same way. Three possibilities now suggest themselves: (1) withdraw the treatment from those already receiving it; (2) retain the treatment for those receiving it but do not prescribe it for new patients; (3) allow all to receive it for whom it is judged appropriate by their doctors, even though it is inefficient. Which option should be chosen? Economics cannot provide the answer though it may provide some relevant information to aid those who have to answer the question. Neither can medicine or epidemiology provide it, since no practitioner of these sciences is especially qualified to make social value judgements, as distinct from clinical judgements, on behalf of the rest of us.

There are a great many attractions to settling ethical matters such as these by reference to an "authoritative" source of value. One is that it opens an ethical debate about what kind of "authority" ought to exist to guide those empowered to make practical decisions about procedures. Another is that it defines roles: the professions involved in making the scientific judgements can provide the essential contextual information to inform those authorised to make, or advise on, the value judgements. Another is that it stops scientists from imposing their own value judgements, using their scientific expertise to lend a spurious authority to their values and preferences. But the principal advantage is that such procedures are open and hence challengeable as regards both procedure and the outcome of the procedure.

Evidence-informed policy and evidence-informed medical practice need, most economists would agree, an evidential base for their value-judgemental content. The ballot box serves only for the broadest of values. At more specific levels, the interaction between those whom it is decided ought to determine the values required for a particular purpose and those with technical knowledge, understanding and the ability to specify (at least some of) the key value judgemental issues, seems to beckon in a new era of what might be termed "empirical ethics". This is not "applied ethics", in its usual sense, but the quantification of particular kinds of ethical value.

Some examples

Economists have played a notable role in ushering in this new era – and in defining the issues that empirical ethics might usefully address. Maynard (2001) is a thought-provoking attack on the implicitness of so much ethics in health care and the arbitrary outcomes that arise in the absence of systematic facing-up to the central issues involved in allocating health care resources: being clear about objectives and analytical about the means of achieving them. He argues pugnaciously for explicitness on the grounds that it is a protection against self-seeking behaviour, is more likely to deliver the objectives sought, and that without it policy makers and practitioners cannot be held to account. Bosanquet (2001) takes economists to task for not adopting a research agenda he prefers. Be that as it may, he is surely right in observing that our understanding of behaviour-governing and regulatory frameworks to promote evidence-based, cost-effective and, come to that, equitable practice is very poor.

Public vs private

A characteristic of nearly all the literature of health economics since Arrow (1963) is its focus on the demand side. Nearly all the theory used to underpin arguments for public health insurance and heavily publicly subsidised services are arguments from the demand side. None of these arguments has any bearing on the relative problems and costs of public provision versus public contracting with private (Chalkley and Malcomson, 2000, for a survey). There remains a big question on the efficiency agenda: what ought the balance between private and public provision within a public, but not necessarily publicly owned, service to be, and through what instruments might an efficient balance be attained? Viewed in terms of outcomes, the ethics in this question are primarily to do with the ethics of efficiency itself: the efficient balance (that is, the balance that maximises the value of outcomes for given resources) and the equitable balance (that is, the balance that delivers equity objectives). This is an interesting and important agenda in a topical area that is still largely dominated by political slogans and untested, usually biased, presumptions.

Market failures

The demand-side nature of the economics of public finance for health care is well illustrated in Hurley (2001). He explores three approaches to the welfare economics of health care: classical utilitarianism, extra-welfarism and Rawlsian contractarianism. He advocates an instrumentalist approach to the meaning of the "need" for health care – the entity asserted to be needed must be needed for an ethical end (such as human flourishing) and the entity must be effective (possibly cost-effective) in serving that ethical end. He identifies the market failures that can prevent the attainment of an efficient allocation of resources for meeting needs as well as the equity desiderata that are hard for market methods to deliver, most of which stem from the universal truth that wealth and health are positively correlated in societies, which means that provision has to be directed at need rather than demand and that health insurance has to find a way of reversing the natural state in which those least able to pay for it are most in need of it. He makes a strong claim on behalf of economics as a taxonomising device: clarifying concepts in relevant ways, breaking them up into specific manageable issues in a classic reductionist fashion, quantifying them where possible, and offering them up as topics for multidisciplinary inquiry.

Rice (2001) considers the standard utility-maximising approach of welfare economics as applied to health care as supplemented by liberal and libertarian arguments for distributive fairness in the context of the rights of individuals to autonomy in choice. This is contrasted with views that give health care (or, perhaps, health) the special status of a primary good and emphasize greater equality at the price of a sacrifice of individual autonomy. Efficiency arguments, let alone equity ones, for market-based freedom of choice fail on grounds of externality – which goes to show that even economic reductionists can provide examples of the whole being greater (or smaller) than the sum of the parts! There is a strong case to be made on both sides but he concludes that one primary good (health) trumps another (freedom from interference) on the ground that endowed allocations of health are inherently arbitrary, as are efforts to separate ill health into that which is self-induced (unworthy of public support) and that which is random (worthy of public support). Not explicitly stated, though it seems implicit, is another ground: that health trumps freedom because it is usually a necessary condition to have the one in order to be able to enjoy the other.

Dowie (2001) uses the ideas of cost-effectiveness and QALYs to open up some ethical issues in both the way health economists do their work and communications across disciplines. The ground is cleared by an uncompromising classification of health economists as "analytical consequentialists" (being neither intuitionists nor absolutists) and by making clear that the oft-misunderstood concept of opportunity cost means health gain deliberately forgone as an act of choice. With this uncompromising opening, he then dissects the objections that have been made to the economic approach in the contexts of both efficiency and equity and concludes that much of the opposition has actually taken the form of a search to achieve a particular form of ascendancy through the application of double standards. Thus, those adopting intuitive approaches to questions of ethics in health care have required those taking an analytical approach (ie economists) to convey the analytical case in intuitive terms (or else they judge it to have failed). Those approaching ethical questions in health with an analytical approach are usually adept at identifying analytical and empirical weaknesses (that is, after all, why they are analysts and they are usually much better at it than the intuitionist opposition). These are then held up as "weaknesses" by the intuitionists, even though their own method masks any specific "weaknesses". Not being analytical, intuitionists are, moreover, not usually very good at tackling weaknesses, for example, by turning them into strengths, or identifying the circumstances under which the weaknesses are likely to mislead, or even cripple, and are hence not to be used.

Empiricism

Williams (2001) argues for an empirical approach to answering the key ethical questions that arise in fairly high level decision making contexts, where ethical impasses are often reached, such as how efficiency and equity ought to be traded-off when they conflict, or which ethical basis for assessing equity ought to be adopted. He observes that views about ethical issues are rarely simply binary (for example, "important", "not important") but reflect strengths of view which vary according to "how much" of an inefficiency or inequity may exist, and its character. They vary across individuals and for each individual over time. The issues then become (again) those of identifying those who are to be the appropriate "authorities", or who may have the "authority" to make recommendations to a higher "authority", and of devising experimental methods to reveal the trade-offs that the selected subjects make when confronted with actual choices. He reviews and rejects a number of objections to "quantification", for example because it lacks sensitivity to the "infinite variety of human experience", and is "mechanistic", which hark back to Dowie's discussion of intuitionist objections to the analytical approach.

Territorial equity

Rice and Smith (2001) examine territorial equity, such as the ethical issues arising in the allocation of budgets to health care commissioners in the UK, or regions in other countries such as New Zealand. They refer to the extensive evidence on variations between areas in terms of health and intervention rates that seem to be explained only by region of residence or treatment and have little relation to any underlying epidemiology, morbidity or clinical need. The issues that arise are problems in both vertical and horizontal equity. They argue for capitation-based systems that distinguish between "legitimate" determinants and "illegitimate" determinants of what expenditure ought to be. Historical utilisation is criticised as a determinant because it fails to take account of need, much of which may have been unmet (to use historical utilisation would imply that inherited unmet needs are unimportant). They conclude that policies to reduce arbitrary geographical inequalities can best be couched in terms of those that tackle variations in the quality of care, variations in the accessibility of care and factors outside the control of health care agencies.

Clinical governance or other forms of performance management may be the primary method for dealing with quality variations; supplementary resource allocations may be the most effective way of tackling variations in accessibility. Tackling variation may require explicit preferential access (and resourcing) and the abandonment of clinical need as an indicator of regional differences in need, together with a more joined-up approach that addresses a wider set of policies directed at health rather than just the health care services themselves.

Wagstaff (2001) addresses an even higher level equity problem: the problem facing the World Bank as to how best to help countries improve the health of the poor and reduce the impoverishing effects of illness. The character of the issues is not, however, so very different from those discussed by other authors: the question of trade-off (here, for example, between overall increases in health and reductions in the differences between the health of the rich and poor) and the use of analysis (here, for example, the properties of different weighting schemes and the degree to which they meet ethical distributional criteria). A matter also touched on by Rice and Smith relates to the question of whether all inequalities are equally bad, to which one answer appears to be that those that matter are those that arise from differences in the constraining (full) prices people confront rather than the choices they make when they have the same opportunities. These "prices" are not just a question of money but also relate to time costs, distances from health care facilities and a host of other factors that cause substantial differences in the opportunities confronting different people in the same country. Such considerations also raise the issue of whether policies directed at health improvements and reductions in health inequity might be better implemented through poverty reduction programmes and other non-health care means, rather than through health care.

There are (even higher) levels of equity to be addressed, for example, inter-country allocation – and the extent to which it is proper to take account of the integrity of local governance structures and practices, the degree of local "ownership" and control that is both fair and effective (and the associated trade-offs that may be inherent here). The issue of public versus private provision in the context of a publicly financed health care system is also raised, as is the Rawlsian issue of whether international agency support that improves the lot of the well-off as a means of improving that of the poorly-off is ethically justifiable (supposing, of course, that there was a firm evidence base for believing that it actually works in practice).

Cost-effectiveness principles

Weinstein (2001) tackles the trade-off issue at a lower level: that of the physician as gate-keeper. At a sufficiently high level, the decisions are not about identified individuals whose personal circumstances are known (perhaps intimately) to the decision maker but about whole classes of persons, such as those in a particular social class, or income category, or those having particular family responsibilities, or having a particular disease. At this level, questions are about the terms on which services are to be made available and to whom. The benefits to one group are compared (at the margin) with those to another (again at the margin) in order to maximise something (such as health) and to secure an equitable distribution of something (such as access or equity). Even if all these issues have been settled in some way deemed to be satisfactory, there remains the issue of how similar types of resource-constrained decision are to be made at the level of the individual, for example, comparing the likely benefit to the patient in front of the doctor with the potential benefit to one who has yet to appear. Weinstein contrasts the agency role of a physician seeking the best for her/his own patients with the physician in a different agency role: seeking the best for society as a whole. His analysis suggests that cost-effectiveness principles, consistently applied, can generate guidelines for decisions that do not involve the doctor in invidious breach of the trusting relationship with patients. He suggests that this is made much more effective if doctors' choices are governed by well-designed incentives (for example, capitation payment may be preferable to fee-for-service), suitably designed budgets (in order to reduce the prevalence of sub-optimising), well-designed clinical guidelines (coupled with a degree of permitted flexibility in their use) and a major attempt at public education and public enlistment in the business of what in the UK would be called clinical governance. It is likely that the kind of "buy-in" he seeks is more easily obtained in the UK and other countries with a tradition of more-or-less open acknowledgment of resource limitations in health care than in the USA.

Finally Culyer (2001) discusses conflicts between concepts of equity. A common focus of economists has been on the potential conflict between equity and efficiency. There are, however, important conflicts between equity concepts, which even a pluralist approach cannot accommodate. Within one approach to equity (meeting needs equitably) the ambiguities of the term "need" are explored and a resolution suggested. Some of the other key issues needing to be resolved are identified, their significance explained, and their consequences for policy outlined.

There are many aspects of medical ethics that economists have not actively considered and, of those they have, the ones discussed here are but a subset. I hope, nonetheless, that the range is sufficiently broad to encourage non-economist readers to enter into more effective dialogues with economists. One reassuring thing ought to be clear: health economists have a good track record of collaboration with the practitioners of other disciplines and recognise the need for such collaboration if the research programmes to which they aspire are to be developed as well as they ought to be. Moreover, there are now policy customers out there for the sort of work to be done, so the environment could scarcely be more conducive to such work than it currently is.

9

Need: the idea won't do – but we still need it[9]

Health care is a commonly cited example of a service that ought to be distributed according to need; but, if need is to be a practical idea, useful in helping people to allocate health care resources more efficiently and equitably, it has to have particular characteristics, the absence of any one of which makes it virtually useless. Unfortunately, in the common contexts in which the term has been taken seriously (political slogan-mongering and, on quite a different plane, philosophical discourse) at least one of these necessary conditions is always absent.

The conditions proposed are these:

1.   its value-content should be up-front and easily interpretable

---

9   This chapter is an amalgam of articles appearing originally as: Culyer, A.J., 1995. Need: the idea won't do but we still need it, (Editorial). *Social Science and Medicine* 40, 727-730; and Culyer, A.J., Need an instrumental view. In: Ashcroft, R., Dawson, A., Draper, H., McMillan J. (eds.), *Principles of Health Care Ethics*, 2nd Edition, Chichester: Wiley, 2007, 231-238. A fuller and more detailed account of the reasoning in this article is Culyer, AJ. and Wagstaff, A. (1993) Equity and equality in health and health care, *Journal of Health Economics*, 12: 431-457 (reprinted in N Barr (ed.) *Economic Theory and the Welfare State*, Cheltenham: Edward Elgar, 2001, 231-257 and in AJ Culyer (Ed.) *Health Economics: Critical Perspectives on the World Economy*, London: Routledge, 2006, 483-509).

2.   it should be directly derived from the objective(s) of the health care system

3.   it should be capable of empirical application in issues of horizontal and vertical distribution

4.   it should be service and person specific

5.   it should enable a straightforward link to be made to resources

6.   it should not, if used as a distributional principle, produce manifestly inequitable results.

The general context is, I shall assume, one of fairly high level resource allocation decisions, that is, levels like those of governments, professional organizations, managed care organizations and third party payers, above one-to-one decision-making in the professional-patient relationship. My conclusion will be that there are helpful and not so helpful concepts of need but that none is *particularly* helpful in making resource allocation decisions.

Talk of need is important for a number of reasons. One is simply that one ought to be as clear as possible about what one means, especially when using nouns that resonate strongly. Another is that 'need' has been and is used both in the slogans used by politicians, patient interest groups and ideologues as well as in more careful academic discourse, but it seems unlikely that the same meaning and significance attach to the word in each of these contexts. Yet another is that the word is commonly used by those actually involved in the process of managing and delivering health care but, again, one doubts that each profession attaches quite the same meaning and significance to it. Finally, need is often advocated and, indeed, accepted as an appropriate moral basis for prioritising choices about resource allocations within health care systems, so one talks of meeting needs efficiently and meeting them equitably or fairly. The last of these uses requires precision and even quantification to be practically useful, and it is that usage with which I am primarily concerned here: what is a need and how ought need be interpreted and used (if at all) in matters of health care resource allocation?

The existence of a need seems always to imply an absence of something, together with an implication that the something that is lacking is not trivial either on account of the severity of the deprivation, which is exemplified in the frequent coupling of 'poor' with 'needy', or, possibly, of the extreme attractiveness of the state achieved if the need is met. However, mere absence is plainly not enough, for there is a wide gap between what we generally imply when using the word 'need' compared to 'demand', yet 'demand' is no less a response to the absence of something. This chapter therefore concentrates on what seems to be special about 'need'.

The distinction between satisfactory (according to canons of fairness and efficiency) allocations of *health care* to people (not just patients but also whole populations, especially in programmes of primary prevention) and satisfactory distributions of *health* is fundamental. It is a common carelessness to assume that there is a one-to-one correspondence between health care (or, more narrowly, medical care) and health. It takes little thought, however, to realise that the one is the hoped-for product of the other and that there is no automaticity about the relationship (Rachlis and Kushner, 1989). Health care can be harmful to health; it can be irrelevant; it can be effective but only at prohibitive cost (when it is more satisfactory to devote resources to other forms of health care or, indeed, to something altogether different, even the development of regional sports facilities). There are large variations in the rates of medical intervention, not only between different health care systems but also within them (for example, Bunker 1970; McPherson et al 1982; Wennberg and Gittesohn 1982; McPherson 1988; Sanders et al 1989). These variations often reflect what has become known as a 'surgical signature' in which the uncertainties, subjective judgements and preferences of particular physicians vary. They are sometimes indicators of wasteful use of resources and at best suggest that in practice there may be considerable empirical uncertainty as to what really is needed.

The concept of need has commanded the attention of philosophers, most significantly Barry (1965), Braybrooke (1987), Daniels (1985), Flew (1977), Gillon (1985), Liss (1993), Miller (1976), Thomson (1987), Weale (1978) and Wiggins (1987). Some have taken an extremely simple idea of need as 'absence'. For example, both Williams (1962) and Gillon (1985) suggest that people who are more ill than others have greater need. While it is obvious that they have a relative absence of health, it is not altogether clear what it is that they need other than health itself. What if no treatment exists or, if it did, but would make only a tiny improvement to their condition? Even if there is a treatment, there may be considerable argument about its efficacy (that is, the way it works under ideal, usually experimental, conditions) and even more argument about its effectiveness (that is, the way it can be expected to work in practice), for which indications it ought to be used (even those for which, if it is a drug, it has been licensed) and for which patients. The idea that a deficit of health generates a need for ineffective or absurdly costly care seems preposterously wasteful. The identification of need at the aggregate level of whole communities with either morbidity or mortality (absolute or relative) has been common among economists (for example, Le Grand, 1978; O'Donnell and Propper, 1991; Wagstaff et al, 1991) and raises similar issues to those just mentioned.

Need vs demand

An early attempt to distinguish need and demand was made by Matthew (1971). He argued thus: "The 'need' for medical care must be distinguished from the 'demand' for care and from the use of services or 'utilization'. A need for medical care exists when an individual has an illness or disability for which there is an effective and acceptable treatment or cure. It can be defined either in terms of the type of illness or disability causing the need, or of the treatment or facilities for treatment required to meet it. A demand for care exists when an individual considers that he has a need and wishes to receive care. Utilization occurs when an individual actually receives care. Need is not necessarily expressed as demand, and demand is not necessarily followed by utilization while, on the other hand, there can be demand and utilization without real underlying need for the particular service used" (p. 27). This approach has been characterised by Williams (1978) as a supply concept. As Williams puts it: "a 'need' exists so long as the marginal productivity of some treatment input is positive" (p. 33). It is plain that the marginal product in question is not to be equated with the usual underlying maximand of demand theory (that is, utility) but something else, not quite defined by Matthew (1971) but apparently health or at least some outcome which someone (again not identified precisely) considers "effective and acceptable".

Bradshaw (1977) adopted a more synthetic approach. He developed a four-fold classification of need:

• Normative need – that which the expert or professional, administrator or social scientist defines as need in any given situation. A standard is laid down and is compared with the standard that actually exists, the difference being what is needed.

• Felt need – people who do not have something are asked whether they feel they need it. It is an expression of hypothetical demand.

• Expressed need – felt need expressed by behaviour, as when a consultation is sought or when one is placed on a waiting list; need turned into action.

• Comparative need – the difference between two individuals or groups who are otherwise the same, but one of which is receiving a service and the other not, the latter being 'in need'.

Each of these definitions is descriptive and empirical, and each clearly captures something of the 'absence' element of need, essentially based on a with-and-without comparison, but, in comparative need, having the additional twist of comparing people with and people without. The definitions are not philosophically normative. Their truth is tested by asking for the opinions of either professional groups or patients, or by looking at their behaviour. Having these characteristics, need is devoid of persuasive power; there is no particular ground offered, for example, for distinguishing it from demand and, indeed, Bradshaw's concept of felt need is similar to the idea of demand used in studies of contingent valuation and willingness to pay (for example, Bateman et al, 2002). So the question arises: why ought we to feel impelled to meet any of the needs thus described? This question takes us beyond the descriptive, technical relationship between health care (input) and health (outcome) (or changes in the one and consequential changes in the other) into the matter of the valuation of the outcomes. It also raises the question of who ought to be deciding such matters. Plainly, it does not follow, just because doctors, nurses and other clinically qualified professionals like physiotherapists may be relatively expert at predicting the consequences for health of various inputs into the process of health care, that they are also expert at assessing the worth of the outcome and of outcomes forgone.

If the productivity approach addresses need essentially from the supply side, the valuation of outcomes is plainly a demand-side matter. It is a characteristic of the concept of need suggested here that a useful concept will entail both a supply side and a demand-side element: supply-side because what is needed must be productive in terms of promoting health, and demand-side because productive effects have value and we must address the question, 'how much value?' Not all care is equally productive nor is all equally productive care equally valued. One must tread carefully here for the standard economic theory of value is built on the idea of *preference*. Whether the analysis is positive (explanatory) or normative (prescriptive), preferences are the fundamental sources from which value is derived (see, for example, Boadway and Bruce, 1984). In the case of need, the source of value is far more ambiguous, though it is plainly not mere preferences, and it will need careful examination, particularly in a context that often asserts that needs trump demands. The idea that some considerations trump others is frequently found in non-utilitarian philosophical literature. It goes against the grain of economic thinking on the grounds that it denies the possibility of trade-off. For example, it entails the view that the meeting of the least of needs ought invariably to dominate the meeting of the greatest of demands and, should there be a hierarchy of needs, that the least of a high order need ought to be met before the greatest of a lower order need. This form of lexical prioritisation is well suited to the organization of telephone directories but unattractive and unhelpful in practical policy discussions of 'what should we do?'

Need: absolute and relative

Some usage of 'need' is not only categorical, like Bradshaw's typology or the identification of need with morbidity or mortality, but also absolute, with the implication that the need described ought, therefore, to be met absolutely and regardless of any other claims there might be on resources. One difficulty with absolutism over need is that health is not itself absolute. It is a variable, for example, in functioning, activities of daily living, experience of pain, mobility and longevity, mental state and it is also largely culturally determined, both with regard to the pathologies regarded as detrimental to living in a particular community at a particular time and with regard to the social construction of living. An extreme example of this is pinta, a bacterial skin disease so prevalent among some South American tribes that it was not regarded as a disease at all: the few single men not afflicted were regarded as pathological to the point of being excluded from marriage. So in such tribes' culture there can be no need for a treatment for pinta; that would not be the case, however, in Scotland (if pinta were ever to arise there). Another sort of extremism to which an absolute approach is prone is illustrated by Harris (1987): "life saving has priority over life-enhancement and... we should first allocate resources to those areas where they are immediately needed to save life and only when this is done should the remainder be allocated to alleviating nonfatal conditions" (p. 120). Thus the smallest possibility of the shortest extension to the most miserable of lives is to receive priority over the most sure and massive improvement in the quality of a life already expected to be long.

Need interpreted instrumentally

The peculiar power of need resides in the combination of two elements, one empirical and the other ethical. The empirical element is the idea of necessity. If something is to be said to be needed, then it must be necessary for some purpose. This is an empirical matter because it is a matter of fact whether the thing in question really is necessary. In medical research, the generally accepted gold standard for knowing whether something is necessary (though it is not a standard that can always be achieved) is the randomised controlled trial, a scientifically designed method for testing the link between an intervention and its alleged effects and for minimizing the intrusion of confounding variables which might bias the attribution of cause and consequence both as to sign (positive or negative) and to effect size (large or small). In popular parlance, the question is 'does it work?' and 'how well does it work?' Positive answers to these questions do not, however, imply that the intervention in question really is necessary. After all, there may be other interventions that also work, or that work even better than the one on which we are currently focusing, or that work similarly but at a much lower cost. In such cases we plainly cannot describe the one in question as necessary because there are substitutes for it, of which one may actually be the intervention of choice. 'Necessity' is nonetheless about the productivity of health care in terms of health outcomes. It is a supply-side concept.

The ethical element concerns values (as does demand) and derives from the association of need with the moral idea that needs ought to be met, at least in part. Now the oughtness of need might be fixed in a number of ways. One view might be to locate it in the ethical character of the end served by meeting it. Thus I, the author, may cheekily assert that I have a need for an SL-Class Mercedes Roadster in order to promote a dashing image (and impress my students) but this object carries little moral weight, even if it is true that my image would become more dashing and that my students would be naively impressed. But if, instead, the end served is better health, and I would escape from a bed-bound and pain-racked life, and there is indeed a procedure that will deliver me in the way described, then the ethics of the claim about need changes in a way that depends not only on the empirical truth of the link between the thing needed and the outcome of the need being met but also, and critically, on the *value* of the outcome, so it is the significance of the end that distinguishes need from preference. This is a demand-side concept, though there is no particular reason to suppose that the value appropriately to be attached to an outcome is based (or solely based) on a person's preferences. The coupling of something being necessary for something else to happen with the ethical value of that consequence is what I mean by the instrumental idea of need.

The view that need is an instrumental concept has been strongly argued by Barry (1965) and Flew (1977). It has been opposed by others (for example, Miller, 1976; Thomson, 1987) on the grounds that some statements using the word 'need' are intrinsic and elliptical, or imply an objective which would be trivial to make explicit. For example, the statement: 'surgeons need manual dexterity' is hardly elucidated by asking 'why', for the answer might well be that 'surgeons need manual dexterity in order to be surgeons'. Similarly the statement: 'Anthony needs open heart surgery' is hardly elucidated by adding: 'if he is to live'. But this is to use trivial examples to cast doubt on the usefulness of the concept. It is easy to think of nontrivial examples that are still service-and person-specific and these usually require that one adds prepositions: something (like a specific medical act) has to be needed (is necessary) for something else to be accomplished. We must ask also for what it is needed (necessary). And we must also ask for whom it is needed (necessary). The first requirement is crucial in health care, for it directs attention towards the question of whether in fact (or whether it is probable that) the act in question will have the effects (for the better) expected. As so much in medical (and health) care is of unknown effectiveness (or is even of known ineffectiveness), directing attention in this way alerts one to the possibility that someone may even be seriously ill without there being any reasonable prospect of medical care effectively changing their characteristics for the better. In such cases, whatever else they need, they do not need the sort of health or medical services that might be available. Too many unsubstantiated assertions of need assume, rather than enquire whether, the acts in question really are necessary.

The 'reasonable prospect' I have in mind is one judged by people, including scientific experts, who have examined the matter via, say, randomised controlled trials, overviews or meta-analyses. One should ask for what it is needed because there ought to be some more ultimate good from which the need in question derives its moral force. It should be person-specific or, at the planning and management level, group-specific as one must be able to identify who it is that needs whatever is asserted to be needed. One can trivialise these requirements as in the cases of Anthony and the surgeon, but the more precise statement "I need prophylactic lignocaine following my heart attack" may be false if I fear the risk of early mortality more than I value the prevention of arrhythmias (Yadav and Zipes, 2004). And the statement "I need intra-gastric hypothermia for my gastric ulcer" is plainly false; for gastric freezing will do me no good at all and may do me harm (Edmonson, 1989).

A major objection to unsubstantiated assertions of need is therefore that they assume that, rather than inquire whether, the thing alleged to be needed really is necessary. Modern technology may indeed make surgery less dependent on manual dexterity. Therefore, if we are to stipulate the skills surgeons ought to have, it becomes important to be explicit in determining how surgeons should be trained-and re-trained. Or, if we are deciding on Anthony's treatment, we really do need to know whether open heart surgery is appropriate for him, what the risks are, what the probability of success is, and what alternative actions might be taken. Moreover, these assertions assume that the objective really is the one sought. If the operation is likely to extend Anthony's life, will it do so only at the cost of a much lower quality of life? Or, how small must the probability of peri-operative death be before Anthony judges the risk worth taking? The assertion that this or that is needed, even though its effectiveness may be disputed or unknown and even though the end sought may rank low in the priorities of those allocating resources or receiving services, is a commonplace of medical politics.

Effectiveness or cost-effectiveness?

It is rare to have a fixed and unique technology of treatment. It seems absurd to suppose that, of two procedures, each with the same expected resource implications but one with a much better expected outcome available, the one with the poorer outcome is as equally needed as the other. Conversely, of two procedures having the same expected outcomes but differing in the amount of resources used, it seems no less absurd to consider the costlier one as equally needed as the other. It makes more sense to say in the former case, that the less productive procedure is no longer necessary (needed) because another, more effective and no more costly one is available and, with regard to the latter, that the more resource-intensive procedure can hardly be said to be necessary (needed) when there is an alternative that will achieve the same outcome but with fewer resources.

It is not absurd to talk of a need for an effective procedure that does not exist. People may have a disease for which there is no treatment of any kind, or they may have acquired a chronic resistance to the only effective treatment there is. Such people have needs and we know the character of the things that are needed but they do not have needs that can be met (yet) and they do not pose an issue in resource allocation (apart, possibly, from resource allocation to research).

143

Need and the flourishing life

Even if health care is indeed effective, it hardly follows that the need ought to be met, let alone provided for, at public expense. Whatever is morally compelling about a need comes from the end served. A need for health services exists only if there are grounds for believing that these services will promote health, restore it, prevent ill-health or postpone death. These are the principal benefits sought from health care (less critical benefits include reassurance, legitimisation of status for purposes of receipt of benefit and hotel services), and it follows that a need for health care can exist only when there is a capacity to benefit in one or more of these ways. More specifically, the need is for the service that might generate the benefit and the nature of the benefit must be sufficiently weighty, ethically speaking, to justify the use of so persuasive a word as 'need' rather than, say, 'preference' or 'demand'.

One can conceive of a hierarchy of goals, especially in the context of health care. One may, for example, speak of health as being needed. The weighty end served by this means might be a 'flourishing life' (Wiggins, 1984), or a 'vital purpose' (Nordenfeldt, 1984) or realizing one's 'life's projects' (Williams, 1973), or being able to operate within the 'normal opportunity range' (Daniels, 1985). But if one speaks, as I do here, of health care being needed, the principal goal in question is, I assert, the improvement of health. What then gives health the special ethical character to warrant the use of need rather than demand for health care?

Le Grand's (1991) answer to this is that people demand health care because they fall ill and that, since whether or not they fall ill is *not within their control*, the demand for health care is qualitatively different from the demand for other commodities where ethical considerations do not feature prominently, if at all. It is for this reason, contends Le Grand, that the term 'need' is applied to health care but not to, say, televisions. But this does not seem to get to the heart of the distinction sought. There is, to be sure, a large stochastic component to the demand for health care. But individuals' health, and hence their demand for health care, is also affected by their behaviour. Once this is accepted, it becomes hard to use this line of argument to draw a meaningful distinction between health care and other commodities whose demand is also subject to uncertainty. An individual's demand for automobile spares, for example, is also highly stochastic, but it is also influenced by the way the individual drives and how carefully they look after the vehicle.

Tobin (1970) thought that services like health care seem to be different in that they are more *fundamental to the good life* than others, which begins to make the beginnings of an ethical grounding for need. Insofar as health is necessary for (or at the least conducive to) the more ultimate human good of flourishing, and insofar as health care is necessary for health, then the ethicality of the ultimate objective becomes transferred to the activity that can contribute to producing the ultimate good. It is that which differentiates the ethical status of health care from that of televisions.

We have now arrived at a point at which it may be seen that there are two necessary conditions that should be met when we speak of a need for a service. One is that the service in question should be cost-effective; the other is that it should be necessary for achieving a high ethical aim. Health care fits both. But *not all* health care fits. Ineffective care is not needed. Cost-ineffective care is not needed. Cost-effective care that meets mere demands without serving the higher ethical end is not needed. It is merely demanded. The definition has an ethical element (it must contribute to an ethical end) and a technical element (cost-effectiveness) which also involves ethical judgements, for example ones to do with appropriate measures of outcome that stand in operational terms for health or change in health.

Need and allocation principles

If we consider resource allocation in the context of a publicly funded or a managed care system, almost any definition of need carries the implication that a service that is not needed probably ought not to be provided, at least not at public expense. Beyond that, however, need turns out not to be an especially useful way of developing allocation criteria.

The claim that health care ought to be distributed according to need comes in two versions, due essentially to Aristotle: a horizontal version (persons in equal need should be treated the same) and a vertical version (persons in unequal need should be treated in proportion to the inequality in need). These principles do not imply that all needs ought to be met but stipulate instead the manner in which resources and needs ought to stand in relation to one another. I shall assume that resource constraints prohibit the meeting of all needs and also the meeting of any single need completely. I shall also assume that we have a well-calibrated and uncontroversial measure of health in order that we may focus on the implications of the principles without becoming entangled in the complexities (and controversies) about the validity of the construct 'health' and its measurement.

Need as ill-health

Horizontal equity requires persons having like ill-health to be treated in a similar fashion. It would plainly be silly to interpret this as requiring each to have the same resource, partly because having the same degree of ill-health does not mean each has the same disease or, even if they did, that the appropriate treatment for each would be the same. As far as vertical equity is concerned, similar considerations apply. Unless there were a coincidental correlation between ill-health and the cost of the procedures for addressing those needs, and a further correlation between ill-health and individuals' capacity to benefit from medical care (which is by no means the case, especially in extremis), the application of a formula using the principle would again cause any actual health gain to the population to be less than the potential health gain (assuming equal weights to be attached to the gains accruing to different people). The full potential is realised if provision differentially favours those needing low-cost procedures and those with high capacity to benefit from the procedures most appropriate for their condition. A difficulty with both the horizontal and vertical equity implications of considering need as ill-health arises because it is hard to see why a group that is sick can sensibly be said to need health care, irrespective of its ability to improve their health. They may need medical research, they may need comfort, and they may, most fundamentally of all, need health, but they may (or may not) need health care.

A related idea is Daniels' (1985) definition of health in terms of an individual's impairment within what he calls the 'normal opportunity range' for a person's life plans. In his view, need depends not only on the ability of health care to restore the range or compensate for its curtailment, but also on the magnitude of the existing curtailment. By this definition, someone can need health care even though health care can make no contribution to the restoration or expansion of the range. According to the definition advanced here, a need exists over the whole range of cost-effective health care, wherever the marginal product of care is positive in terms of health. Imagine that the capacity of a population to benefit from health care is ordered so that the person with the highest capacity to benefit is placed first in a parade, the person with the next highest capacity is placed second and so on until individuals with zero capacity are reached.

Only the individuals ahead of those with zero capacity are in need. Or, considering a single individual, imagine that by the application of one 'unit' of health care, a given 'pile' of health can be obtained and that we order incremental units in such a fashion that the biggest pile per unit is placed on the left, the next biggest immediately to its right, and so on until the piles have become tiny. Need exists only in the range in which the piles are visible.

Need as capacity to benefit

Capacity to benefit is the difference between what a person's health is predicted to be over a period of time, with and without care. It is not a before-and-after but a with-and-without comparison. On the face of it, capacity to benefit is a more attractive allocation principle than the mere fact of ill-health. It is not subject to the objection that it could entail allocating health care resources to people who cannot benefit from them (at least in terms of their health). It also implies that care is needed only if it is a necessary condition for the more ultimate goal to be attained. Capacity to benefit is therefore a condition for a need for health care to exist. It does not itself amount, however, to need. Despite this, capacity to benefit could plainly, at least in principle, be used as a principle for allocating health care.

But it is not immediately apparent that this is an attractive criterion. It will favour those with relatively high capacities to benefit, even if they are already relatively healthy. Conversely, in a situation where people start off with equal health, it will generate health inequality. These considerations suggest a need to dig deeper into the real distributional concern that may underlie talk about need. If, for example, that concern actually relates to the distribution of health, or ill-health, in the community, then the appropriate allocation rule would be to allocate resources neither in proportion to the prevailing distribution of ill-health nor in proportion to capacity to benefit, but in relation to the contribution made to redressing health inequalities. That contribution will depend in part on the initial distribution of ill-health and in part on capacities to benefit, but neither alone suffices. The need is for disproportionately more health for those with low health and the 'derived need' for health care will flow from the effectiveness of the technologies that are available.

Need as health care expenditure

A technological breakthrough which makes it possible to treat a particular condition at a fraction of the previous cost clearly leaves a person's capacity to benefit the same (in the sense that the improvement in health achieved by treatment is the same) whereas the amount of resources the individual needs is much reduced. This suggests that the definition of need for health care for which we seek is best conceived as the resources (or the expenditure on them) required to effect the maximum possible health improvement. In more general terms, the amount of any service that is needed is that which is sufficient to exhaust capacity to benefit. If marginal capacity to benefit is zero, need is also zero. Where marginal capacity to benefit is positive, assessment of need requires an assessment of the amount of resource required to reduce capacity to benefit to zero. This definition captures the instrumental nature of need by defining it in terms of what is needed: resources. It also relates the need for resources to the ethical objective sought (health, to enable flourishing) which gives need its special ethical status. It also defines a finite quantum of need (namely, that which exhausts capacity to benefit) without building in distributional values about how much need ought to be met, a question still to be resolved. This definition is also not subject to the objection that it could entail allocating health care resources to people who cannot benefit from them. Like the capacity to benefit concept of need, it implies that care is needed only if it is a necessary condition for the more ultimate goal to be attained. Unlike capacity to benefit, it specifies that it is health care resources that are needed.

But again it is not immediately apparent that this is an attractive criterion. It will favour those whose marginal capacity to benefit falls to zero only after very large expenditures have been incurred. The application of such a distributional rule could, as in the previous cases, increase the inequality of the distribution of (ill-) health and, again, does not address what may be the real underlying concern of distributive fairness in health care: promoting a fairer distribution of health.

None of the three allocation principles discussed so far is in conflict with the principle of efficiency, in the sense of using resources to maximise the impact of health care on the health of those receiving it (see Culyer and Wagstaff, 1993; Culyer, 2006). The conflict in question arises in health care policy chiefly if one seeks to apply the efficiency criterion across individuals in the manner of classical utilitarianism and makes the value-laden assumption that increments of health, however measured, count for the same whoever gets them. Assuming this is to make a very strong, and not obviously acceptable, distributional value judgement. It is this judgement that creates the conflict with other distributional criteria.

Five important implications of need

The instrumental approach to need has several important and potentially radical implications, not only for the way we speak about need but also for the ways in which we use it in resource allocation decisions. First, need and ill-health are not synonyms and one should not imagine that in measuring the latter, one is also measuring the former. The only kind of health care that might be held to be needed is that which promotes health, reduces or postpones deteriorations in health, or extends life.

Second, capacity to benefit is not identical to need. On the one hand, capacity to benefit is defined in terms of outputs (improved health compared to what would have happened without the health care intervention). On the other hand, my preferred definition is need as the resources required to exhaust capacity to benefit. It is possible, in a comparison of two individuals, that their capacities to benefit will differ but be exhausted by the same resource expenditure on each. Hence, the need for resources is the same, even though capacity to benefit is not.

Third, need is forward-looking rather than backward-looking. It is prospective rather than retrospective. It emphasizes what can be done for people rather than what has previously happened to them or what their current situation is. Past and present are important only in so far as they may affect what can be done. The inadequacy of a definition of need based only on past or current sickness, impairment or disability is thrown into sharp relief (although a long history of suffering might be held to be a ground for weighting one person's need more highly than another's); so too is the need for evidence about effectiveness.

Fourth, it will usually be both efficient and equitable for some needs to go unmet. This implication arises out of resource constraints. If resources are insufficient to exhaust all capacities to benefit and if it is deemed efficient, equitable and otherwise desirable not to divert resources from other (non-health) uses, then the question arises as to what is the most equitable way of distributing existing resources across the range of needs. Some individuals may receive none and those who receive some may not receive all they need. Either can be compatible with equitable resource allocation, whether directed at achieving an allocation proportionate to need or one that will be conducive to a more equal distribution of health.

Fifth, need, even when it relates directly to a need for health care derived from the technological possibilities and an acceptable set of social value judgements, is probably at root not an appropriate criterion for resource allocation. In any version of it that can be linked to resources, it bears no systematic relationship to distributions of health that are likely to be considered to be equitable. It has no bearing on desert and it has no systematic bearing on health equality; indeed, its application might both reward the undeserving (if desert matters at all) and enhance social inequalities.

Conclusion

I conclude that need is most usefully construed in an explicit way as being a need for resources when individuals have a capacity to benefit, the resources are used in a cost-effective way and the benefit is a part of a socially determined ethical objective. It is sharply to be differentiated from demand by virtue of the source of its value content, demand being a function, inter alia, of preferences rather than moral values that are independent of individuals' preferences. This does not necessarily, however, place any specific need higher in an ethical hierarchy than any specific demand. If the objectives of health services include having maximum impact on the community's health and doing so in an equitable fashion, then need is not a helpful guide and can, indeed, be a mischievous one. Focus in that context is more appropriately directed to establishing the cost-effectiveness of services with resource allocation designed to increase equality in the distribution of health.

Although need is insufficient on its own as a distributional principle, having a need remains a necessary condition for receiving anything at all. And to establish whether needs exist, one must determine capacities to benefit for, as has been seen, absence of capacity to benefit implies no need at all. So needs and capacities to benefit must be assessed. For them to be assessed requires that access to initial assessment (diagnostic) procedures be as cheap as it can be made. As *cheap*, not as *equal*, as possible. Indeed, for some individuals, positive inducements might be necessary for them to make the initial contact with the health service. Here seems to be a fundamental case (given the values assumed) for having universal, zero (possibly even negative) price access to health care. Finally, should the ethical focus indeed fall ultimately on the post hoc distribution of health, the question will arise as to whether the needs that should be searched out are needs only for medical care (or indeed for medical care at all). The quest then stretches out beyond the medical services into the wider realm of the determinants of health, the cost-effectiveness of policies that might affect health through these alternative pathways, and the possibility arises that equity in health is best achieved through entirely different routes from medical care.

10

Equity – some theory and its policy implications[10]

Theoretical discussions of equity are often distant from the practical world of policy. In this tract, I try to bridge the gap. What is equitable in health care policy, as in other arenas of policy, is a question of ethics. I am not concerned with descriptive ethics (which depicts the values people seem to hold) but with analytical ethics (which asks what we ought to do), and with the equitable allocation of health care resources. I am, therefore, concerned with questions like: 'what is an equitable distribution of the available health care resources among residents of a country?', 'is the present distribution of health care resources equitable?', and 'how might the distribution might be made more equitable?'

Any idea of equity must embody value judgements about what it is that makes for a good society. There will also be contextual

10 This chapter originally appeared as: Culyer, A.J., 2001. Equity some theory and its policy implications. *Journal of Medical Ethics* 27, 275-283 but it has been substantially adapted and abridged.This paper originated as a discussion paper for the Ontario Premier's Council. I am grateful (without implicating them in any way) for discussions with and comments from Martin Barkin, Peter Coyte, Amiram Gafni, Jonathan Lomas, Lesley McTurk, Gavin Mooney, Fraser Mustard, Owen O'Donnell, George Pink, Terry Sullivan, Adam Wagstaff and Alan Williams. I am also grateful for the hospitality of Peggy Leatt.

and other empirical questions of fact: we are likely to want to know what the present distribution of resources is, what the health experience of different socio-economic groups is, and (as a matter of fact) what it is that ordinary people think about such distributions. The questions of fact are not questions of value. To determine whether they have been satisfactorily answered certainly requires *judgements* but they are not *value judgements*: for example, judgements about whether the number of hospital beds counted in England and Wales is accurate or whether the population sampled was representative of the groups whose opinions were sought.

A pluralist approach for a pluralist society

There is disagreement about the meaning of equity among and between the general public, philosophers, political theorists and economists. All include the word in their vocabularies. There are some who deny that it has any relevance to public policy whatsoever and others, even more extreme, who deny that it has any useful *meaning*. The first task, therefore, is that of definition, enabling the reader to form a judgement about the significance of equity in public policy toward health and health care.

Why is health care important?

Why be concerned about equity in health care distribution? Part of the answer is that health care serves a significant end (individuals' health) although health care is not the only means to serve this end. Moreover, health services serve other ends: providing information, reassurance, counselling, certification, legitimisation of sickness states for those seeking insurance benefits, and a variety of other services marginally connected with health. It is, however, the link between health care and health that is important in equity because health is important in ways that the other needs served by health care are not. What is this particular significance about health that raises its status in equity above other services? The answer seems to be that health, like the cognitive skills developed by educational institutions, is one of a special set of characteristics (sometimes called primary goods) about whose distribution people are particularly concerned. Tobin (1970) uses the term 'specific egalitarianism' because health care services are regarded as fundamentally necessary to the good life. Aristotle termed this concept 'eudaemonia', which is usually taken to mean 'flourishing'. This is not the same as the naive utilitarian notion of 'satisfaction', whose limitations are well highlighted by John Stuart Mill's famous remark: "Better to be a human being dissatisfied than a pig satisfied" (Mill 1962, p.260). In a very basic sense, one cannot flourish at all if one is dead or diseased. Care that postpones death, diminishes disease, or eliminates destructive influences on the quality of living, improves the capacity for savouring all that life has to offer, *and not merely its pleasures*. Entities such as health derive equity significance because of their ability to enable people to flourish in the societies they inhabit. Health and sickness are, moreover, culturally contingent: the things and attributes you need to flourish in Britain today may not be the same as those you needed in the middle ages, nor are they necessarily the same as are needed now in Bangladesh. This does not, unless one is going to give ethical rank to cultures, affect the ethical primacy of flourishing as an ultimate human 'good'.

If it is felt that all residents of a political jurisdiction ought to have equal opportunities for their lives to flourish, then it follows that health care is one of the goods and services whose right distribution must be ensured. Precision in the meaning of flourishing is less critical than agreement that the concept captures diverse but fundamental aspirations that are dependent on better health. This idea of 'fundamental' requirements, for example, that bread is more basic than jam or that needs trump desires, has received scant attention in the mainstream economics literature. Sen (1979, 1980, 1986), a cogent critic, criticises conventional welfare economics for attaching social value only (a) to goods and services and (b) to the utility they afford consumers and externally affected parties rather than, say, to capabilities, such as the ability to flourish, that exist and that can be further developed.

What is equity?

The treatment of individuals is invariably judged to be inequitable if it is capricious or relates to irrelevant characteristics. This is common to all notions of equity. Commonly cited characteristics of this sort include race, religion and gender. These may sometimes become relevant – for example, dietary restrictions and other prohibitions of some religions may be regarded as legitimate grounds for patients to be treated differently. What is less frequently perceived, however, is that equality and equity, and inequality and inequity, are not the same, although they are intimately related. Equity in health care requires that patients who are alike in relevant respects be treated in like fashion and that patients who are unlike in relevant respects be treated in appropriately unlike fashion. In short, there can be equitable inequalities. These requirements correspond to a familiar distinction between horizontal and vertical equity.

Horizontal equity requires the like treatment of like individuals and vertical equity requires the unlike treatment of unlike individuals, in proportion to the differences between them. Some of the ways in which people are generally considered like or unlike, such as health or need, are taken up later. But supposing that need is selected as the only relevant factor, then the two principles would imply that like needs should receive like attention and resources (horizontal equity) and that greater needs should receive greater attention and resources (vertical equity). Horizontal and vertical equity considerations apply also to entities other than health. One closely related entity is the financial contribution to health care. A horizontal principle here might be, 'equal contributions from households having an equal ability to pay' and the corresponding vertical principle is 'higher contributions from households with a higher ability to pay'. Such principles clearly separate payment for medical care from the willingness of households to pay for it. In considering need, these principles also separate receipt of care from willingness (as conditioned by ability) to pay.

There is a prevalent view in the wealthy world that policy ought to concern itself only with the distribution and redistribution of income (and wealth), leaving it up to individuals to determine their preferred consumption of goods and services, including health care, by appropriate purchases, taking into account such taxes and transfers necessary to satisfy the requirements of vertical equity in the income distribution. There are, however, two difficulties with an equity focus on purchasing power alone. One is that people care more about the fairness of the distribution of 'important' commodities like health care than they do about other purchasable items (Tobin 1970), so that even an equalisation of incomes may leave substantial inequities in the 'important' entities. The other is the difficulty of identifying the principles that ought to guide income distribution independently of the moral significance of their purchases out of that income. For example, if it is said that health care ought to be allocated in proportion to need, then the income redistribution required to achieve this must account for the different needs of, say, those with ischaemic heart disease, those needing continuous nursing, those chronically disabled, and the costs of services required. But, if there are specific distributive concerns, why not focus policy specifically on them, the things needed, rather than the means of purchasing them?

What is 'relevant' 'appropriate' 'treatment'?

Two problems arise in interpreting 'treatment'. First, not all health care is intended to serve health. For example, it is possible to conceive of the hotel services of hospitals being offered at different quality levels, without this having much impact on the effectiveness of medical care. The range may be from one star to five, with private and semi-private rooms or ward-based care, different quality food menus, and so on. Thus, if equity of distribution derives from the ethical importance attached to *health*, then not all health-related services have equal equity significance and some may be irrelevant. One might, for example, envisage a system in which individual choice and the power of the purse (usually via insurance arrangements) determined the level of hotel services, with equity focused on the distribution specifically of health-affecting care. Second, not all health care intended to be effective is actually effective. Unequally distributed ineffective care will not command the same equity concern as inequalities in the distribution of effective care. Moreover, some treatments that are effective may not be cost-effective. Such treatments are also irrelevant in equity, for they are not needed and ought not to be provided at public expense. Health care that is not related to the protection, promotion, and restoration of health may have ample justification in terms of the satisfaction of consumer preferences, but it ought not to be evaluated by equity criteria.

Is merit 'relevant'?

The equitable distribution of health care that has appropriate characteristics, like effectiveness and cost-effectiveness, is one realm of equity. Several writers (for example Mooney 1983) have enumerated the characteristics of people that are relevant to equity judgements. According to one argument, a relevant characteristic is the 'merit' or 'desert' of individuals, based on judgements about their contribution to society. Here further judgements might also be involved, for example, whether their economic contribution is unusually significant, or whether they are at a stage at which they are supporting young children or elderly persons, or judgements about their stewardship of their own health. Horizontal equity, if 'merit' is relevant, requires there to be equal treatment for those of equal merit, and vertical equity requires more favourable treatment of those with greater merit.

Merit based on income or economic productivity strikes directly against several other relevancies considered below and usually arises from a view of health care as a service no different in kind from any other to which monetary wealth gives access. The question is at root whether health care is one of the goods and services within the general incentives and rewards system in a society. The overwhelming evidence is that the citizens of most countries have thoroughly rejected the rewards approach to health care. This approach has, however, a residual and continuing presence in the policy of some physicians of preferring males of working age to others (including females) when rationing access. This policy is ad hoc, however, and is not enshrined in any statement of public policy.

A second version of the merit argument relates to number of dependents, and is more frequently heard, for example from physicians and surgeons when defensible local priorities are required. There is also survey evidence that people attach special significance to the health care needs of those with dependent children (Williams 1988). This may, therefore, be a (vertical) principle of differentiation that a pluralist synthesis might incorporate into judgements of equity and policies to attain it.

A negative version of the merit argument dominates and conflicts with several of the other relevancies. Its main role is to justify differential contributions by smokers. The most telling practical argument against it is that it is exceedingly difficult to think of any aspect of ill health which is not influenced (albeit indirectly and partially) by the lifestyle choices of individuals. Thus, if it were to be adopted as a relevant principle for equitable distribution, it would apply very widely and there would be formidable problems in assessing the contribution of each individual's past negligence to current ill health and penalising each accordingly.

Need is relevant

Medical care is a commonly cited example of a service that ought to be distributed according to need (for example, Culyer 1976, Gillon 1985, Braybrooke 1987). Let us suppose that what we mean when we say that something is needed is that it is needed for what it is able to accomplish. The thing asserted to be needed is instrumental – a necessary condition if a more ultimate objective is to be met. The view that need must be an instrumental concept has been strongly argued by Barry (1965), Flew (1977) and Culyer (2007). It has been opposed by others (for example Miller 1976,

Thomson1987). The main reason for objecting to unsubstantiated assertions of things needed is that they assume, rather than inquire whether, the thing needed really is necessary. The assertion that this or that is needed, even though its effectiveness may be disputed or unknown and even though the end sought may be unclear or, if clear, rank low in the priorities of those allocating resources, is a commonplace of medical politics. So there is much to be said for explicitness about the instrumentality of any resources asserted to be needed.

Capacity to benefit

Whatever is morally compelling about a need must come from the end served. I propose that there can be a need for health services only if there are grounds for believing that these services will enhance health, prevent its deterioration, or postpone death. These are the main benefits sought from health care, and it follows that a need for health care can exist only when there is a capacity to benefit from it (Williams 1974: 1978). It is rare, however, to have a fixed and unique technology of treatment. Thus, of the various possibilities available, the treatment needed is that judged to be the most appropriate in the particular circumstances of the case, which is that which is the most cost-effective. The amount needed is whatever is sufficient to exhaust capacity to benefit. More than that amount is unnecessary and not therefore needed; less than that amount is needed, though the need may diminish the more of it is met. This definition captures the instrumental nature of need by defining it in terms of what is needed – resources. It also relates the need resources to the moral objective sought (health for flourishing) which gives need its special moral status. It also defines a finite quantum of need (namely that which exhausts capacity to benefit) without building in distributional values about how much need ought to be met, a question still to be resolved.

As well as saying that health care is needed, one might say that *health* is needed, asserting another instrumentality, that health itself is needed to achieve some more ultimate state, such as the enjoyment of a flourishing life. The ultimate end is ethical in its own right, and this moral worth is transmitted back down the line to all the things that are necessary for its attainment. It is the end that imbues 'need' with moral urgency and affords it priority over mere demands. It is also the crucial criterion in determining whether, and which, needs ought to be met.

Need is culturally determined

The use of the word 'need' is often categorical or absolute and the need described ought, therefore, to be met categorically and absolutely. However, health is not categorical or absolute. It is a variable, for example, in functioning, activities of daily living, experience of pain, mobility and longevity and it is also largely culturally determined, both as regards the pathologies regarded as detrimental to a flourishing life in a particular community at a particular time and as regards the meaning of flourishing. A sort of extremism to which a categorical approach is prone, is illustrated by Harris (1987) "Life saving has priority over life-enhancement and... we should first allocate resources to those areas where they are immediately needed to save life and only when this is done should the remainder be allocated to alleviating non-fatal conditions" (p. 120). Harris's point is made without qualification. Thus the smallest possibility of the shortest extension to the most miserable of lives is to receive priority over the most sure and massive improvement in the quality of a life already expected to be long. Such is the cruel possibility inherent in a devotion to absolutism: a moral commitment held irrespective of its consequences and the harm those consequences inflict.

Meeting needs equitably

Is it true that (as Miller 1976 claims) egalitarians are committed to the view that justice consists (minimally) in a distribution of resources according to need? Or more generally, what kind of equality is right for a health care system that emphasizes need? Miller's claim is equivalent to the needs version of horizontal and vertical equity – those in equal need ought to be treated equally and those in greater need ought to be treated in proportion to the greater need. It is quite easy to see that distribution according to need may worsen the distribution of health and, at best, will improve it only incidentally. Consider the following cases.

In the first case, Anthony and Betty are judged to be equally sick and also to have an equal capacity to benefit. The resources available will permit either Anthony or Betty, but not both, to be restored to full health, and the same resource allocation for each is needed to accomplish this. An equal distribution of resources between the two will afford to each an equal increment in health. Since they started out with identical health states, the end state will also be identical. Here, then, is a case which is solidly egalitarian in that the individuals began equal, have equal capacities to benefit, have equal needs, are treated equally, and end up equal, though neither has needs that are fully met. The road to equity is clearly signposted.

In the second case, Charlie and Dawn, too, start off with equal ill health. Suppose also that the amount of care (measured as expenditure) required to eliminate the capacity of each to benefit is the same – their need is equal – and, as before, suppose that resources are insufficient for each to receive the maximum benefit of which he or she is capable. But suppose now that, whereas Dawn can be restored to full health with the available technology and resources, Charlie's health can be only modestly improved. Since need is the same, the horizontal equity principle requires expenditure to be divided equally between them. However, since Dawn's capacity to benefit is higher than Charlie's, she will receive a larger increment of health. Since the two started off with the same health, the result is that Dawn finishes up healthier than Charlie. Moreover, the reason for this is not that Charlie has exhausted his capacity to benefit, but that some resources which would benefit him are being devoted to the care of Dawn. Here the starting states of health were equal but the outcome is a more unequal distribution of health.

There are several other possible conflicts between equity in terms of meeting needs and equity in terms of the final distribution of health. It is quite possible, in a starting situation of unequal health to have a needs-based distribution of health care that actually exacerbates this initial inequality (see, for example, Culyer 1993, Culyer and Wagstaff 1993). The important point is that there can be conflict between rules such as 'distribution according to need', 'distribution according to capacity to benefit', 'distribution according to initial ill health', and 'distribution designed to reduce inequalities in health'. It is therefore necessary, except in special cases that cannot usually be expected, to choose between rival principles.

Distribution of health

Is there any reason to prefer any one of these distributional principles? Recall that the fundamental reason for caring about the distribution of health care is for its effect on health, the ethical significance of which hinges, in turn, on its role as a foundation for the flourishing of individuals in society. If this is indeed the reason for concern about the distribution of health care, then it is perverse to select need, capacity to benefit, or initial health as the characteristic in proportion to which health care should be allocated. None of these will necessarily result in the more equal distribution of health. They are not all equally faulty, although none is as egalitarian as it may initially have seemed. Distribution according to initial ill health is most likely to be egregiously inequitable, since it may waste substantial resources on those who will derive no benefit whatever while denying their application to the correction of rectifiable inequalities. Distribution according to capacity to benefit will produce anomalies when the relatively healthy have higher capacities to benefit. Even distribution according to need is flawed. What ought to dominate is the distribution of health and how health care interventions can alter that for the better.

An equitable health care policy should seek to reduce the inequality in health (life expectation, self-reported morbidity, quality of life in terms of personal and social functioning) at every stage of the life-cycle. Such a policy must meet needs, but in proportion to the 'distance' each individual is from the population average. Constraints may be desirable, some of which might be based on merit arguments. Moreover, it is probably not ethical to seek greater equality of health by reducing the health of the already relatively healthy. But the principle underlying the selection of those needs that are to be met will not be a simple, proportionate one in terms of needs. Instead, needs will be met in such a fashion as to reduce the dispersion of ill health in the community.

It also follows that judgements about some of the process-oriented conceptions of equity in health services, such as equity of opportunity to consume and equity of access, do not translate into equality of these processes, but have to be informed by judgements related to the contribution each can make to the ultimate objective of an equitable and, as far as possible, equal distribution of health. In judgements, for example, about the equity of introducing (further) user charges or about distributing health care facilities so that the time and transport costs of attending the facilities are reduced for patients, a decision again has to be made as to whether such policies are conducive to meeting those needs that contribute most to reducing inequalities in health.

It is unlikely that precision is possible in such judgements, but the force of equity insists that these are the relevant considerations. The fact that there will never be sufficient information for the judgements to be reached with absolute confidence should not stand in the way of policies which push the system in the direction that equity demands. The perfect should not be allowed to become the enemy of the merely good.

Who should make these judgements about needs and the best ways of meeting them? Ultimately, it ought to be policy-makers accountable to the public, because the principles and priorities they select are quintessentially political matters of public policy. But the concept of need has as one crucial ingredient, the effectiveness of health care, and top-level policy makers may be expected to know little about this. Conversely, those who know a lot about effectiveness are ill-suited, through lack of accountability and training, to make the value judgements required in trading off the rival claims of articulate and powerful provider interests within the health care system. It is therefore clear that judgements about need and meeting needs at the macro level have to be made in a multidisciplinary fashion and, given their significance for public policy, in a publicly accountable way.

From theory to policy

In this section, I tease out what seem to be the practical implications for policy of the foregoing. The implications are organised into four groups: policy assumptions; target groups; information, and research.

Policy assumptions

The first set of implications relates to the underlying mind-set that the foregoing seem to require:

1. there may be no single, overriding, equity principle to guide resource distributions. Policy-makers should be prepared to juggle with several, for example by including merit as well as equality of health

2. in view of the possibility of multiple deprivation, policy-makers should watch for compensating inequities in non-health areas in terms of health care and vice versa

3. need should be seen as a necessary condition for the receipt of equitably distributed public care

4. equity requires, in the first instance, equal and universal access for assessment, especially in primary and emergency services

5. access for 'approved' treatments ought to be unequal

6. 'approved' treatments will be those that (a) are needed and (b) make the most contribution to reducing inequalities in health

7. slavish devotion to principles of allocation in proportion to need and equal universal access should be avoided, time-honoured though they may be. They are misleading principles.

Target groups

The next few implications are conjectured to be helpful ways of categorising patients and programmes:

1. since multiple deprivation is likely to be common, there needs to be a powerful focus in policy-making and management structures so that a broad view of 'basic goods' can be taken, their distributions monitored over time, and policies developed and likewise monitored. The simplest, though imperfect, way of doing this is to monitor the distribution of health, or ill health, and other significant 'basics' by family, household, or by income, socio-economic class, or known risk factors such as ethnicity, single parenthood, disability, and exposure to environmental hazards

2. geographical distribution is usually an important dimension because regions, as well as individuals, can be multiply deprived and because there are usually significant variations in the ill health and in the avoidable or remediable ill health of regions

3. medical specialties are important provider groups, some of which speak with voices that are more powerful than the voices of others. However, their voices rarely speak of inequities and the potential of each for contributing to greater equality in health has hardly been investigated at all. Finding out more should be a priority

4. such popular slogans as 'prevention is better than cure' or 'community care is better than institutional' ought to be tested in terms of the impact on the distribution of health that expansions or contractions might have, in addition to the prime requirement that each should have *demonstrable* (and not merely *assumed*) effectiveness

5. simply because of their vulnerability, those members of the community most at risk from changes in health care policy and those least likely to take advantage of the effective services available should be identified.

Information

Equity, like efficiency, demands particular forms of knowledge for its implementation. Moreover, the knowledge each demands is essentially the same.

The main items are:

1. information on the current distribution of resources and health (or sickness) in relation to target groups above and any other groups perceived as ethically significant. Prior agreement on the meaning of 'health' and 'sickness' is necessary as is agreement on the appropriate statistical measures of inequality to be employed

2. informed judgements about the effect of changes in resource distribution on the health of individuals and especially target groups

3. information on the time and monetary costs faced by patients in accessing the system, and subsequently using this information to form judgements about the impact of user-charges, long travel times, and so on.

Research

The principal types of research needed are as follows:

1. data and information collection of the types enumerated above and further research into concepts and theories of equity and efficiency directed at the policy and management needs of the ministry of health and other related divisions of government and the health services

2. more research into the non-health care determinants of health, which may have a greater (and more cost-effective) impact on health than health care

3. further epidemiological and economic studies into effectiveness and cost-effectiveness, including the development and refinement of outcome measures of health. A major priority ought to be research directed at the quantification of the potential health gains from alternative delivery strategies, changes in programmes defined by disease and changes in programmes defined by targeted groups.

4. research into avoidable deaths may provide a rough but workable set of clues as to where there are major, unexploited health improvements. An immediate task might be to commission a comprehensive and authoritative review of the existing epidemiological evidence on the relative cost-effectiveness of medical, including diagnostic, procedures

5. research into the actual distributions of health and sickness, performed in advance of policy initiatives so that the initiatives be informed by the results; and routinely performed at an aggregate level for key groups, to monitor distributional changes over time and their likely determinants

6. research into appropriate statistical measures of inequality and into practical survey/census procedures, with the empirical measures based on agreed concepts (health, equity, need, access, etc) and tested for content validity.

These policy proposals constitute a formidable agenda. The question is whether it is worthwhile welding the talent that usually exists in the developed world into a purposeful programme of interrelated and multidisciplinary activity, a programme in which policy and statistical branches of government, researchers, health care providers, health care users, carers and the public at large, are all interwoven and share a common purpose. Some Perestroika. Lots of Glasnost. And the goal? The most efficient, humane, and equitable health care system yet devised by humankind!

11

Equity of what in health care?
Bad slogans; good slogans[11]

Introduction

There are many deep philosophical issues regarding equity that I shall avoid in order to address some practicalities of equitable policies in health and health care (for deeper material, see Olsen 1997). I intend, however, to link theory and policy, rather than keeping them in separate silos, as is all too usual. This has dangers. My amateur ethics will not impress serious philosophers, while my policy strategies will strike serious policy makers as innocent of any reality. But if we cannot discuss ethics as a foundation of policies in health and health care policy, then I doubt that it will be possible elsewhere. And the emphasis is on 'discuss' rather than 'assert', which is all too often what the ethics of health care policy comes down to: slogan-mongering by interested parties who have a commitment. So the intent is serious and the consequences of the approach turn out to be not always what one may have expected. I shall also provide some new slogans.

11 This article is an adapted and shortened version of Culyer, A.J., 2007. Equity of what in health care? Why the traditional answers don't help policy and what to do in the future. *Healthcare Papers* 8, 12-26. The hospitality is gratefully acknowledged of the Department of Health Policy, Management and Evaluation (as it then was) at the University of Toronto while I was a visiting professor.

Here are some familiar assertions:

1. Health care ought to be allocated in proportion to a person's need.

It has a group or regional counterpart:

2. The group or geographical allocation of health care resources ought to be in proportion to the population's need in each group or region.

Here is another:

3. Access and utilisation of health care ought to be equal for all members of society.

And another:

4. Equity and efficiency in health and healthcare usually conflict and, when they do, equity trumps efficiency.

These slogans fail to help policy for four main reasons: first, they are not good ethics; second, even if they were better ethics, they would still be confused and confusing; third, following these precepts can easily generate situations that we would all agree are neither more efficient nor more equitable than what we have now; and fourth, the principles are not practical: it is unclear what policy steps follow for any who wish to embody them in practical actions such as measuring the size of the problem, or the likely outcome of policies intended to do something about a problem, or managing a process intended to deliver a solution.

I have already argued against the bogus claim that there is a conflict between equity and efficiency (Culyer 2006). The point is simple but often ignored. The usual economic definition of efficiency states that an allocation of something between persons is efficient when no re-allocation is possible without imposing an uncompensated 'harm' on any one person. If we are speaking of health, and we assume that the relevant notion of 'harm' is 'loss of health', then the appropriate definition becomes this: an allocation of health care resources between persons is efficient when no reallocation is possible without imposing a net loss of health on any person. The criterion is known as the 'Pareto criterion'. It leads to the notion of a 'health frontier' indicating the highest level of health attainable for any one person given the health of the others. There is a near infinity of points on this frontier, each of which is efficient in the sense just described. Choosing between them requires one to value the health of persons relative to one another. Those who claim that there is a conflict between equity and efficiency, however, generally assume that efficiency exists not when one is at the frontier but when one is at a particular point on the frontier – usually a point associated with valuing each person's increment of health equally, or where the notional frontier has a slope of minus 1. Under the circumstances, it is scarcely surprising that a conflict may arise, for it would only be by coincidence if this point were also one at which health itself was relatively equal – by coincidence or through making the untenable assumption that all people are clones of one another. There is indeed a clash but the clash arises because an inequitable assumption has been improperly built into the definition of efficiency. They are no longer clearly separated criteria for evaluating the health of the people and the acceptability of their health care system.

Setting aside, then, this spurious conflict, we can address a truly big conflict, or suite of conflicts, between rival notions of equity. These rival notions hardly ever receive explicit discussion in policy frameworks. The common assumption, much embraced by bio-ethicists, many of whom have fallen innocently into the mis-definition of efficiency exposed above, is that equity trumps efficiency in general and possibly always. Of course, outrageous inequity might rightly command more concern that mild inefficiency but there is no obvious ground for not supposing also that outrageous inefficiency might rightly command more concern than mild inequity.

To address the weaknesses of the other principles enumerated above, let us go back to first principles.

Equity as fairness

It seems attractive to treat equity as a matter of fairness (as does, for example, Rawls 1971). It seems unfair whenever people who seem to be the same in some relevant comparison (say, their need or their income) are treated differently (say, one gets more care than the other, or one pays more than the other for the same care). It also seems unfair when people who seem to be *different* in some relevant comparison (again, say need or income) are treated the same (say, the one with greater need gets less care than the other, or the one with lower income pays more than the other for the same care). The first kind of unfairness is commonly called 'horizontal inequity' and the second 'vertical inequity'. Horizontal and vertical equity exist when such unfairness is absent.

Health or health care?

Underlying all issues regarding equity in health and health care are a distinction and a concern. The distinction is between health and health care: they are not the same and, in general, the latter is there to improve the former. Health care is not an end in itself; health is. Health care is a means (just one means) to better health. In particular, there is no reason to suppose that equality in health care will generate equality in health. Whether it will depends on a host of factors, like regional or group genetic differences between people, their early parenting experience, their patterns of disease, the effectiveness of the means of treating them, cultural variations that affect rates of utilisation and attitudes to prevention. The concern arises from the fact that health and wealth are positively related. There is a social class gradient: in the case of almost every disease the higher the socio-economic group to which a person belongs, the longer their life-expectancy and the better their health at each stage of the life-cycle. It follows that those who are the most in need of health care are also those worst placed to buy it in the market either directly or via insurance. To all other concerns about equity we need, therefore, to add a concern that the financing of health care is fair. Unfair financing both enhances any existing unfairness in the distribution of health and compounds it by making the poor multiply deprived. This is not, moreover, just a question of rich vs. poor. The gradient implies that at every socio-economic rung of the ladder those on rungs further down die sooner and suffer more ill-health than those on higher rungs.

Efficiency and equity – twin moral principles

Why bother? There are two fundamental reasons, each of which is worth exploring. Both are principles.

One says
> *more health is a good thing, ethically speaking;*

the other says
> *fairly distributed health is a good thing, ethically speaking.*

The 'ethically speaking' qualification is important, for the principles are not saying that more health is a good thing simply because it is preferred, nor more fairness if that is simply preferred. The underlying reason for their ethical desirability is due to Aristotle (as are the two principles of horizontal and vertical fairness). This is the proposition that the ultimate human goal for which we ought to strive is to be a society of flourishing individuals. By 'flourishing' I mean something more than the economic-cum-utilitarian idea of 'welfare', which is essentially merely the satisfaction of preferences through the consumption of goods and services regardless of what the preferences are for, or whether they are worthy preferences. But nor do I mean the somewhat elitist ideal of Aristotle: the active life ruled by reason. Flourishing may mean different things to different people; all I require is that it be a high goal whose accomplishment gives a deep satisfaction to the one living it, and perhaps others too, as when it is said of someone who has died 'that was a life well-lived'. In the general case, I expect good health to be a necessary condition for whatever version of flourishing one may have in mind. Here are two factual propositions: that there is a range of concepts of 'flourishing', all of which have it in common that they are ethically compelling (for example, more compelling than any concept of preference or taste satisfaction); the other that they all require, or usually require, good health for their full realization.

Now add a third factual assertion: effective health care is one of the means through which health is promoted; not any health care, only *effective* care, and not *only* health care, for there are many other determinants of health that could also be targets of policy.

We now have a value judgement: the ultimate aim ought to be 'flourishing'. There may be several notions of 'flourishing' but each of them can be an ultimate aim for human society. That is a factual proposition (we can ask people if it is indeed so). There are other factual propositions: good health is necessary if one is to flourish. That too is a factual proposition (we can find empirical markers for 'flourishing' and 'health' and see if the latter predicts the former well). Effective health care enhances health (again not uniquely). That too is a factual proposition (we can conduct trials and other empirical exercises to test the effectiveness of medical interventions, as well, incidentally as variations in many of the other determinants of health). So, combining the value judgement and the factual statements, effective health care is an ethical objective, since it promotes good health (albeit not uniquely) and good health is an ethical objective, since it serves the ultimately ethical end of flourishing.

The next steps in the argument are plain and bring us closer to policy. If it is good to encourage flourishing, it must be good to be efficient at it. For example, if we were using more health care resources than were necessary to achieve a given health gain, that would be inefficient and we would be less ethical than we could be. Resources devoted to morally compelling causes ought to be used so as to have maximum impact on the cause served. Hence the first moral principle: *more health is a good thing, ethically speaking.*

Moreover, if having 'flourishing citizens' is the fundamental characteristic of a good society, how can it not be maintained that avoidable inequalities ought indeed to be avoided? Enter the second moral principle: *fairly distributed health is a good thing, ethically speaking.*

There are some immediate policy implications. One is that health care that does not contribute to health (ie is not effective) has no place in an ethical policy for health. It also implies that cost-ineffective health care has no place in it either, even if it is effective, because providing cost-ineffective care implies that a redistribution of resources could increase the health of at least one person without reducing the health of any other. Ineffective, and cost-ineffective, care may still be produced and consumed but simply as any other good or service that is bought and sold in the market place to meet people's wants.

On the fairness side, inequalities of health ought not to be manufactured without ethically compelling reasons and ought not to be allowed to continue if they can be removed by reasonable means. By 'ethically compelling reasons' I mean countervailing ethical arguments that carry sufficient moral weight to overpower the flourishing argument. By 'reasonable means' I mean actions and policies that do not have costs or undesirable downstream consequences that might morally outweigh the gain in equity.

Equity and equality

Equity is not the same as equality, although they are often carelessly thrown together as though they were. However, they are connected. Equity often requires the equality of something. The critical question is 'equality of what?' It has been common to consider equity as principally requiring broadly equal availability of resources: hence the unfairness of 'post-code rationing'. In the past, however, there has been a remarkable degree of complacency. In the UK, the first study of the territorial distribution of resources occurred in 1970, twenty-two years after the inception of an NHS dedicated to the principles of egalitarianism; moreover that study was sponsored by the British Medical Association and not an official one (Cooper and Culyer 1970, 1971, 1972, Maynard 1972, Maynard and Ludbrook 1980a,b). Sometimes, however, equity is found in just inequalities and the question then is 'what is the criterion for deciding which inequalities are fair or unfair?' As we have seen, equity means treating likes alike and unlikes appropriately differently. So what are the respects that might be ethically relevant in determining the appropriate treatment of people, whether equal or unequal in that 'relevant respect'.

Rival relevant respects

Here I enumerate seven commonly stated 'relevant respects', the principle (horizontal or vertical) to which it seems to be connected, and then make some comments about it. In what follows, I take 'treatment' to mean the provision of health care resources, for convenience expressed in monetary terms (i.e. representing health care purchasing power).

1.   Need. Populations with equal needs should receive equal treatment and populations with greater needs should receive more favourable treatment.

A disadvantage of this principle is that it is far from clear what 'need' means. It might mean one or more of the respects that follow.

2.   Ill-health. Populations that are equally ill ought to be treated the same; those that are sickest ought to get more.

A disadvantage of this principle is that it seems to assume what might not be the case – that the conditions in questions are effectively treatable by health care and that all conditions are equally costly to treat. In reality the effectiveness of health care varies widely (iatrogenesis is the term used when the effect is actually negative on health). It cannot make much sense to require a population to receive the same treatment regardless of its morbidity characteristics, the effectiveness of relevant preventive and restorative medical care or the cost, whether high or low, of delivering that care.

3.   Desert. Populations of equal desert ought to be treated the same and those of greater desert ought to receive more.

Common elements that advocates of this principle have in mind are life-style choices such as smoking, drug abuse, poor diet, dangerous sporting activity and promiscuous sex that increase the chances that someone will need health care, that might react negatively on the health of others and that might reduce the chances that health care will be effective. The principle suffers from the problem that it is virtually impossible, empirically, to distinguish lifestyle effects from other effects and that it assumes, anyway, that lifestyle differences are avoidable, not socially conditioned and, if deleterious to health, that the patients in question are culpable. Another, more positive, argument holds that groups with higher productivity such as high earners, those with dependent children or who do much voluntary public service work, deserve a high priority. The argument again suffers from the problem that the claim of desert rests heavily on a claimed contribution to the well-being of other people, which is hard to measure without arbitrariness and is, at best, only a partial measure of anyone's deservingness.

4.   Resources themselves. This is usually presented as a purely horizontal equity proposition – since all people are to be regarded as equal, each ought to have equally available resources; the per capital distribution should be everywhere the same.

A disadvantage of this principle is that, like the previous ones, it ignores the *productivity* of resources. Why ought there to be any equitable concern for a more equal distribution of ineffective services, or even if services are effective, why ought people who have different needs receive the same? It denies the possible fairness of equitable inequality.

5. Capacity to benefit. People with an equal capacity to benefit from health care ought to be treated the same; people with higher capacities to benefit ought to receive more.

This principle addresses the productivity issue. However, if it turns out that those with the greatest ability to benefit are also initially healthier people, then the application of the principle will lead to greater health inequalities and, because such people are also likely to be relatively wealthy, they will be made relatively wealthier too. A double inequality.

6. Health. This principle aims at greater equality of health by giving priority to those with relatively low health or who are furthest from the average.

A disadvantage of this principle is that it could imply awarding huge resources for those who are both very sick and have a low capacity to benefit. The same resources could generate much more health if they were distributed to appropriate others (i.e. those with a greater capacity to benefit).

7. Equality of access. This principle is perhaps the most frequently encountered type of equity encountered in discussion of health care policy.

A disadvantage of this principle is that it is satisfied even at very high levels of price – just so long as the cost of access is the same for all. A $1,000 co-payment for a family doctor consultation may be what each must pay but is unlikely to be regarded as equitable on the grounds that it will be to the marked disadvantage of the poor sick and the poor with a high risk of sickness. Equal access is not the same as *cheap* access and it is cheap access that matters.

Only one of these seven even begins to address the heart of the matter, which is the distribution of health. It is health inequality that is inequitable. The other inequalities may be relevant but each is unsatisfactory alone as a principle and if so used is likely to generate both waste (inefficiency) and further inequities. Despite this, current morbidity and mortality continue to be widely used in resource allocation formulae, and measures of the 'burden of disease' continue to be used as indicators of priority in service allocation and research, even though these measures tell us nothing at all about the productivity of either services or research (Mooney and Wiseman 2000).

The right way forward

Addressing inequity in health requires two difficult tasks to be accomplished. One is the development of acceptable statistical measures of 'health', suitable for creating targets and for monitoring the impact of various patterns of resource allocation on the distribution of health. Although statistical, any such measure inevitably embodies social value judgements, which it is hardly for the statisticians (or any other professionals) to make. The other is an understanding of the kinds of intervention that will have the biggest impact on health inequalities. Armed with this information, some of which is likely to remain dependent on professional judgements of effective impact (in principle, these are scientific and, though involving judgement do not involve *social value* judgements and they will often be only approximately quantifiable), it becomes possible to bring together both the inequality of concern and the productivity of resources in redressing it. The solution is unlikely to be available through the application of formulaic means as distinct from deliberative processes with wide consultation.

Some preferable slogans

Rather than the assertions with which the article opened, I suggest the following alternatives, based on the foregoing arguments.

1.   *Only needed health care ought to be provided free. Health care that is not needed should – if demanded – be paid for privately.*

Equity is a factor in determining resource allocation decisions only in respect of health care that is needed; ie of the health care that it would be technically possible to provide only that which is (a) necessary for a person's timely health improvement and (b) cost-effective, may be said to be needed. Not all care that is needed may be afforded.

2. *Access should be as cheap as is necessary to enable utilisation of needed health care.*

Equality of access is not specifically equitable but policies should seek to ensure that access is cheap by lowering barriers (financial, geographical, cultural, linguistic or social) to service use. This is because diagnosis is a necessary stage in establishing whether there is a need for health care. The larger the barriers to the receipt of care, the more likely it is that genuine health care needs will go undetected and untreated, to the detriment of both efficiency and equity. Without *cheap* access, the community's need for health care goes unassessed. *How* cheap it ought to be will depend on the elasticity of demand for diagnostic services and the impact of copayments and other costs of access and use on a person's overall purchasing power (if other inequities are not to be undesired side-effects of health policy).

3. *The main inequality is inequality in health.*

Addressing other inequalities (eg of resources per capita) is a distraction and can lead to greater health inequality.

4. *Equity in health is impossible without an empirical measure of health.*

The measure required does not have to be perfect nor suited for all decision contexts. It must, however, have construct validity and enable the making of politically acceptable comparisons between differing population groups. The values embodied in it ought also to be clear.

5.   *Avoidable gross inequalities in health are intolerable moral outrages.*

Good health is normally necessary for people to flourish as human beings. Gross inequalities in health imply gross inequalities in people's flourishing. Policy targets for reducing health inequalities should be set by the ministry.

6.   *The largest differentials between persons and groups should command the highest priority.*

In seeking to promote the health of all through cost-effective health care, policy should address the biggest disparities in people's lifetime experience of health through selective resource allocation and specific policies aimed at having maximum impact on the health of the least healthy.

7.   *Unavoidable gross inequalities should be accompanied by generous palliative provisions and other compensating variations.*

Avoidable gross inequalities ought to be avoided. Although unavoidable inequalities may not be fully compensatable through other policies, other policy opportunities for promoting more equal flourishing ought to be considered. This is but one policy element requiring inter-ministry collaboration.

8.   *Achieving equity in health requires a policy implementation process that is deliberative.*

Achieving the equitable allocation of resources requires a combination of judgements about social values and judgements about the contribution that various interventions and types of care are likely to have on population health and its distribution. Interventions ought ideally to include public health interventions and other nonhealth care determinants of population health. The combining of scientific judgements about the evidence with social values probably requires a deliberative process with a wide representation of stakeholders of all kinds.

9. *Equity in health is impossible without an information base.*

A policy for the thoughtful eradication of gross health inequalities routinely requires: information about the current distribution of health across relevant groups; information about the current distribution of resources across relevant patients groups; and information about the technical potential of health care and other services to improve health: incremental impact ratios of resources on health.

In short ...

In this chapter I have criticised four common points of ideology, disparaged seven grounds commonly put for discriminating between people when allocating health care resources, and contributed nine coherent slogans that are built upon what I conjecture to be the real values held by most people whatever their country of origin. They are founded on the twin beliefs that both efficiency and equity in health and health care are important and that neither automatically trumps the other. I hope these new slogans prove conducive to more transparent policy making and will promote contemporary moves towards greater efficiency, fairness and sustainability of our health care systems.

Part Four:

Health Policy

12

The principal objective of the NHS ought to be to maximise the aggregate improvement in the health status of the whole community[12]

Caveats

It seems a pity to compromise what seems uncompromising, but let us nonetheless begin with some health warnings. First, 'principal' does not mean 'only', and some of the other things the National Health Service does (and ought to do) like inform, advise, comfort, validate and authorise, turn out to be necessary anyway, if it is to achieve this prime objective. Moreover, efficiency, which is what maximising is about, always needs to be tempered by the consideration of equity in both process and outcome. Second, let us remind ourselves that most moral objectives (of which this is one) do not lose their force by virtue of being impossible to attain. One of the reasons for having moral rules about anything is that they provide bases for judging how well one is doing with respect to what one ought to be doing. Failure to be consistently outstanding

---

12 This is an adapted version of: Culyer, A.J., 1997. The principal objective of the NHS ought to be to maximise the aggregate improvement in the health status of the whole community, *British Medical Journal* 314, 667-669 (reprinted with changes in New, B. (ed.), Rationing: Talk and Action. King's Fund and BMJ, London, 95-100) and of Culyer, A.J., A rejoinder to John Harris. In: New, B. (ed.), *Rationing: Talk and Action*, loc. cit. 106-107.

does not detract from the value of having a tough criterion for judging how outstanding one is. Third, let us remember that there are good reasons for having taken health care out of the 'ordinary' market place. These include: a solidarity case that ensures no one is excluded from benefit on grounds of lack of portable, transparent, and comprehensive entitlement; protection from professional dominance in the determination of both general healthcare priorities, and specific patient-doctor relations. This is a risk, since in any system of health care it is primarily the doctor who determines the demand for care, not the patient. They also include equity in funding arrangements, processes, and outcome (which I take to be mainly health) and the provision of care that is more likely to confer benefit than harm. Fourth, maximising such an objective involves not only a commitment to the ethicality of the maximand (health), but also embodies within it a host of other ethical issues. These often take the form of trade-offs, whose exposure, discussion, and resolution by people with legitimate rights to be involved is important. Moreover, 'maximising' does not imply 'regardless of any constraints', some of which may be resource constraints while others may be ethical or arise because of conflict with other potential maximands. Fifth, maximising anything implies the need for particular sorts of knowledge – for information about health status, changes in it, its decomposition into relevant population subgroups, and believable attribution of such changes to causes (whether they lie in the delivery of health care or through other means). Finally, the desirability of measurement in general ought to be distinguished from the suitability, reliability and acceptability of any specific measure.

One desideratum of any measure of health or health gain is that it should enable interpersonal comparisons of health gain (or loss) to be made; this is one of the striking departures from the more general utilitarian objectives customarily set by economists in evaluating the advantages and disadvantages of various institutions and policy options. A common objection to health measurement is not so much an objection to outcome measurement itself as to either a particular measure of it (for example, that the measure in question misses out something important) or to a particular way of using a measure (for example, not adjusting prospective health gain or prospective beneficiaries of health gain differentially according to potentially morally relevant factors, like their history of disease or their degree of handicap). One of the attractions of explicit measures of prospective outcome is that they clearly expose sins of commission and omission. Thus, they enable the explicit discussion and implementation of ethics-based desiderata, rather than leaving them to the uninformed whim of committees and individuals with influence.

The NHS ought to be about maximising health

There can be no doubt that a principal objective of the NHS is to maximise health. We have ministerial authority for that. The more interesting, nonfactual assertion is that it *ought* to do this. The ethical underpinnings for the view that it ought lie in the importance of good health for people's flourishing lives, which I take as an ultimate good. We can all think of individuals with terrible handicaps of ill health who seem to flourish, but these are not persuasive counter examples. Such people excite our admiration and are seen as exceptional. In general, I take it that flourishing is indeed an ultimate good and that good health is normally a necessary condition for achieving it. In short, health is needed in the twin senses that it is both necessary and serves an ethically commendable end. This gives an otherwise merely technical relationship between means (health care) and ends (health) and between means (health) and ends (flourishing) its ethically persuasive quality and raises the need for health to high ethical significance. This is not true for my need for a Rolls Royce, even though owning a 'roller' would undoubtedly be an effective way of achieving one of my life's ambitions: impressing my students.

To take the argument further, health care (including medical care) may be a necessary (though not sufficient) condition for realising better health. If so, it too is needed (that is, is necessary if improved health is to be attained) and it too derives its ethically compelling character from the ethicality of the flourishing that is the ultimate good. So, not only may it be reasonably assumed that being accepted, maximising the health of populations becomes an ethical objective, as does being efficient so that the resources used in health care are used to maximise health outcomes. This is not the same as maximising the use of beneficial health care. It differs from it principally in that delivering only the care that is most effective takes no account of the opportunity cost of such care (a highly effective but very costly treatment may rightly be given lower priority than a less effective but much cheaper one) when both cannot be delivered to all who might benefit.

Distributive justice also acquires a high priority: in my view this is best tackled in terms of seeking to identify and move towards a more equal distribution of health across the population, while at the same time ensuring that each procedure offered to patients is that believed (on the best evidence available) to be the most cost-effective. This will not usually imply an equal distribution of resources, nor will it imply a curmudgeonly equality in which everyone gets nothing (equally). It actually implies, given current knowledge of the way medical technology is deployed, both a rise in peoples' average health and a more equal distribution of health.

There are twin problems for social decision-makers here. One (for healthcare commissioners and providers) is the selective use of their resources to be efficient in their achievement of objectives. Others (for higher level decision-makers) involve trading off other ultimately good things that we might legitimately seek in pursuit of flourishing lives, but compete with health care in the battle for resources. There is no room for absolutism here, for there is more than one means to the great ethical end of flourishing. Nor can every desirable thing be done for everyone. Conflict, and the need to choose, are inevitable.

Efficiency and equity aren't always in opposition

Conflicts can, however, be overdone. One that is commonly overdone is the alleged clash between efficiency and equity. If we define efficiency in a health service as being the maximisation of probable health outcomes from given resources, and if there is also an acceptable quantification of these outcomes across the variety of activity we call 'health services', then there exists, as a matter of logic, such a maximum for every possible distribution of resources to individuals. All these possible distributions are efficient. But all are most certainly not fair or equitable. Choosing between these possible distributions, all of which are efficient, cannot involve any conflict between efficiency and equity, unless you make the additional ethical judgement that the marginal unit of outcome is always of equal value, whoever is accruing it. I see no compelling moral argument for such a judgement.

Talking theoretically, although difficult, can sound glib. In practice, one is in a sea of uncertainty, even in a world as conceptually simple as that just described. There is a deficit of usable relevant information on health itself, its distribution across population groups, on health gains (actual or projected), on the links between the activities of the NHS and their final impact on health, on the reasons for the huge variations that can be measured between practitioners and the variations in outcomes that individual practitioners achieve. As a practical example, the enormous clinically inexplicable variations in general practitioners' referrals within and across health authority areas, are a source of both deep inequity and substantial inefficiency, which only health authorities can address.

For many in the research and development commissioning communities, these lacunae provide the ethical momentum for changes that have recently been set in train in the research and development programme, for the intelligent use of evidence based medicine, for outcome measurement, and for the partial separation of the activity of healthcare commissioning from healthcare delivery. There is an act of faith involved here, which requires one to believe that more evidence relating to the components of the links in the flourishing healthcare cascade is a good thing, and also involves the conviction that more (relevant) information is better than less and a commitment to the principle that the best should not be allowed to become the enemy of the good.

Information not a substitute for judgement

Undoubtedly, the mere provision of information is insufficient. At the very least it will need interpretation in particular contexts by patients and professionals who understand enough of its limitations not to fall into the trap of supposing that information can ever be a substitute for judgement (including clinical judgement). Moreover, there is abundant evidence that the mere provision of even very good information is not itself sufficient to persuade professionals to act upon it. Further, issues of value pervade the entire decision structure. At one level it is impossible to define 'health' without value judgements (whose should they be?). At another level, it is usually impossible to determine the appropriate course of medical actions for a particular patient without making patient specific value judgements (whose, again, should these be?). There are values to be selected at all points in between.

As I wrote at the beginning, improved health is not the only business of the NHS. In relations with patients, a common task in both primary and secondary care is to provide information and nothing else: for example, information that a person does not have the disease he or she feared, where, outside the NHS, should one go for help with a problem, or about healthy lifestyles. Plainly, such information serves an ethical end. It may also serve the end of health maximisation. The institutional side of the NHS also provides hotel services, which ought to be provided efficiently but which may not raise questions of distributive equity of the same compelling nature as does active medical care itself, and might be left to private purchasing power and insurance arrangements without damaging the objectives of the NHS.

Similarly, equity in the distribution of health (or of health gain, or of healthcare resources) does not exhaust what ought to be proper equity concerns in the NHS. Procedures and processes must also be fair. It is not fair: to keep similarly placed people waiting avoidably different times; for professionals to be rude or inconsiderate to social inferiors; to treat professionals within the system as though they were employees in a command economy, or to set them professional targets without also supplying the means by which they might meet them; or to exclude those for whom the NHS exists from decisions about the values that are to be incorporated in the layers of this many tiered cake.

Work on measures is needed

Setting an objective of the sort postulated here is not the usual way that economists have approached issues of efficiency and equity. They have more usually had a particular and rather sophisticated branch of utilitarianism to set the conceptual rules for resource allocation which goes under the name 'Paretian welfare economics'. The Paretian view holds that decisions ought to maximise subjectively perceived welfare, that the only identifiable improvements are those where no one loses such welfare and at least one makes some gains, and that in situations where some gain and others lose, one can only sit on one's hands. Some of us have rejected this framework for health and health care not because we want to reject the respect for individual values which is enshrined within its ethical frame, but because it fails to deliver practical guidelines with practical consequences and, where it does, does so with severe limitations. A particular weakness of the traditional Paretian approach is that it affords no leverage on choices that have to be made which involve some people losing while others gain – sadly, the general situation. The usual evaluative framework is also silent for choices that are based on considerations of equity.

This is not true of the object set here (maximising health), provided that a suitable measure of the thing to be maximised is available. Twenty-five years ago there was no such measure. That is no longer true. A battery of claimants exists, each having its advantages and disadvantages and some more appropriate to certain types of choice than others. We need appropriate measures for all the outputs of the NHS that are of prime concern and indicators of the varied dimensions that equity takes. We also need a community of users of this information who can interpret and use it towards the NHS's objective and who can feed problems back to the consumer and the professional, managerial, and research communities so that improvements and refinements can be made and lacunae filled. All this entails comprehensive partnerships and dialogue across a spectrum of communities and interest groups. It also requires education, training, and research.

The practical problem at all levels of the NHS is to be able to apply consistent and acceptable principles to answer questions like: which services shall be available and to whom, and on what conditions shall they be available? These questions all concern rationing and the principles need to be useful in a practical sense and defensible by those using them. If you don't find mine acceptable, at least they meet the requirements of consistency and applicability and are derived from a set of explicit ethical considerations, and you need to have an alternative and to explain how you would expect ministers, the NHS Executive, NHS managers, and NHS professionals to implement them.

13

Markets for R&D in the National Health Service[13]

The Report of the Research and Development Task Force (Culyer 1994) was quite deliberately long on principle and short on detail. This was not merely due to the pressure of time. It was also because it was something for which we consciously strove, partly because we felt that there was a real need to set out the basics of a new framework for supporting research and development (R&D) in the National Health Service (NHS) and partly because we realised that the final details of the arrangements eventually to be adopted would depend upon a lot of specific work in the office of the Director of R&D (DRD) at the Department of Health (DoH) and upon much further consultation.

The general purpose of the Task Force was to set a strategic framework for the Central Research and Development Committee (CRDC), to advise the DRD, and through the DRD the NHS Executive Board, on:

1. the overall pattern of funding for R&D, and the plans and priorities of individual research funding agencies

---

13 This chapter first appeared as Culyer, A.J., 1995. Supporting research and development in the National Health Service. *Journal of the Royal College of Physicians of London*, 29, 216-224 but has been abridged. It was based on a lecture given at the first Forum Supporting R&D in 1995.

2.   the need for NHS support for externally sponsored R&D within the NHS

3.   progress on the establishment and operation of new systems for funding and supporting R&D in the NHS.

The inheritance was that R&D was being publicly supported by a variety of streams of funding that, like Topsy, had 'just growed', sometimes with one stream being added to rectify anomalies in another. They included the NHS R&D budget, the research element of the Service Increment for Teaching and Research (SIFTR), the special funding for London postgraduate teaching hospitals, the special funding for other major centres, and the 'implicit' research generated by institutions out of their own resources. The central recommendation was that the existing multiple channels through which training and research in NHS institutions were supported should be replaced with a single funding stream.

We were not charged with the task of considering the support of medical and health services research in its entirety, let alone that of the fundamental sciences (natural science or social science) on which all else depends, whose interface with the more applied sciences of medicine and health services research is absolutely essential, and whose various sources of support are highly complementary.

Basic science and (not versus) applied science

That the fruitful interplay between basic science and the more applied sciences is crucial can scarcely be emphasized enough. Few major innovations in health care do not have their roots in core disciplines such as physics, biochemistry or economics. Basic science, whether in physics or economics, is rarely targeted at any specific use. It is speculative and inventive, addressing questions generated by the imagination of the scientist in the search for greater generality, consistency and the solution of puzzles that may be absolutely fundamental. That kind of work is less common among clinical academics, who are more concerned with solving clinical problems using the paradigms, theories and experimental methods developed within the parent disciplines. Clinical researchers are trained in the clinical investigative skills and the laboratory methods required to address such problems, and they usually need access to patients. *Mutatis mutandis*, similar patterns can be observed in some at least of the social sciences which provide much of the core of health services research, for example, the axiomatic structures of both the behavioural theory and normative methods being developed by basic scientists, then applied and developed over many years in statistical empirical work and then further developed for specific purposes in health services research. Health services research sometimes involves the application of only medical science, as in clinical trials, sometimes the application of only social science, as in estimating the demand for health care, and sometimes it involves both types of science, as in many cost-effectiveness studies of medical procedures. I am not implying any meritocratic ranking to the activities of colleagues working in these various fields; the fruits of science, beyond the sheer intellectual delight of puzzle solving and the invention of explanations for phenomena (which is reward only to those engaged in it) inevitably depend upon a quite extended team of people having different skills and motivating passions.

The fruitful interaction, however, between the constantly developing 'science base' and its application along a continuum, at the other end of which lies the practical implementation and use of procedures, is not linear. It is much better seen as a loop, and I conjecture the more of a loop it is made to be, the greater and more valuable the eventual fruits. While the ideas, concepts, theories and so on that are 'applied' clearly have to predate their application, it does not follow that the organisation and support of research should follow in a compartmentalised or linear fashion. Applied science must apply, test, or develop the ideas and theories of basic science. The invention of valid ways of doing this testing and application, whether laboratory-based in environmentally controlled experiments, or statistically-based and using the variation observed in nature, is a part of the imaginative excitement that draws many fine minds into points along the continuum that are not 'basic'. It therefore follows that applied scientists have much to learn from basic scientists and that, given the dynamic nature of scientific development, means must be found for frequent briefings and intellectual interaction, lest the more applied run down the intellectual capital which they acquired as graduate students and become incompetent in comprehending, interpreting and applying the work of researchers in more basic science. But a flow goes the other way too. While serendipity and curiosity drive much research that has revolutionised medicine and health care, the needs of health policy, which are broader than those of NHS policy, ought also to inform the research agenda in the basic sciences, or at least that science which is one step nearer the applied end of the spectrum than the most abstract. When difficult questions of method, or empirical puzzles and apparent contradictions arise in applied research, we need mechanisms through which those at the 'basic' end can be briefed and brought into the search for solutions. Some 'basic' questions might even be supplied by applied research.

Two issues in particular arise. One is largely for institutions, especially universities, which must find ways of ensuring that the dialogue in the scientific loop is developed and nurtured. The ways in which we organise research, the geography of our universities, and the managerial leads given by deans, pro-vice-chancellors and the like are all crucial here. In general, our various quality control systems, or external scrutiny methods, or internal forward planning mechanisms typically pay little attention to these interactive issues. They tend to be left to serendipity. The second is the question of who should pay for what. In the Task Force we were concerned only with the NHS's own R&D and its support for particular forms of applied research by others. This must include the hospital infrastructure that underpins research endeavour, or at least part of it, through maintaining patient flows of the right kind. But it needs also to keep the big picture firmly in view; research activity is not easily, nor sensibly, unpicked into parcels, each with its own separate support and funding structure. Much of the structure is shared. Moreover, there is also a sharing with the teaching function, especially postgraduate teaching. The training of the next generation of researchers is one of researchers' principal tasks. Moreover, teaching, even at quite elementary levels, is commonly a source of inspiration for good research ideas.

This has important implications. One is the undesirability of creating walls between researchers within institutions. Another is the undesirability of creating walls between teachers and researchers (quite apart from the personal tensions and jealousies that might otherwise arise). Another is the creation and maintenance of a 'market' for research resources that encourages the best and assures public accountability.

The Service Increment for Teaching and Research (SIFTR)

How anyone was supposed to understand the proportions of support funding in SIFTR that was intended for teaching and research is far from clear. Not surprisingly, the DoH, in seeking to advise ministers on the appropriate division of SIFTR into its T and R components, conducted some multivariate econometric analysis. Its results were not very helpful and for good reason. Consider a sheep farmer producing sheep meat and wool. Some variation in the quality and quantity of meat and wool might be possible in the short term by, say, varying the diet of the animals but, short of selective breeding, or mixing breeds in one's stock, meat and wool are produced in pretty fixed proportions and, to all intents and purposes, jointly. It makes no sense to ask 'is the fodder the cost of the wool or the cost of the meat?' By variation in feeding, one might be able to estimate the marginal cost (in fodder) of more or better meat, or more or better wool. But that is *marginal* cost and not the same as apportioning the total between the meat and the wool. Much the same is true of teaching and research, and also of the different types of research alluded to before. The proportions may not be strictly fixed, but in centres of research excellence and postgraduate education they are variable only within fairly strict limits. In SIFTR, how much is T and how much R is not a good question.

So what should one have done? The sheep market can give us some clues. The approximate fixity of the proportions of meat and wool produced, and the impossibility of separating the total cost of rearing sheep into the costs of wool and the costs of meat, do not prevent each commanding its own price. The prices are determined by the interaction of the costs of rearing sheep *and the demand for the various sheep products* (plus, of course, much meddling in the form of the Common Agricultural Policy). In our case, what we need to resolve the puzzle is a *revelation of the demand for teaching and research*. This is not so much a matter for markets to determine as for the public sector funders, who are our principal demanders in the sense that they determine on behalf of the public in general what T and what R shall be purchased. And this, of course, is what happened in the case of SIFTR. In the end, a public judgement by the accountable minister determined what R should go into the new single stream.

The new arrangement proposed by the Task Force

The NHS's R&D strategy is chiefly focused on health services research. The new funding stream will add to this the now-determined R of SIFTR combined with the 'internal research' of hospitals and the special research funding of the London postgraduate teaching hospitals. In allocating the latter, it will be essential to recognise the complementarity between T and R and the infrastructure support of both. It will also be necessary to recognise that the research infrastructure also supports a wide variety of R&D activity, most of it in fact the NHS's own programme.

Different criteria will need to be borne in mind in allocating what the Task Force called 'facilities support' and the NHS service costs of research on the one hand, and support for projects and programmes on the other. None of this implies a narrow or philistine approach. The NHS R&D strategy has long supported fundamental research in outcome assessment; it is funding a set of projects on methodological topics; it has recently set up the Manchester-based research centre in primary care with a long-term contract. The usual way in which R&D has been commissioned has been by inviting tenders for somewhat generally defined topic areas which afford researchers an opportunity for developing or piggy-backing their own research priorities on to those of the strategy. Regions have often supported the imaginative establishment of new research centres and specific academic posts with general briefs that satisfy the most jealous guardians of the principle of academic freedom. So let us not dismiss the R&D strategy of the NHS for what it is not.

Special centres

Some scientific concentrations, combining aspects along the scientific spectrum from basic to applied, benefit from being very large indeed. They have usually been developed with the combined support of the Higher Education Funding Council for England (HEFCE), the NHS, the MRC and one or more major charities such as the Wellcome Trust, and in such cases this collaboration is essential and highly beneficial, provided the internal management plays its role appropriately. They should not, of course, be supported simply because they are there, regardless of the outcome of on-going quality scrutiny; nor should the emergence of other centres be prevented simply to protect those that are established but unable to compete in open competition. Moreover, a very large scale is not always either necessary or desirable. One of the emphases of the Task Force's report was that in the future support should focus more on individuals and teams and not be solely institutional, the latter being justified only when many individuals and teams worth supporting were all members of the same institution or a set of collaborating institutions. But some of these centres have not been successful at developing the multidisciplinary health services research arm that would fully complement their clinical and basic natural science strength. Indeed, I doubt whether some have tried very hard. Further, some of these institutions have made no serious attempts to extend their research significantly into the community, or train cadres of researchers of the first rank capable of doing it. I am not suggesting that every institution, or indeed any single one, ought to invest across the whole spectrum; I am merely observing how few, especially in London, have invested in non-clinical health services research.

The senior partners

There are four major interested parties with stakes in this matter. On the research sponsoring side they are the NHS R&D directorate, HEFCE, the research councils, especially the MRC, and the major charities. On the other side is the research and training community, especially the universities. We seem to have lacked in the past a formal mechanism for (a) debating these various issues (who should be supporting what, on what scale, by what criteria and in what kind of partnership?) and (b) agreeing on a broad policy between them. The Forum Supporting R&D in the NHS, which was the first recommendation of the Task Force, would be just such a body (a kind of comprehensive research liaison group), perhaps with a working party supplemented where necessary with members representing other interests, to consider the matter.

At another level, basic scientists must listen to the applied researchers to find out what holds them back from making even more effective contributions. In my own field, a good example of this sort of interaction has been the development of outcome measures, which is now quite a thriving industry involving applied researchers as well as engaging the interest of theorists in various social sciences. An area where we urgently need work if the fruits of science are more effectively to be brought to the advantage of ordinary people, concerns the question of how to change the behaviour of practising doctors and other medical professionals in ways that are consistent with what good theory and good empirical research have shown to be effective (my examples from sciences that are neither natural nor medical are deliberately chosen to illustrate the generality of what I am claiming).

Facilities support

The Task Force recommended that future financial support from the single funding stream should take three forms, that the R&D Information Strategy, with its emphasis on dissemination of research results and the promotion of their uptake, should be supported and that research capacity be further investigated and supported.

The three forms of financial support were the direct and indirect costs of research projects and programmes, the 'excess' service costs of approved peer-reviewed non-commercial research, and support for research facilities in trusts and other NHS research providers. Facilities support is intended to cover the costs of maintaining or creating particular research facilities and staff to enable R&D projects to take place which cannot reasonably be attributed to a specific project or programme. We envisaged that some programmes would themselves entail facilities support that would be embodied in the contract for such programmes, and this meant that the future system had to guard against the possibility of double counting by supporting any particular activity twice over.

An unresolved facilities issue

One issue, about which the Task Force itself made no recommendation, related to capital, especially funding for buildings. Some of the major centres of excellence (not all of which are large) face severe constraints in their capacity to take on additional research activity, particularly through a lack of suitable space to accommodate the researchers and their associated other space needs. Several important issues need to be resolved in this connection. One is whether Treasury rules would permit the use of what I understand to be recurrent money for capital purposes; another is the question of the ownership of any such estate created in this way (especially when it is not a part of trust property), and another is the question of whether the conventions about investment appraisal procedures ought to be (or, indeed, could be) followed in such cases, supposing that the other two problems were resolved.

This problem may become acute for health services research that does not depend upon a specifically NHS base and which would be unsuitably located on trust property, such as research based in universities or in fundholding general practices. It is not clear whether the answer lies in developing some supplementary capital funding sources within the NHS for such support, or for extending loan arrangements or rental agreements.

Service costs

One of the issues that led to the establishment of the Task Force was a perceived threat to clinical trials, especially multicentre trials and trials in highly specialised units with difficulties in recruiting patients in sufficient numbers, and to major centres dependent on tertiary referrals. The threat came in the form of a reluctance of the new NHS purchasers to buy services at prices that had been inflated by research costs and a related reluctance by trusts to accept service contracts that made no allowance for research costs. A necessary if not sufficient condition for resolving this issue is to identify both the research and the service costs and to ensure that these are built into service and research contracts in ways acceptable to the institutions on whom the costs would fall. They should be seen as fair and acceptable to service purchasers and research sponsors. A set of conventions will need to be developed to cover the various ways of sharing the patient costs between service purchasers and research sponsors. It is unlikely that a simple and standard formula will do the job. There is, after all, a major difference between a research project in which an entirely new procedure is being investigated, where the entire exercise might be considered to be 'research', and one where there is a relatively minor additional cost in the form of extra patient investigations and, say, only marginally longer spells of hospital inpatient stay. Any such future conventions are likely to be highly dependent on the brokering role of regional directors of R&D (RDRDs) and the depth of their relationships and the trust they have established with their local research communities and health care commissioners.

Quality assessment and assurance

Peer review is the main plank of quality assessment and assurance. However, peer review is not only a costly exercise, especially of the time of researchers themselves, but some of the 'Cinderella' areas of research – say in community care – might be vulnerable through inexperience to the early application of a fully rigorous system of peer review. In time, however, I expect that these tender fields will be treated no differently from any other. There are notable lacunae in the present scope of peer review which are less defensible and which protect that which ought not to be protected. All R&D which uses NHS resources (including patients) should be subject to peer review, including the 'implicit' research funded out of trust funds, or by the smaller charities, or industry, which has often not been subject to quality assurance. Moreover, peer review need not be seen as focused solely on *projects*; there is much to be said for concentrating, where appropriate, on *individuals* whose track record or promise suggests that giving them a relatively free hand would be a productive way of spending some R&D funds.

Some alarm has been expressed at our proposals for an HEFCE Research Assessment Exercise (RAE) type of quality assessment that included researchers not currently eligible for inclusion in it, to back up the facilities support element of our proposed financial package. My own view is that, without the cooperation of the HEFCE, any such independent exercise would indeed be far too costly. However, preliminary discussions between the NHS Executive and the Funding Council give cause for hope. The simplest and least bureaucratically costly thing would certainly be for the HEFCE to agree to extend the range of its enquiry by creating appropriate new units of assessment or extending existing ones, especially into applied topics, and to consult the R&D Directorate in the composition of the panels.

Cinderella subjects

The Task Force drew attention to the importance of R&D in community settings for health care and in developing research strengths in the main disciplines likely to be involved. Some of our recommendations were directed to making the funding stream more accessible for these purposes and to support service costs of such research. Without this, we can hope for little in the way of any transformation of the culture of the NHS towards awareness of relevant research outcomes and the implementation of practice informed by them, especially given the increasing role of general practitioners as purchasers. Culture change is needed not only for medical practitioners but also for the nursing profession and the other allied professions. The community is increasingly the setting for health care, and it is therefore a matter for concern that of the 29 nursing units assessed in the last RAE, none scored 5 (the highest), only three scored 4 and two 3; and that of the 34 units of assessment in other studies allied to medicine, there were only two 5s, five 4s and one 3. My own feeling is that we shall have to target a few of the best existing centres in order to develop both the necessary training and the community research partnerships. This might well be an early matter for the newly constituted Central R&D Committee to consider. We were told that there are technico-legal difficulties in offering facilities support to fundholders. At the very least I would hope to see some major support of a programmatic sort for work in this field and a workable way of supporting any service costs of such research.

Contracts and bureaucracy

Whatever arrangements are adopted in future, they should minimise the costs of bureaucracy and management both for the NHS and the research community. While it seems inevitable that some of our proposals, such as the new costing arrangements for R&D with service cost implications, will create further expenses on both sides, it was our judgement that they would be worthwhile provided that they were kept at the minimum necessary, especially if the alternative were for good research never to get off the ground or to wither once it had. One must not allow the perfect to become the enemy of the merely good, especially if the 'perfect' is ultimately self-destructive. The increased use of contracts for R&D does not necessarily imply rigidity or short-termism. The Task Force saw no reason why contracts should not be as flexible and embody as much individual discretion for researchers as the circumstances and common sense demand. Moreover, we saw no reason why contracts should be perceived as inherently short term. They could be (as indeed some have been) awarded for long periods, ten years or more, especially where senior posts are being supported. Nor does a contract have to be artificially specific. The advantage we saw in an intelligently interpreted system of contracting was its explicitness about what was going to be done (there is virtue in making it explicit even that a research project may sometimes be essentially a 'fishing expedition'), how success or failure would be judged, and what the work ought to cost. None of us in the research community ought to have the right to use public money in a casual manner and for implicit purposes with no attempt to assess the value of that activity.

Declaring 'implicit' research in trusts

One of the quantitatively most difficult issues, which the Task Force did not attempt to resolve, was the size of support for research that service providers fund on their own account, partly out of special trustee accounts, or out of patient care contracts partly with the agreement of purchasers, and partly only implicitly so. We had no hard evidence on the size of this last component of funding, which we called 'implicit' research, but were advised that it was a very large sum. It includes R&D sessions in consultants' and other staff contracts and much work by clinical scientists in trusts. In the internal market for patient care, this funding is plainly at risk. We were told that such research is often an important preliminary to more substantive and explicit research, but much of it may also be substantive (though hardly ever peer-reviewed). It seemed to us important that these funds be protected for R&D and we proposed that they should be progressively declared by trusts and added to the single funding stream.

Special treatment for London?

London undoubtedly contains some of our finest research institutions and largest concentrations of expertise across the spectrum and along many relevant branches of science, though it has by no means a monopoly of excellence. Most of the best health services research is not done in London at all: there are many 4 and 5 rated clinical units of assessment in universities outside London. Moreover, London is relatively costly. That is true not only for service provision but also for teaching and research. Nonetheless, excellence in London is evidently worth preserving and the various forms of support for R&D which the Task Force proposed should be sufficient to ensure the future of the best institutions, departments and units that are there, as well as any that might develop, provided that R&D costs and expected outcomes can be explicitly evaluated, and provided that the allocation of facilities support gives due recognition to the demonstrated needs of nationally important centres. However, neither the market for patient care nor the evolving market for R&D will be sufficient to produce sensible results if left to operate without some further controls and central direction.

These issues arise particularly for those groups which depend on tertiary referrals, and for other centres of specialist excellence. Arguments can be made on both sides for keeping some centres of expertise in the capital or for developing them further in major research concentrations in other parts of the country. But what would be intolerable and have disastrous effects on morale would be for such responses to market pressures and individual initiatives to take place in dribs and drabs which debilitated extant teams of researchers and slow down the ability of others to develop the necessary critical masses. That way lies mediocrity and second-ratedness and the destruction of some of our best institutional reputations.

There is no case for general institutional subsidies whose ultimate destination and effects are untraceable and which cannot be accounted for. Properly handled, facilities support is there to meet this need, and could do so in a more sensitive and carefully targeted fashion than the R of SIFTR or the current temporary arrangements for the London postgraduate teaching institutions. After all, cost-effectiveness in R&D is justified by the same ends as cost-effectiveness in inpatient care: the more efficiently R&D resources are husbanded, the more R&D work they can do. This is not a policy for cheeseparing. As mentioned earlier, research that is merely cheap is not necessarily good or cost-effective. There is no reason why facilities support, or indeed either of the other two forms of support, should not recognise that some centres are inherently costlier than others. The best groups have nothing to fear from a purposeful attempt to address these issues. They need to be considered against a background of policy towards concentration of specialist centres, their needs for particular sizes of flows of patients, the academic quality of the institutions (and its within-institution variance), and the relative costs and quality claims that can be mounted by competitors. This is not something for the R&D programme of the NHS to solve on its own: it also particularly involves the Funding Council, the research councils, and the large research charities. It also involves health service purchasers whose willingness to pay their share needs to be assured.

Can purchasers be persuaded?

It has been said that the Task Force's strategy of developing the single funding stream as a levy on purchasers (including fundholding general practitioners) is highly risky, given their extremely uneven commitments to (and experience of) R&D, for which there was much evidence from our consultation. I have to agree with the riskiness of it, but take the view that the risk is there anyway. It would only be window-dressing to fund R&D support by, say, top-slicing the budget centrally. Purchasers, collectively and individually, will be perfectly well aware that R&D funding comes at the opportunity cost of current health care purchases, whatever the mechanisms. Indeed, current health care is already purchased at the opportunity cost of R&D. We were anxious to strengthen the voice of purchasers in the priority setting process, both centrally and at regional levels, so as to ensure that the priorities of the NHS R&D programme reflect the needs of the NHS, partly because their collaboration is essential (for example in ensuring that adequate numbers of suitable patients are available) and partly because they must be involved in the strategy for promoting evidence-based health care (which should be more than just an information strategy). The levy symbolises the seriousness with which the voice of purchasers is to be taken and is also a signal to central R&D managers and to the research community in general that the task of creating a widespread research-oriented culture in the NHS has to command a high priority. If we fail in this task over the next few years, the consequences could be very grave for the future of R&D in the NHS and would have been so whatever the precise form in which the funding stream was presented. We hope to have given it a sharp focus and to have concentrated minds.

Envoi

The work of the Task Force seems in general to have received an uncompromising welcome and commands the interest and commitment of the Secretary of State herself. We are plainly into serious business. However, its successful implementation will also require the support and collaboration of the research community. Much of the environment in which we operate today is not particularly friendly to the research community. Decision makers need to be convinced that there is a pay-off to R&D and that we have our research houses in good order. The Task Force's framework should enable us to offer these assurances but, in the end, it is the research community which has to provide the proof of the pudding. *Mere assertion* of quality, relevance, timeliness, and so on will not do. It will be especially important for us to convince purchasers too, and to enlist their support and commitment in a world where the levy will be seen to be in direct competition with current health care funding. I hope you will not bring to this a frame of mind that hearkens back to some past, and probably mythical, halcyon era. There is no point in wishing the problems away or regretting the history that makes the proposed changes necessary. There is no point in comparing today with things a decade or two ago. But there is every point in comparing what you imagine the research world would have been like in five years' time, had we merely gone on as we are, with what it can be like post-Task Force.

Disaster almost certainly lay ahead, not only because of the effects of the internal market for patient care on research but also because there was so much that was opaque, creaking, unfair and inappropriate in the accretion of history. For us all to realise the opportunities in the sort of world envisaged by the Task Force requires us all to promote a dramatic culture change, to get the national framework right, and to ensure that our own institutions are poised to take full advantage of it. *Carpe diem*!

14

The internal market and demand-side socialism: an acceptable means to a desirable end[14]

Only an end can justify a means

Let us assume, even though it is plainly an over-simplification, that the objective of health services is to promote health, and to do so, moreover, in such a fashion as to maximise the impact on the nation's health of whatever resources are made available to that end, while satisfying various equity constraints to do with geographical availability and individual terms of access. If you accept that premise as a properly moral point of departure, then a number of major implications flow from it:

1. the health service should be as efficient as it can be made

2. we need better information on health needs and health outcomes than we currently have

3. competition among financing (viz. insurance) agencies is inconsistent with these aims

4. provider competition may be the most effective means of attaining the efficiency objective

---

14 This article is an edited version of: Culyer, A.J., 1990. The Internal Market: An Acceptable Means to a Desirable End. Centre for Health Economics Discussion Paper 67, University of York, York.

5.   provider competition need pose no threat to the traditional equity objectives of the NHS.

The rest of the chapter seeks to explain these inferences. It is worth emphasising at the outset, however, that the fundamental touchstone relates to the meeting of the health needs of individuals: the patient (actual or potential) 'comes first'. It is in terms of this end that means such as provider competition are to be evaluated. It is in this sense that means are to be justified (or not, as the case may be) by the ends. Indeed, it is hard to see what, other than ends, could ever possibly justify any means. This is not, of course, to say that any means can be justified by reference to an end. It is all too easy to imagine some means so awful that no end could possibly justify them. It is also easy to imagine some ends that are themselves so awful that we would immediately reject all means of attaining them. But if we agree on a morally acceptable end (or ends), then the question becomes one of selecting the most appropriate means of achieving it (or them). In this sense, it is only the end(s) that can justify the means, if anything can. I hope, therefore, that we can for present purposes accept the ends I have postulated (and, at least for the time being, bear with their imprecision) and discuss provider competition in internal, or even wider, markets in terms of its appropriateness as a means.

The morality of efficiency

The ethicality of efficiency has been a theme I have emphasized over the years, not least because it seems to be an attribute that is despised in some quarters amongst health service researchers and bio-ethicists, and partly because, when it is grudgingly allowed some ethical merit, that merit is quickly quashed by assertions that considerations of equity will always trump any of efficiency.

Let us begin at the beginning. Efficiency has three meanings, the second and third of which cumulatively embrace those that go before:

1. not using more resources than are necessary to achieve an end

2. not incurring a higher cost than is necessary to achieve an end

3. not incurring a higher cost than is necessary to achieve an end plus attaining an appropriate rate of throughput or output.

Not using more resources than are necessary to achieve an end

This is sometimes referred to as efficacy or effectiveness. It enjoins us not to squander resources. Given an objective, such as returning the patient to normal functioning as speedily as possible, one should therefore seek those combinations of diagnostic procedures, medicines, surgical procedures, inpatient and outpatient care, health service and social service and family caring, and the patient's own time, that are most effective. To use more of any of these resources than is necessary is wasteful and inconsistent with the objective of maximising the impact of resources on health in the community. For, if more than is necessary is used, the excess could have been used at no additional cost to the patients in question in order to further the health of some other patients. Thus, overall community health is lower than it need be. Overall community Standardised Mortality Rates may also be higher than they need be.

While this definition seems fine, so far as it goes, it does not really go terribly far. There is usually more than one combination of resources represented in more than one method of case management that satisfies the definition. There are substitutions between drugs, between medicine and surgery, between institutional and community care, and so on, which can be made. This gives rise to the great variety of practice that can be observed within health districts, between them, and across national boundaries. Although some of these variations may represent inefficiency, many of them may be equally efficient in the sense of effective. We therefore need a tighter definition. The second meaning of efficiency meets this requirement.

Not incurring a higher cost than is necessary to achieve an end

This is usually termed cost-effectiveness. It requires the selection from among the effective modes of case-management of that which is judged to be least costly. To incur a higher cost than is necessary is again wasteful and inconsistent with the objective of maximising the impact of resources on health in the community. If a higher cost than is necessary is incurred, the excess could have been used at no cost to the patients in question in order to further the health of some other patients. Thus, overall community health is lower than it need be.

The trouble with this definition is that, although it affords a clear criterion for evaluating the efficiency of whatever it is that one is doing so that, for a given expected outcome and other patient-oriented attributes of the procedure, the cost is minimised, it does not tell us whether the procedure is actually worth what it costs and, in particular, whether there are not other programmes of care whose health payoffs may be higher at the margin (given the resources currently committed to them) than those of the programme whose cost-effectiveness has just been considered.

The notion of 'cost' that I am employing is no simple financial concept but it is the economist's standard notion. If benefit is to be seen in terms of health outcomes obtained (or expected), then cost is the benefit (similarly defined) that could have been obtained had the resources in question been applied in the most beneficial alternative way. In transactions in a well-functioning market, prices tend to signal the value of these lost benefits by virtue of the fact that competition for resources requires those who demand them to outbid other demanders, so the price reveals the alternative value in use. But without a market – for example, within a hospital – direct judgements have to be made about such opportunity costs, which should again, if they are to be consistent with the objective, be couched in terms of benefit to the patient.

Although the concept of cost may, therefore, be quite consistent with my point of departure, the second meaning of efficiency is still deficient for it fails to specify the rates at which each of the services ought to be produced. We need a still tighter definition. The third meaning of efficiency meets this requirement.

Not incurring a higher cost than is necessary to achieve an end plus attaining an appropriate rate of throughput or output

This meaning of efficiency requires not only cost-effectiveness but also an appropriate workload, which may be higher, lower, or the same as the current rate. The judgement that needs to be made here is usually a marginal one: is the gain to be had in the form, say, of added community health from a cost-effective programme worth the additional cost or, in the case of a possibly reduced scale of activity, is the value placed upon the lost health smaller, larger, or the same as the costs thereby saved? The general idea here is that a fully efficient health care system will have sufficient resources devoted to it that, at the margin, the gain in health is judged to be of equal value to the additional costs incurred in creating it, and that the resources within the health care system are so distributed that their payoff per additional pound of cost is equalised across all programmes of care (see Culyer 1976, passim).

The morality of this definition of efficiency is again clear: if the condition is not met, then either resources used elsewhere would be better employed in health care or resources used in health care would be better employed elsewhere. The 'elsewhere' may, of course, be in programmes that affect health but that are not themselves health services but they could also be resources used or to be used anywhere in the economy.

When a good or service commands a market price and is allocated amongst end-users in markets, a further (again cumulative) element of efficiency can be defined, which is that, in the absence of any market imperfections, the amount of the entity per time period going to each consumer ought to be such that the willingness of

217

the consumer to pay for a little more at the margin be equal to the cost of producing that extra. However, we have generally and for good reasons cast aside this principle in the case of health care and adopted instead the principle that health care ought to bear some relation to people's need for it, or their ability to benefit from it in terms of their health, or their health deficiency relative to some expected norm. For this reason, I propose to extend the idea of efficiency no further than the 'supply' side, leaving the inter-personal distribution of health care to be determined by other considerations, principally equity and health gain maximisation.

Health needs and health outcomes

The NHS, like all health care systems, has been handicapped in its pursuit of both efficiency and equity by a desperate shortage of information about needs and outcomes. On the efficiency side, it is only recently that it has become possible to make approximate assessments of the health pay-offs from alternative packages of care. The main reason for this has been the absence of quantitative measures of even an approximate type that would enable more subtle comparisons than can be made by means of relative mortality or survival rates. In the UK, one such new instrument that has proved useful in such fields as the care of the elderly and clinical practice is the Quality-Adjusted Life-Year (or QALY). The QALY has the great merit of highlighting the value content inherent in any outcome measure. While it is pretty obvious that there are important value questions embodied in the notions of both benefit and cost discussed earlier, it is less obvious precisely what the crucial judgements are that need to be made and who should be making them. The QALY sets this agenda out very clearly. It also indicates that there are quite substantial variations in the average costs per QALY across programmes (see Table 14.1). Although these are not the marginal costs one would ideally prefer, data of the sort indicated in the table suggest pretty strongly that current resource allocations are not making their maximal impact and they also suggest the general directions in which it may be sensible to try to redistribute resources.

Table 14.1 'League Table' of costs and QALYs for selected health care interventions (1983/4 prices)

Intervention	Present value of extra cost per QALY gained
GP advice to stop smoking	170
Pacemaker implantation for heart block	700
Hip replacement	750
CABG for severe angina LMD	1040
GP control of total serum cholesterol	1700
CABG for severe angina with 2VD	2280
Kidney transplantation (cadaver)	3000
Breast cancer screening	3500
Heart transplantation	5000
CABG for mild angina 2VD	12600
Hospital haemodialysis	14000

Notes: CABG-coronary artery bypass graft
LMD-left main disease
2VD-two vessel disease
Adapted from Williams (1985).

Developments of this kind can also afford ministers an enhanced bargaining power with the Treasury in the Public Expenditure Survey round, as evidence for the expected payoff of judiciously targeted additional public expenditure. They also offer (at least in my judgement) the most satisfactory means of reaching a view on that very vexed question as to whether the NHS is under-funded.

A need for health care can exist only if a patient has the capacity to benefit from the consumption of health services. If the care is not effective, it cannot be said to be needed. If the technology that would improve someone's health for the better does not currently exist, current services cannot be said to be needed (though it may well be that research is needed). In deciding what needs shall be met, however, it is essential to be able to form a judgement about the likely size of the benefit (in terms, say, of enhanced health). So, if needs are to be fairly met (for example, equal treatment for equal need) it becomes important to be able to prioritise need. The important thing about capacity to benefit is that it must be seen in terms of changes in health status. An absolutely or relatively high mortality or morbidity rate does not in itself indicate a high need: that depends on whether there is a capacity for the rate to be reduced sufficiently by the application of the relevant resources for it to command a priority relative to other needs. Moreover, it is the contribution of health care to the potential health improvement that is important. Many conditions are, for example, self-limiting, so one is concerned with the faster recovery that health care enables rather than the probability of recovery itself. In other cases one may not actually expect a payoff in terms of better health than before, but rather in terms of better health than would otherwise have been the case: amelioration rather than cure, reduction rather than elimination of disability, slowing rather than stopping deteriorations.

There may also be a 'big trade-off' (Okun 1975) between efficiency and equity. For example, in remote areas where the population is thinly distributed, the cost per unit of effectiveness may be relatively high, implying that community health could be increased by redistributing resources away from such localities towards those where population density is greater and cost per case lower. This is, however, likely to offend against any equity principle that requires approximate equal geographical accessibility. If such is the case, it is natural to allocate general resources (say, in the form of regional or district budgets) on a capitation basis, with the pursuit of efficiency in the meeting of local needs being conducted within the constraints that the equity rule imposes, and accepting that the ultimate cost of equity may be higher overall mortality and morbidity than it actually lay within our power to attain.

I have focused on health status in talk about efficiency, equity and need, it is because this is the prime business of the NHS (I make no apology for asserting that) and because it is only relatively recently that it has become possible to assess effectiveness and cost-effectiveness in such a fashion that decision-makers like doctors and purchasing authorities are going to be able to use these ideas and real evidence to evaluate their practice and to frame the terms of contracts. Fortunately, there is now lots on which people can build.

The NHS and demand-side socialism

The traditional arguments for why health care is 'different' from other goods and services are almost exclusively demand-side arguments which argue in particular for a low or zero user-price, for low-cost subsidised insurance and for preserving so far as possible the integrity of the agency role of the physician, in particular for helping the doctor, whether in general or hospital practice, to form professional judgements about a patient's needs and how best they might be met out of available resources, without being contaminated by other professional (provider) interests (especially those determining doctor's pay).

These arguments amount to a pretty unassailable case for a health service having the following characteristics:

1. the insurance function is monopolised by the state rather than by competitive private insurers, thus avoiding premium-loading through failure to secure scale economies on the finance side, the possibility of monopoly premium setting, extensive billing and fraud-checking administrative and legal costs, adverse selection through community premium-setting, inequity through experience premium setting, a host of "gaps" in coverage arising from employment status and inability to pay, and publicly unaccountable methods of controlling the excess demands that all insurance systems throw up (such as indemnity

limits, co-insurance, and privately determined quantity
limits on the supply side) (See Culyer et al 1988b)

2.   access to care should be determined by need rather than (for
example) insurance status, income, social or ethnic group,
or any other non-health related factor

3.   the bargaining and regulatory power of the state should be
used to countervail the monopoly professional and supplier
organisations and to enforce standards of safety and quality
determined in publicly accountable procedures

4.   professionals should be rewarded adequately but primarily
by salary and capitation rather than by fee for service.

While these desiderata all require the partial rejection of free
market solutions, they do so for demand-side reasons and for the
most part involve a heavy rejection of market-determined resource
allocations only on the demand-side. The relevance of the collective
expression of demand (demand-side socialism) lies in its ability to
specify and regulate need. It is appropriate therefore that health
authorities, for example, should specify a demand for the care
of their client populations. None of these traditional arguments
for health care being different requires the public ownership of
the means of production (viz. doctors' practices or institutional
care providers). Not least among the benefits of *Working for
Patients* (Department of Health 1989) is the clear distinction
between purchaser and provider that it has introduced into public
discussion. All the major ideological strengths of the NHS relate
to characteristics of demand. The job of the supply side is to be
cost-effective at meeting whatever demands are placed upon
it by the (partly publicly expressed) demand side. Its ownership
and structure ought to be whatever pattern of ownership and
structural features prove as a practical matter to be cost-effective
and responsive in the way just described. Nothing less than
this, but also nothing more. What matters is what works. What
matters is what means are best suited to the ends determined by
the collective demanders. The supply-side is not to be judged by

ideological but by practical criteria. Whether directly managed units, or trusts, or private organisations (for-profit or non-profit) best satisfy the requirements of NHS demanders is something to be determined by experience and judgement, not judged a priori. The NHS is essentially a demand-side organisation – or so it should be. Muddling supply-side features inside the public NHS not only begs the question as to the most effective means of delivering what is needed, it also exposes it to the serious hazard of domination by supplier interests that are independent of, and may be inconsistent with, the true objectives of the patient-oriented demand-side.

Provider Competition

If competition between providers of finance has scarcely any redeeming features, the same cannot be said for competition between providers of care. The particular attraction of competition on the health care provider side is that it provides the very systematic incentives for efficiency and innovation that are so conspicuously lacking in the NHS and dispenses with the need for the periodic sledgehammer strategy of financial squeeze (which has penalised the efficient and the inefficient rather indiscriminately).

Two forms of competition can be exploited, though *Working for Patients* emphasizes only the first of these: competition within a market and competition for a market. The first of these is competition between existing or incumbent providers for contracts offered by purchasing authorities, fund-holding GPs, other GPs, local authorities, private demanders, and even overseas demanders (increasingly one may expect from the rest of the European Community). The second is competition between incumbents and potential new entrants to the market for the right to provide service. It is a competition for franchises and, in the economics literature, it goes under the generic term of 'contestability' (Baumol et al 1988).

Three aspects of provider competition are worthy of particular attention: the rather poor performance of competition in the USA; the problems arising from possible monopoly behaviour by providers and the attendant need (though this is not unequivocal) for some form of price, quantity and quality regulation; and the problems that may arise from having multiple demanders under the arrangements in *Working for Patients*.

The US experience

Competition between providers in the USA has led, not to greater efficiency and lower costs, but to the duplication of services, excess capacity, higher costs (and hospital cost inflation persistently above general inflation) and (though the evidence is somewhat ambiguous here) inferior clinical outcomes. These adverse results are less due to provider competition per se than to the particular market environment in which US providers operate. One factor is that comprehensive insurance (despite the fact that 50 million US citizens have either no private or public cover, or extremely inadequate cover) reduces the incentive for demanders, whether patients or physicians, to select providers on the basis of quality balanced by cost, and generates pressures on providers to compete on a non-price basis. This is only partially constrained by the consequential upward pressure on premiums, because premiums are not prices of using the service.

Premiums enfranchise people to use a range of services at a user-price less than their cost. Hence premiums serve to reduce demand as they increase only through the effect they have on residual disposable income, rather than the direct disincentive that a rising user-price would have. Premiums are, anyway, subject to tax-relief and are normally part paid by employers. Moreover, rising costs arising from one's own use of service are borne by all policyholders. In the NHS, by contrast, purchasers are effectively expenditure capped and are to make contracts in the interests of entire resident populations or an entire GP's list. Demand, in general, is expressed in a collective fashion which sets the availability of resources into which the individual demand decisions expressed (mostly) by doctors as agents has to fit (and which is to be planned in conjunction with such expected individual demands).

Moreover, in the USA, the retrospective cost-based reimbursement system has enabled most providers to bill the insurer for whatever costs are implied by the services it has been decided (by physicians and hospitals) to provide, usually on a fee for service and per diem basis. Third party reimbursement plus retrospective compensation at a rate determined by providers has confronted demanders with an effectively open-ended budget constraint which has been widely held responsible for the substantial hospital cost inflation experienced over many years in the USA (and to the visitor is most apparent in the spectacular atriums and lavish parklands that greet one on entering hospitals). This cannot happen under the prospective budgeting arrangements in *Working for Patients*.

Monopoly

Monopoly arises when there is a single provider or a small group of colluding providers. It affords them greater discretion over price, quality and output than they have under competition, and is generally associated with higher prices, lower output or throughput, and higher unit costs. The latter is particularly to be expected in non-profit organisations in which 'profit' is taken in the form of a higher rate of use of some inputs than is necessary (especially highly skilled human ones and the technical equipment that every able technician can never get enough of). This enhances the job-satisfaction of the providers themselves and can easily be passed off to the innocent public as better quality. (The question is altogether begged as to whether the extra costs incurred actually benefit patients or, even if they do, as to whether the benefit is large enough to justify the expense.)

The policy response to these problems can be of two kinds. The first seeks to suppress the operation of the market via centrally determined price schedules, based on Diagnosis Related Groups (DRGs) for example, and myriad other controls. The second seeks to encourage the effective operation of the market via information dissemination (eg. about historic cost patterns locally and elsewhere, DRGs, performance indicators of various kinds, and prices struck elsewhere in the system between purchasers and providers) and by exposing incumbents (especially monopoly incumbents) to the threat of entry of new providers by making markets more contestable. The second of these two responses is likely to be the stronger, partly on grounds that any suppression of the working of the market tends to destroy beneficial as well as adverse effects (this is very evident in the case of centrally determined price schedules), partly on the ground that such regulation is costly and may also come, through customary political processes, to be dominated by provider interests, and partly on the ground that a strategy aimed at making the market operate more effectively is more likely to deliver cost-effective contracts, especially if there were a greater emphasis on contestability, which can be a complete answer to a monopoly problem posed by one or a few collusive incumbents.

However, contestability, selective contracting, openness in costing and prices, can all impose an awkward dilemma for politicians, who may not be able to escape a residual responsibility for poor performers (in a world in which poor performance becomes increasingly easy to identify) and who may, in particular, come under intense political pressure to prevent some incumbents from going out of business even though, in extreme cases, they offer services that no one wants and which purchasers have been able to purchase satisfactorily elsewhere with no net loss either of employment or of service for client populations.

Multiple demanders

Under the new arrangements of *Working for Patients*, a collective demand is not expressed solely (as may have been preferable) by a single purchasing agency acting for its population catchment area, purchasing from a wide variety of potential providers (including voluntary agencies and local authority social services) and able to exert considerable monopsony power to hold down prices for maximum throughput of contracted caseloads with contracted arrangements for quality assurance, and the ability to stipulate the providers to whom GPs would normally be able to refer. What we have instead is the clear possibility of different local judgements of need being reached by health authorities and local authorities, which may be difficult to reconcile and impossible, even if agreed, to enforce. With competition between GPs, moreover, (particularly non-fundholding GPs) there is the danger that they will be under greater pressure than hitherto to refer to non-contracted providers offering relatively attractive packages of services but whose cost consequences the health authority has little power to control. It is not possible to assess the likely practical significance of this at the present time, but there is clearly the possibility that some of the adverse features of competition in the USA may arise in Britain since the demand decision and the bearing of the financial consequences are effectively separated.

As the number of fundholders increases, the problem in one sense will become less because the demand and its financial consequences will become increasingly localised on the same decision-making unit. However, by the same token, the bargaining power of health authorities will also fall as this process takes place and their recurrent funding becomes increasingly top-sliced. As the principal agencies responsible for assessing a district's needs and determining the most cost-effective means of meeting them, health authorities may find themselves increasingly unable to implement the strategies that would seem most appropriate. These problems will be the more pressing in a world in which local authorities feel their budgets to be under great pressure and might decide to allocate resources to non-health priority areas.

Equity

Provider competition poses in itself no particular impediment to the attainment of whatever equity objectives are set. Indeed, if its effect is to increase cost-effectiveness and better matches of case-mix, workload and quality to population needs, equity is likely to be enhanced. Budget allocations within regions can clearly depart from a strict capitation basis if regional needs assessments suggest this would be more equitable. Regional initiatives in clarifying and implementing appropriate local notions of equity will be needs-rather than supply-based. If district funding is needs-based, decisions at that level about the place of treatment of patients will need to weigh the advantages of treatment close to patients' homes against the possibly lower unit costs and/or higher quality and/or shorter waiting times that may be available elsewhere. This partly involves equity issues, but it also involves judgements of effectiveness and efficiency in matters like the integration of community, GP and institutionally based services that are entirely appropriately made at local levels within the general equity constraints set by central government and region. Purchasers will have to bear equity issues in mind when formulating and placing contracts. For example, the notion of 'equal treatment for equal need' has implications for hospitals' admissions policies that will need to be made explicit and to be monitored.

The development of better information about community health care needs and the most cost-effective means of meeting them is one of the most promising parts of *Working for Patients* and will eventually enable much more explicit judgements to be made at all levels about both equity and efficiency. It can also be expected that, within regions and districts, not all will reach the same view of equity, how best to implement strategies designed to improve it, and the way in which trade-offs should be made. Perhaps this is as it should be for, if the notions of effectiveness and efficiency are reasonably clear – at least in principle – the same cannot be said for equity, for which many criteria vie for supremacy. It may therefore be neither surprising nor undesirable if different criteria and different judgements in their application emerge in different places.

Conclusions

The strategy of *Working for Patients* seems to be one that can be welcomed by all who care about the NHS. It does not prejudice the equity objectives of the NHS and it offers considerable scope for enhancing its efficiency. This is highly acceptable morally because inefficiency implies that some patients necessarily go without the care that a more efficient system would, with the same resource base, have provided. It also promises to be a more responsive service: more responsive, that is, both to the collective expression of need by authorities and to the individual preferences of patients. The NHS is, however, already relatively cost-effective in general – so far as one can tell from international comparisons. So whether the new strategy will generate sufficient cost-savings and sufficiently substantial resource reallocation between patient groups according to the best evidence of effectiveness, as markedly to improve the impact of NHS resources on the nation's health, remains to be seen. However, at the very least it will, over time, make more clear what has previously been extremely opaque: the link (at the margin) between resources and outcome.

Any major change brings major uncertainty and major worry. I have alluded to my worries about the fragmented demand-side. The pace is also frenetic. Indeed, the biggest threat to the strategy's success is probably that insufficient time will have been allowed to ensure that the early stages operate smoothly and without delays being imposed on patients and their doctors in the prompt matching of need and care.

I was once (in 1987/88) an advocate of regional experiment. I recognise now that experiments could all too easily have served, as ministers have claimed, to postpone or sabotage any real change. But even were that not so, such major experiments are quite extraordinarily difficult to evaluate independently of the vast array of confounding incidental pressures and changes that inevitable accompany them. It is also always necessary to compromise in the design of any experiment based only on part of a system but intended to model the working of the whole (for example, by omitting regional interactions). So we have an all-or-none experiment. A more limited experiment might (at one time) have been a sensible way of proceeding. It may not have told us much. It might have been used for destructive purposes. In any case it is now too late. But the all-or-none game implies that we (especially of the research community) will have to monitor what goes on extremely carefully, and the government should be prepared to invest substantially in such monitoring of the system's behaviour. Policy makers at every level must be adaptable so as to close off avenues that are destructive of the ends of the strategy and to open up new avenues that might help.

Provider competition is likely to be a reasonably assured success. The adverse effects of competition as seen in the USA are unlikely to emerge in the UK. The strategy is has much to commend it in principle and, even if it is less than perfectly consistent on the demand-side, we shall have time enough to monitor progress and make the required changes.

A final area of uncertainty lies with the behaviour of politicians. The combination of better evidence of effectiveness in meeting need and of better quality (or of their absence) and the ruthless judgement of markets on poor performers is going to make politicians accountable in all sorts of ways from which the opacity of the present system protects them. If they prove chicken, their ability to compromise the good that the internal market can generate is, of course, limitless. So too is the power of politicians having an outdated and unwarranted commitment to supply-side socialism (though not the other kind). But if you really believe in 'communism in health' (to each according to his/her need and from each financially according to his/her ability) then the prospect of a tax-financed NHS in which demand is collectively expressed and providers are constrained by market forces to meet the needs thus specified, and the funding is at worst proportional to ability to pay, is a prospect that all should be able to welcome.

15

Chisels or screwdrivers: deforming the NHS[15]

A market is like a tool: designed to do certain jobs but unsuited for others. Not wholly familiar with what it can do, people often leave it lying in the drawer when they could use it. But then, they also use it when they should not, like an amateur craftsman who carelessly uses his chisel as a screwdriver.
(Lindblom 1977, p. 76)

Financing Health Care, prepared by National Economic Research Associates, (NERA 1993) runs to 1,453 pages, reviews the experience of 12 countries, develops a prototype model and a phased strategy by which the UK might approach it. I shall not review the descriptions and analyses of the health care systems of other countries but shall focus on the UK, making occasional reference to other countries where it may be helpful.

---

15 This chapter first appeared as Culyer, A.J., 1995. Chisels or screwdrivers? A critique of the NERA proposals for the reform of the NHS, in A. Towse (ed.) *Financing Health Care in the UK: A Discussion of NERA's Prototype Model to Replace the NHS,* London: Office of Health Economics, 23-37. It has been abridged and edited.

The diagnosis

There is no single place in the study at which the reader can find a convenient summary of the problems faced and so there is some risk of having missed some crucial element in the diagnosis. However, a trawl reveals the following:

1. government is predicted to relinquish the roles of health insurer and health care provider to the market, which forces the issue of change and reform dramatically (p3)

2. the demand for health care will continue to outstrip the supply due to aging population and technical advance (p3)

3. bureaucracies are inherently less responsive to demands for new treatments than market orientated systems (p22)

4. governments will choose to spend less on health care than individuals prefer (p3)

5. centralised systems, such as the NHS, create distortions which seriously compromise the delivery of appropriate levels of service (p5)

6. patients and physicians do not have the correct incentives or information for making well-informed and efficient choices (p6).

The treatment

The recommended treatment is to move the existing UK system towards that of the NERA prototype over the long term (p1127). The main prototype components are to:

1. establish an agreed Guaranteed Health Care Package (GHCP) consisting initially of the current range of NHS services (otherwise unspecified) (p1132), but with a 'target' (unspecified – it is not clear whether the services ultimately to be included would curtail or extend the current range of NHS and community care benefits) (p1127)

2. create a market for health care insurance for the GHCP (plus top-ups at customer discretion) with insurers being denied the right to turn away clients at prevailing premiums (pp1127-8)

3. make health insurance compulsory (p1128)

4. set premiums in two parts: one, a function of (family?) income payable to a central agency for redistribution to insurers after adjustment for risk, the other risk-rated and payable directly to insurers (p1129)

5. establish a public National Health Insurance Fund (NHF) for those 'unable to manage their own health care insurance' (p1130)

6. make all services within the GHCP subject to mandatory co-payments, initially with exemptions but 'increasing the rigour' over time (p1133)

7. by implication, abolish the National Health Service Executive, its regional offices and health care commissioners (it is not clear what implications there are for services outside general practice or hospitals, such as community, blood transfusion or ambulance services)

8. make contracts between insurers (purchasers) and providers (public or private, primary, secondary and tertiary care) legally binding and enforceable at law (p1131)

9. deny insurers (purchasers) the right to own providing institutions (p1131)

10. create unregulated entry for providers (subject to 'medical qualification requirements') and permit providers full access to the capital market (p1131)

11. reduce the role of government to accrediting insurers, enforcing compulsion in insurance and the way the insurance market works, collecting premiums for the central fund and specifying the GHCP.

Is the diagnosis correct?

It is clearly one central objective of the current NHS to increase the scope and range of patient choice. Another, on which I shall for the present concentrate, is to maximise 'health gain'. What this means is not entirely clear and neither 'health' nor 'gain' are easy either to conceptualise or quantify. However, the issue needs addressing. Indeed, a good starting point would have been an analysis of the *efficiency* issue of what the NHS ought to be maximising (and what limits its success in accomplishing that objective), complemented by a parallel analysis of *equity* in resource distribution and what limits success in accomplishing that. It would be possible to develop both some principles to guide distributional judgements and some practical suggestions for improvements on where we are now. The implications for organisational and financial structures would not be terribly radical but, then, the structures currently being developed (which I characterise as 'demand-side socialism') are already broadly appropriate.

So what are the underlying objectives for the health care system of the UK as seen by our authors? They are elusive. And who are the ultimate clients for the study and what are their objectives? Are their objectives likely to be shared by the British electorate? Even if we pick the diagnosis apart, these issues do not become any clearer. But let us look anyway at the diagnosis in more detail.

The diagnosis in detail

The role for government will decline

As a diagnosis, this resembles wish fulfilment rather than careful prediction. As a prediction, it is implausible. Its theoretical foundations are not given and the empirical trend has for long been in the other direction. The issue might be better put as whether the government ought to relinquish or take on roles, and why.

Demand for health care will outstrip supply

This is hardly news. All it is saying is that, with insurance (of any kind), user price falls, so health care has to be rationed by other means. The issues are the levels to which demand (or need) is to be rationed, the criteria that are to be used in the rationing and the means used to do the rationing. Should these be market-led or subject to public deliberation and decision?

Our authors also claim (quite conventionally) that there are two main drivers of the overall medical bill: an aging in population and changing technology. They treat these two factors as exogenous when they are in very large part endogenous: that is, determined within the overall economic system. If health care expenditure per head of elderly is rising relative to health care spending per head of the rest, that is the result of decisions taken within the system. Chucking high-tech medicines and inpatient care at the elderly regardless of true cost-effectiveness is not something that we have to do. Nor do we have to adopt every latest mark of imaging technology the moment it appears. More deeply, the character of the research that produces the sorts of technology that are held to drive costs ever upwards (relative to constant price GDP) is itself endogenous, it too is driven by knowledge of what is likely that the finance of medical care will pay for, so research is driven in part by expectations about what the system will buy and is hence ultimately endogenous and influenced by system design.

Some technological change is cost-reducing rather than cost-increasing. The development of an effective vaccine for polio was a classic example that eliminated the need for the iron lung; or that for rubella, which led to a greatly reduced incidence of babies with birth defects. But, in general, technological advance in medicine does tend to be cost-increasing. A notable example is modern neo-natal intensive care which has increased the survival chances greatly of low and very low birth-weight babies but which has major cost consequences not only of the neonatal care itself but also of the subsequent long term care of these children as they survive into adulthood. But this bias towards cost-increasing technological change is hardly accidental. None of these things is inexorable. They are themselves generated by the systems we have and the incentives they embody. No successful business is going to embark on the development of products if it believes there is no market for them. Whether or not there is such a market depends on the willingness and ability to pay of those with power to decide what technologies they shall use, and the criteria to be used in selecting technologies.

Bureaucracy is unresponsive to new technology

It is poor analysis simply to assert that 'bureaucracies are inherently less responsive to demands for new treatments than are market-orientated systems' (p22). Market-orientated systems of competing funders have immense bureaucracies of their own which respond, as do all bureaucracies, to the organisational goals that are set for them and the rewards systems in operation to promote those goals. It may be that public bureaucracies are less efficient than private ones but one should ask (again): efficient at what? And in what way is their inefficiency 'inherent'? Are shareholders inherently more capable of disciplining their managers than public agencies are theirs? What theory suggests this and what is the evidence? If a public bureaucracy like a purchasing health authority has more rigorous standards of effectiveness than a private health insurance agency, then the difference between purchasing decisions will reflect something quite different from 'inherent' lack of responsiveness. After all, there is abundant evidence that competition between health care providers in the US operates less through price than through 'quality', and this is why there are under-utilised (and probably misused) scanners in neighbouring 50-bed hospitals in the US. If this is not the sort of responsiveness which our authors want to see in the UK, one must wonder at the (necessarily bureaucratic) mechanisms that competitive insurers might employ to counter the very real inherent tendencies that such competition is likely to evoke.

Beneath these prejudiced assertions there is, however, a fundamental and real difficulty: what is the optimum rate of diffusion of a new technology? It is not enough to reply; 'let the market decide' because the market is extremely imperfect and the element of public accountability for expenditures is going to be high even under their prototype. In essence the problem involves a trade-off between two uncertain elements: the postponement of possible (but uncertain) benefits while effectiveness and cost-effectiveness trials and analyses are done, against the greater assurance that what is adopted will have real benefit and constitute value for money. I do not pretend to know what the right general answer is except that it is unlikely to be 'leave it to the market'! The issue is a serious one and demands a serious analysis.

Macro and micro efficiency

The nub of our authors' diagnosis probably lies in the last three bullet points. They tell us that governments spend too little on the NHS (macro inefficiency) and that what is spent is not spent efficiently (micro inefficiency) through centralised distortions and inappropriate incentives. Efficiency is, of itself, a pretty emotionless term. It means simply maximising outcome per unit of input. The big issue here is: what should we be maximising? One possibility is to take the (economically) conventional view that we should be maximising individual welfares, as perceived by individual clients. This is traditional 'welfarism' (Sen 1979). Put more crudely, health is like most other things, so let individuals choose subject to the prices they confront and their incomes. This tends to fit with a pro-market presumption towards efficiency. But this may not be what our authors have in mind.

Their discussion of performance (pp 13-15) leaves much to be desired. They tell us (p13) that health care expenditure (HCE) as a percentage of GDP, and HCE per capita, are measures of the 'macroeconomic efficiency' of health care systems. They also tell us (p29) that the amount of health care services should reflect the informed preference of consumers. These assertions are unambiguously wrong. It is a matter of definition that HCE as a percentage of anything or per head of population tells us nothing at all (even as a proxy) about efficiency of any kind, nor would a monetary estimate of benefit as a percentage of something or per head. 'Macroeconomic efficiency', if it means anything, must mean that the total spend is set so as to optimise the social benefit relative to the social cost. The fact, as reported by our authors (p13), that HCE as a percentage of GDP has been rising in the United States cannot credibly be held to imply that the macroeconomic efficiency of US health care has been *rising*! The fact that the UK spends less on health care as a percentage of GDP or per head than many other developed countries, does not imply anything about efficiency unless one assumes that, by some magic, everyone else has their shares at the optimal level and the criteria for determining cost and benefit are identical in all comparator countries. Plainly, neither is the case. Our authors' index of microeconomic efficiency is physician visits per head. This is also crucially flawed. The ratio is neither a cost nor a benefit indicator, but a measure of utilisation or, if turned upside down, a workload measure for physicians. This, in international comparisons, can reveal neither relative efficiency nor inefficiency in the NHS to other countries. Nor does it have any clear bearing on the issue of whether these quantities reflect the informed preference of consumers ('informed' one wonders by whom?).

Back to the objective of 'efficiency'

Depending on the scope of the analysis, the constraint might be taken as the resources available to the NHS, where the system is judged efficient if it maximises the postulated value function given these resources or, at a broader level, the resources of the whole community, where the health care system is judged efficient if it allocates an optimal share to health care *and* maximises the value function given the share allocated to it. Economics has only one concept of efficiency, not a micro one and a macro one. Central to this concept is the idea of maximising some value function, such as utility, welfare or health.

The idea is at once so important and easy to lose sight of when one comes to try to apply it, that it is worth spending just a little time getting the theory straight. We can use a model for this purpose (Culyer and Wagstaff 1993). In Figure 15.1 we assume, for simplicity, that there are just two people (A and B) and that there is a fixed sum annually available for spending on health care. This budget is shown in quadrant III of the diagram as sum of money, which could all be spent on A (in which case A gets X_{Amax}) or on B (X_{Bmax}). It could also be divided between them at any point on the straight line connecting these two points, which is called the budget constraint. The outcome of applying health care resources to A or B depends upon what economists call the production function. A production function shows the maximum rates of outcome that can be obtained at various rates of use of the inputs. These functions identify 'productive efficiency' (p. 150). I have supposed that the production functions exhibit diminishing returns so that, for constant increases in resource commitment under prevailing technology, additional health outcome becomes smaller and smaller. Production functions for A and B are shown in quadrants II and IV, where I have assumed that B is relatively sick and also has a greater capacity to benefit from health care over a wide range of expenditures. The model also assumes that 'health' is the relevant outcome and that we have an acceptable measure of it. Each production function has its origin at the relevant individual's current health status and the outcome is the expected *change* in health that results from the application of health care resources. The co-ordinates of point S in quadrant I, the 'starting point', indicate the presenting states of health of the two individuals.

If we were to trace round the maximum health gain for A and B for different divisions between them of the budget in quadrant II we trace out the convex locus in quadrant I. This is called the health frontier. It shows the maximum increases in health that are possible, given the budget in quadrant III, the presenting states, and the two production functions determined by prevailing technology in quadrants II and IV. In the sense of production efficiency, any

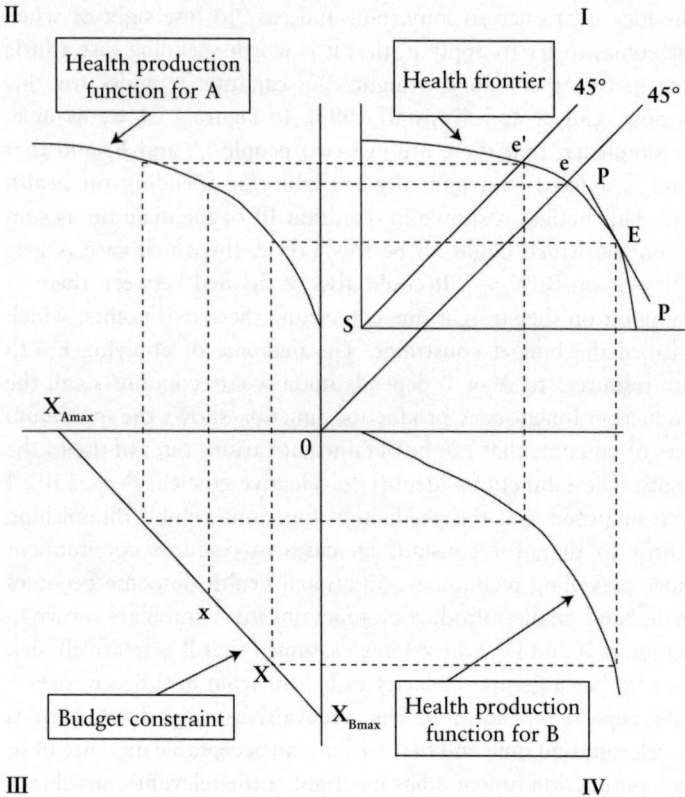

Figure 15.1 Health care efficiency and equity

point on the health frontier is an efficient point. It follows that a system is inefficient if, for whatever reason, the allocation of resources between individuals (in quadrant III) results in a point in quadrant I that lies inside the health frontier. This is most likely to arise because the most efficient production technology is not being used so that, given any amount of resources devoted to, say, A, the health gain is less than that indicated by the production function in quadrant II. In common parlance, such treatments would be seen as inappropriate, inefficacious, ineffective, or not cost-effective (Evans et al 2011). A failure in any one of these respects for either individual will result in an outcome that lies below the health frontier. This source of inefficiency is the most prevalent in all systems of health care including the NHS. The epidemiology literature is replete with examples of wide and inexplicable variations in clinical practice, continued use of proven ineffective procedures, and the use (this is the largest category) of procedures that have never been subject to careful critical scrutiny, let alone tested for cost-effectiveness (eg Chalmers 2005). A concern for this aspect of efficiency lies at the heart of the government's drive for a 'knowledge-based' health service and which is also driving its research and development programme, the meta-analytic function of the UK Cochrane Centre, and the no less important activities of disseminating best practice (the York Centre for Reviews and Dissemination) and trying to secure a contracting and incentive environment that maximises take-up of cost-effective methods of health care, which mainly means educating purchasers so that they can better identify true needs and then purchase truly effective services to meet them.

Some economists would push the idea of efficiency further, beyond that of *productive efficiency*, so as to embrace the idea of exchange efficiency: an efficient allocation of outcome across individuals. In the market system, individuals ('consumers' in the language of our authors) would form a judgement of the value of additional health to them and express this in terms of the purchase of appropriate inputs, given their income and wealth, insurance status, and so on. The relative marginal valuations of health implied in such a system can be indicated by the prices individuals would be willing to pay for additional health and these relative prices are shown by the slope of line such as the one labelled PP in quadrant I. If these were indeed the implied relative marginal valuations of health in our community of two people, then E on the health frontier is the allocative efficiency point and this would entail a distribution of the health budget between A and B shown by point X on the budget line on quadrant III.

However, a better way of addressing matters of interpersonal allocation may be to employ judgements of fairness or equity. Let the idea of efficiency in health care be restricted to the supply-side. In this way one may prefer points closer to e on the health frontier in quadrant I, which, since it lies on the 45° line through the origin in quadrant I, indicates (complete) equality of health between A and B. Less strongly, one might prefer points on the frontier closer to the 45° line than the starting point S is. Note, incidentally, that aiming at greater equality of health will generally involve an unequal allocation of resources between individuals (tracing back from point e to the budget line does not bring you to the half-way point along it, X_A is not equal to X_B) but to x. Note also that going for equal health is not the same as going for equal health gain, which would involve preferring a point e where a 45° line passing through S cuts the health frontier.

We can now make some quite important distinctions, for example, about efficiency in production compared to efficiency in interpersonal allocation, or that going for a more equal distribution of health in the community may involve quite unequal allocation of health care resources within the community, or that the final distribution of health in the community depends upon presenting health states (and the non-health care determinants of these), the relevant production functions, and the distribution of health care expenditures. It also enables us to frame a discussion of the efficiency or inefficiency of the NHS more carefully and avoid mistakes.

'Macroeconomic efficiency' revisited

'Macroeconomic efficiency' can now also be seen to be a question of the location of the budget line in quadrant III. Greater resources for health care will push it out further from the origin and fewer would move it towards the origin. As it moves away from or towards the origin, so the health frontier moves away from or towards the origin in quadrant I, assuming that efficient technologies only are used. And there is the rub. A British government would be reluctant to expand the health care budget if the increases went into income increases for existing resource owners (such as doctors and nurses) rather than additional inputs, or if any real increase in resources increased the use of ineffective health care technologies. In such cases, the budget line might move out but the use of inefficient production functions would still result in an outcome point beneath the health frontier in quadrant I of the diagram. In these cases, additional health care spending yields no ultimate additional benefit to the clients of the system.

Is the treatment appropriate?

Consider the general character of the 'prototype'.

A Guaranteed Health Care Package

The first striking feature is the proposal for a Guaranteed Health Care Package (GHCP). The issues here would be to do with its contents, a matter not discussed. It may indeed be a good idea for the NHS to adopt a GHCP (though its definition would be very contentious).

Compulsory competitive health insurance

Competitive insurance coupled with a much more aggressive use of co-payments is proposed. The arguments seem to be advanced on efficiency grounds, though they are not systematically set out. Where are the efficiency gains likely to lie? One possibility would be that our authors expect their proposals to generate a more optimal overall expenditure on health care. They expect the budget line in Figure 15.1 to move out and that this will, in turn, push out the health frontier. Since the compulsory two-part premium is effectively an ear-marked tax, it is certainly possible that this will happen. But it is far from certain. It would depend on political judgements about acceptable premium levels and public subsidy as well as the avoidance of the effects discussed above.

They also expect that such insurance would enhance the productive efficiency of the system by weeding out inefficient technologies. The mechanism through which this would happen is not spelled out. Would the new insurers somehow be more effective purchasers for the needs of their clients than current purchasers. One main reason for productive inefficiency lies in the availability of information on best practice for maximum health gain and the absence of an environment in which purchasers have the ability to create incentives for providers to use best practice and providers the means of controlling (mainly) physicians so as to adopt it. Our authors have nothing to suggest that is additional to current policy or structure in this respect. Premiums, of course, are not a cost of using the service and so they themselves will not cause much movement, though they may have important (and probably regressive), consequences for the sharing of the burden of health care finances.

We are told nothing of the billing and monitoring mechanisms to be used (or the bureaucracies required to administer them) under 'competitive' insurance. The transactions costs of competitive insurance are bound to be high, setting aside the costs to government of monitoring and regulating the industry in order to maintain its competitiveness, if the dangers of cream-skimming are to be minimised. There are countless ways of erecting informal mechanisms to cream-skim in ways impervious to any regulatory correction (for example by having user-unfriendly application forms, unhelpful responses to telephone enquiries, discourteous front office staff). Detecting such outrages would involve, needless to say, a costly, and presumably public, bureaucracy.

Co-payments

Would the more 'rigorous' use of co-payments for 'consumers' (including co-payments for components of the Guaranteed Health Care Package) shift the distribution of health in a way most people would think desirable? Further, and more fundamentally, who is the consumer? One of the odd things about the economics of health systems is that nearly everyone agrees that the principal character who determines what resources shall be used, and for whom, is a doctor. Patients have very little understanding of medical technology and effectiveness. They are usually worried and anxious at the time of consultation, most are elderly, some are confused, and many are frightened. While they have the right to have their values and personal circumstances better understood and respected by their doctors, in most cases decisions about resource commitment are actually taken by the doctor. Patients may receive care and, in that sense, be consumers, but they are unequal partners in the decision to consume. It is misleading to extrapolate from other walks of consumerist life, when personal judgements about what to buy are much less clouded by fear and anxiety, and are less likely to be delegated in whole or part to a professional (who may have his or her own personal agenda to pursue which may conflict with the patient's) and, via this extrapolation, suggest that financial brakes (we are now trying to reduce expenditures, not increase them) be applied to the patient. Why not the doctor? What are the grounds for supposing that the greater use of patient out-of-pocket payments would enhance the efficiency of the system? None are presented. The patient is a victim of ill-fortune or self-induced calamity. Why saddle him or her with further burdens, even though there is no perceptible reason for supposing that these burdens will, even in subtle indirect ways, lead to substantive improvements in either welfare or health. The rationale is obscure. Modest charges are one thing but 'rigorous' charges? If we are to deter people from early consultation with GPs, which is the stage at which preliminary (and sometimes final) judgements about the need for medical care are made, then there is the grave risk of introducing a feature that would substantially impede the system's ability to deliver health gain – for it would become increasingly difficult to identify the existence of the very needs the system is there to meet, let alone set about meeting them. So, how rigorous is 'rigorous'? And whose bureaucracy would manage a system that had exemptions?

A part of the study's case for co-payments is 'to make patients more aware of the cost of treatment' (p 1133). This argument is at best incomplete in that paying only *part* of the cost at the point of use is in fact to receive a false signal about cost. If anything, then, the message received by patients would be that the care they receive cost much less than it actually does. This proposal does *not,* then, produce the transparency claimed for it and the desirability of reducing 'demand' at the point of use depends very much on which needs would go unmet as a result.

Enforceable contracts

To advocate enforceability is much too bold in our current state of knowledge. It is not clear what the relationship between purchasers and providers would be in terms of contractual obligations, statutory obligations, and obligations arising out of tort and restitution. Effective contract enforcement is crucially dependent upon information being available that will stand the test in determining whether or not obligations have been carried out. Such information concerns, among other things, information about service mix, quality, and risk. A further complication is that the status of patients in the contracting process is problematic. The traditional contract doctrines of privity and consideration preclude third parties like patients from enforcing contracts even when such contracts are made to further their interests. The current arrangement is that contracts between purchasers and providers are not legally enforceable as *contracts* but are subject to arbitration by the Secretary of State. This is itself a murky legal area and incompletely thought-through by our authors.

Insurance, moral hazard, externalities and agency

There are many other important unanswered questions. For example, will premiums be set for individuals or families? Whose income would count in the income-related part of the premium? Whose health experience will count in the health-related part of the premium? Are these matters to be left to the market? If the government chose to have a health policy, as it might wish, what would be the mechanisms by which such a policy might be implemented? How would the vexed interface between the health services, conventionally defined, and local authority services be managed?

All systems of health insurance have their own ways of resolving moral hazard problems of various kinds: those that arise *ex post* at the consumption end when insured parties have an incentive to demand more because the user-price falls as a result of insurance, those that arise (also *ex post*) when providers see opportunities for billing practices that inflate the true costs of effective care, and those that arise *ex ante* when insured parties face a reduced incentive to avoid the circumstance that may lead to their making a claim on the insurer.

There is an undoubted potential inefficiency inherent in moral hazard but is 'excess' demand truly excess in relation to policy objectives and, if so, how is it best managed: through publicly agreed criteria and transparent processes, or privately and programmatically? The NHS is far from perfect in handling moral hazard but to put right what is wrong hardly requires private insurance as the remedy. It requires thoughtful criteria for prioritisation, thoughtfully applied. These questions need to be asked because the onus is on those who propose change to be clear about what's wrong, how significantly wrong it may be, what's needed to put it right, and how much improvement it may be reasonable to expect as a result. Reformers do not have to promise the earth, but we do need to know the approximate shades of green of the grass on the other side.

Patient choice

Another objective of the NHS is to widen patient choice. Here we confront a large number of difficult issues, most of which have to do with the 'doctor-patient relationship'. In its idealised form, this relationship consists of two individuals coming together to determine a course of action. The doctor is supposed to bring to this relationship an expertise in the probable consequences of alternative courses of medical action and a skilled judgement as to what procedures are likely to be effective. The patient brings personal circumstances, values and preferences, perhaps occasionally some medical knowledge, and is frequently confused, frightened and having difficulty articulating his or her perceptions, even to a GP with whom he/she may be very familiar. The art lies either in the patient transmitting the relevant personal circumstances and values for the doctor to fit them into his or her portfolio of medical knowledge so as to make a recommendation, or in the doctor transmitting the medical knowledge for the patient to fit into his or her personal knowledge so as to make a decision.

Which are the choices our authors wish to see expanded and why are their proposals needed in order to bring this expansion about? Again, these are not rhetorical questions. They need answering before one can enter in to a useful dialogue on the meaning of patient choice, those elements to which greatest importance is attached, the principal deficiencies of the NHS that need putting right, and the various means at our disposal for putting them right. There is no discussion of these matters in the Report, even though it is plain that 'competitive insurance' could militate against the ideal relationship, by for example encouraging the use of treatments that are to the doctor's but not the patient's advantage, or by encouraging hospitals to invest in 'me-too' technologies that involve hospital doctors operating too low on their learning curves for effective (let alone cost-effective) care.

Final comments and conclusions

These radical proposals generate a host of important questions to which sound economics can actually provide answers. These include: definitions of 'need'; means of promoting effective medical care; managing the transaction costs of competitive insurance; identifying the sorts of patient choice that need expanding; dealing with adverse selection, moral hazard, cream skimming and externalities; promoting the equitable distribution of benefits;

designing meaningful contracts; and so on. The questions deserve better answers than mere assertion.

There are alternatives. I prefer the UK Cochrane Centre to competitive insurance as a means of raising and sharing the knowledge base with *both* doctors and patients for securing greater efficiency, public purchasing health authorities to private health insurers as a means of revealing need and meeting it, and GP gatekeepers to co-payments, and low-cost access to the entire system, as a means of investigating *prima facie* need and determining where and by whom it is best met.

Part Five:

Health Technology Assessment

16

Social indicators: health[16]

Introduction

There are broadly two purposes for which a health indicator might be useful. First, they are useful in recording the state and progress of groups of individuals. Second, they are useful in formulating policy: at what targets shall we attempt to aim; what interventions shall we provide? It has not always been recognised that indicators designed to fulfil the first function will in general be different from those which are constructed with the second purpose in view. In particular, indicators that are to be of use in the formulation of policy must take account of the values of society (mainly preferences, ethical judgements and ideas of fairness) and the costs involved in accommodating these values. Since the policy functions include the purely recording function, it is convenient to consider indicators in the context of the requirements of social policy decisions. This suggests that the decision-taker requires

16 This paper is an amalgam and adaptation of two papers: Culyer, A.J., Lavers, R.J., Williams, A., 1971. Social indicators: health. *Social Trends* 2, 31-42 and Culyer, A.J., Lavers, R.J., Williams, A., 1972. Social indicators: health. In Shonfield, A., Shaw, S. (eds.), *Social Indicators and Social Policy*. Heinemann, London, 94-118. Thanks are due to the Nuffield Provincial Hospitals Trust for a grant to the Institute of Social and Economic Research at the University of York for the study of social and economic problems of health services which financed part of the research.

three different kinds of indicator, each serving a different function and each complementary to the others but none sufficient alone for policy making. These three requirements are:

1.   a measure of the 'output' of social policies, eg the 'amount' of education, health, etc

2.   a means of deriving the social valuation placed upon different 'outputs'

3.   a measure of the technical possibility of increasing 'output'.

Together, adequate information on each of these measures is sufficient to form policy: (1) provides the units in which policy objectives are to be defined; (2) values increments (in terms of social worth) in each objective; and (3) specifies what it is physically possible to do. For example, how much of one good thing must necessarily be sacrificed in order to obtain more of another. Each can be used at a more or less aggregated level, whether referring to society as a whole or to groups within society, like unmarried mothers, retired persons, specific social classes or ethnic groups, or patients suffering from particular disorders. Each is necessary for proper planning. Each raises important problems in conceptualising the kind of actual numbers needed and the extent to which the practical corresponds to the ideal, and each raises problems of ambiguity of interpretation.

This chapter is concerned with measuring the state of health. We discuss the ways in which the measure could be used to assess the size and value of health care interventions in cost-effectiveness studies, and then, briefly, how it might be used in population surveys of a nation's health.

A proposed health indicator

In order to generate a state of health indicator, it is necessary to devise an algorithm which will encompass both (a) medical data and judgements and (b) social judgements, with each expressed numerically in a standardised manner, yet clearly distinguished one from another. In this section, we outline such an algorithm and discuss some of its implications. If we are to build up an index of health (or, in this case, of ill-health) we need to measure both intensity and duration. 'Intensity' is here interpreted as having two dimensions, 'pain' and 'restriction of activity', and for the purpose of exposition, the discussion here is conducted throughout in terms of these two dimensions only. In practice, however, it would probably be desirable to extend the number of dimensions to include other factors thought relevant, such as distress. The fundamental problem, however, of how to combine the relevant measures of ill-health into a single index can be illustrated without loss of generality in a two-dimensional example. The first step would be to experiment with simple standardised descriptions of painfulness and of the extent to which activity is restricted, to see if there is any consensus among medical personnel as to the degree of pain and restriction in particular conditions, using these descriptive categories.

The initial descriptive stage may be represented as in Figure 16.1 below:

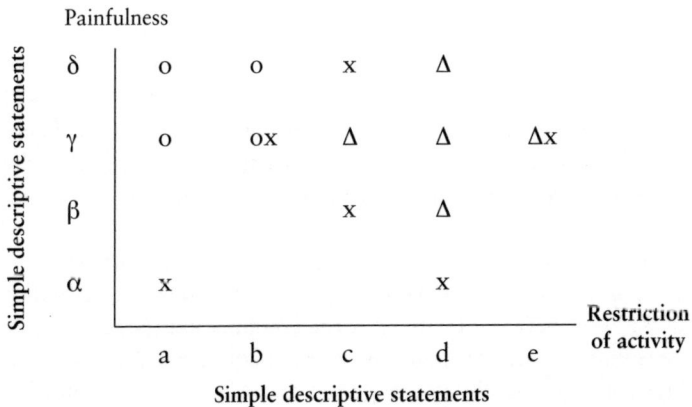

Figure 16.1 Descriptive stage in constructing an index of health

The symbols α, β, γ and δ represent simple descriptive statements concerned with painfulness (such as 'mildly uncomfortable', 'very uncomfortable', 'extremely painful' etc); a, b, c, d and e are simple descriptive statements concerned with restriction of activity (such as light work only, confined to house and immediate vicinity, confined to house, confined to bedroom, confined to bed). The symbols o, x and Δ each represent descriptive statements made by different observers about different medical conditions or different combinations of medical conditions. For example, the medical condition o in Figure 16.1 is regarded by one observer as involving, for a patient suffering from it, degrees of painfulness and restricted activity described by the statements δ and a respectively. Of the other four observers who place the condition o in the 'painfulness-restricted activity' space, one agrees with the statement of the first observer on painfulness, but categorises the degree of restricted activity by statement b. Two agree at assigning level γ to condition o, but one assigns a low level or restricted activity (a) and the other a higher level (b). Similarly each x represents corresponding judgements by six other observers of the most appropriate descriptions of those conditions. The specification of medical conditions may, of course, have reference to age, social class and other attributes, and the degree of articulation would have to be such that patients suffering from each condition formed a relatively homogeneous group, If there is any consistency in these judgements (as there is in o and Δ in the example), some 'norm' will be indicated as the standard description for that condition. Where no consensus exists (as with x in the example), it is likely that the condition under study needs to be more closely specified.

Supposing that we now had each condition clearly ascribed to a pain and a restricted activity level, we would then need to establish the trade-off between them, eg is the combination (β, b) better or worse than (δ, c)?. This pair-wise comparison is essentially a social judgement and should be recognised as such. The first evaluative step is set out diagrammatically in Figure 16.2, where each combination of pain (α, β, γ, δ) and restricted activity (a, b, c, d, e)

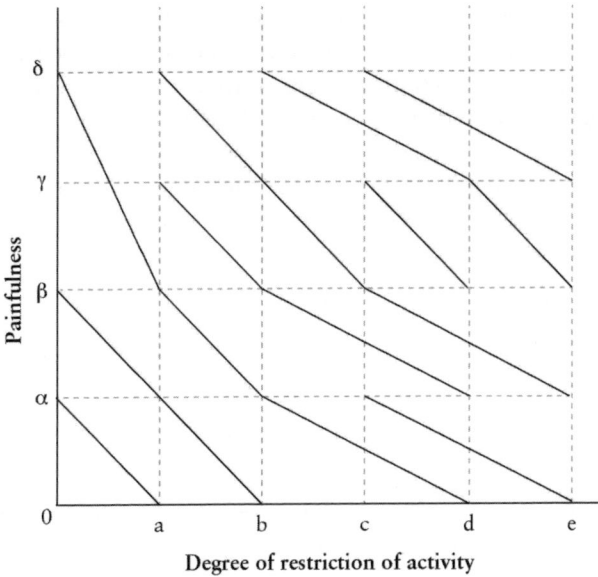

Figure 16.2

is compared and those that are regarded as approximately equal, in terms of the social-humanitarian benefit of avoiding them, are linked together by contour lines. In the example shown in Figure 16.2, (β, 0), (α, a) and (0, b) are equivalent to one another but better than (α, b) and any on its contour line which is, in turn, better than (0, e) and any equivalent combination. Because the contours only rank combinations, there is no presumption that the contours are concave from above. If numbers are attached at this stage, they are ordinal – indicating no more than order.

However, since it is intended to use these numbers as weights, and not simply as rankings, it is important to stress that society's judgements concerning the relative importance of avoiding one state rather than another are represented by the actual numbers attached to each respectively, eg state 2 is twice as bad as state 1, and state 10 is ten times as bad. This implication must not be shirked, and must be regarded as a statement about health policy (and is to be made by whoever is entrusted with that responsibility, for example, 'the Minister'), not a technical statement about each medical condition. In terms of Figure 16.2, this would be represented by attaching cardinal numbers to each of the contour lines. These will indicate how much better or worse one is, relative to each other. A ten point scale of intensity of ill-health might be constructed along the following lines:

0   normal

1   able to carry out normal activities but with some pain or discomfort

2   restricted to light activities only but with little pain or discomfort

3-7   various intermediate categories reflecting the various degrees of pain and/or restriction of activity

8   unconscious

10   dead.

Cost-effectiveness studies in the health field are plagued by the difficulties encountered in measuring the effects of various input changes on the health status of clientele. An index of the type we are suggesting might be used in the following manner for such studies.

Suppose a health care intervention is to be appraised relative to the 'best alternative' procedure. Figure 16.3 starts at a point of time 0 when the condition for which the intervention is to be used is diagnosed. The dashed line represents the expected pattern of ill-health (prognosis) with the conventional intervention; the continuous line represents the prognosis using the intervention being evaluated. The time up to t_1 is spent in further observation, deciding on an appropriate treatment, and waiting for therapeutic facilities to become available. The patient's health is the same under either regimen. The prognosis with conventional treatment gets worse as time passes, in a series of steps until death (score of 0) occurs at time t_5. This might be the standard prediction for this class of case. The prognosis with the intervention being evaluated (say a new treatment package) is represented by the solid line, and may be described as two weeks of severe restriction of activity after t_1 and t_2 (the pre-operative, operative and immediate postoperative phases) plus, possibly, considerable pain, with a steady improvement in condition after t_3, when the patient is expected to be already in better health than with the alternative treatment.

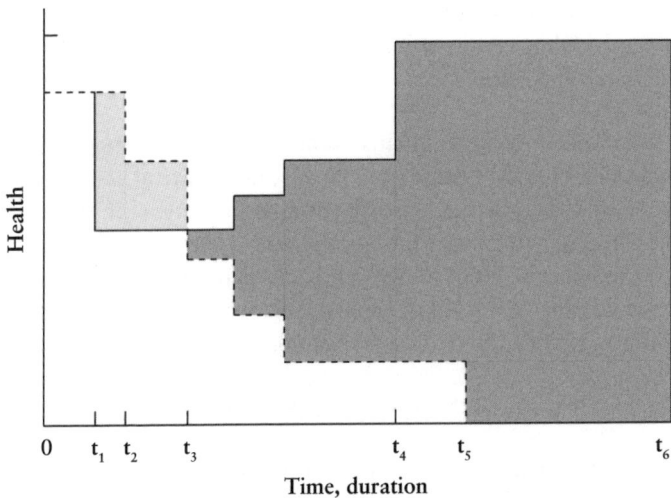

Figure 16.3 Time profile of health index with alternative interventions

There follow periods of convalescence, leading to full recovery at t_4 and full health thereafter until t_6, which we take to be the normal life expectancy for patients of this type.

The index score (representing the effectiveness of this treatment) is the dark shaded area minus the light shaded area. The net sum of the two areas is the health gain expected from using the trialled intervention rather than usual care. This particular example would obviously be a highly effective treatment, especially if applied to people with long life-expectancy, but less so for those with shorter life-expectancy. Both the time profiles used should be derived from statistical analyses of clinical results, or experimental data if the former is lacking. It is up to the medical statisticians and clinical triallists to provide these key data. A further sophistication that could be introduced would be to apply a discounting factor that would give less weight to future states of health compared with present states, and hence reflect the greater weight people seem to attach to the 'here and now' rather than to more distant prospects. In this way, the use of the indicator would serve to narrow the area of uncertainty about the consequences of alternative patterns of resource allocation.

As a measure of a community's state of health, the same categories could be used as a basis for a large-scale statistical survey, aiming to measure both the intensity and the duration of the various conditions affecting the population. Repeated periodically throughout the year (to allow for seasonal fluctuations) and from year to year (to establish trends), this would provide the kind of information required as a contribution to general social indicators.

Certain features of this system are noteworthy:

1.　in principle it enables preventive as well as therapeutic activities to be incorporated

2.　although much more difficult in practice, in principle it can embrace mental illness

3.　it treats one week of suffering at any particular intensity level as being equally undesirable, irrespective of the identity of the patient and while distributional assumptions are possible in principle, they would make the analysis much more complicated

4.　it relates only to patients, and does not include infectivity, or the pain and suffering caused to others by the patient's condition. Neither of these shortcomings is insuperable in principle, but as a practical matter they will be difficult to overcome in the near future

5. the satisfaction felt by patients themselves (or their friends and relatives) is not regarded as an independent consideration in this formulation. To do so would raise such enormous difficulties for any health indicator that the matter is mentioned here only so as to not lose sight of it.

Conclusions

The chief aim of this chapter has been to devise a conceptual scheme that will assist in the construction of health indicators designed to measure the quality of life and the effectiveness of health care interventions in improving health. State of health indicators should be as free of contamination by health care inputs as possible. They are also inherently imbued with policy values. As Moser (1970) has pointed out, "in practice the weighting of the components of quality of life according to some set of values is taking place all the time." We have sought to make the process explicit, keeping our examples simple for expositional reasons. There are many extensions that would need to be made in practical cost-effectiveness studies and health surveys, only some of which are mentioned here. Other key questions include methods for handling the inevitable uncertainty attached to the alternative profiles, determining the different competencies required of those making scientific, clinical and value judgements, and the ultimate question of whether the gains thus calculated are 'worth' the costs necessarily incurred in realizing them – costs that are ultimately reflected in resources drawn away from other patients and hence in turn reflected in reduced health gains elsewhere.

Perspective and desire in comparative effectiveness research: the relative unimportance of mere preferences, the central importance of context[17]

If economists could manage to get themselves thought of as humble, competent people, on a level with dentists, that would be splendid!

(Keynes 1932, p.373)

It might not surprise some readers that economists could be charged with lacking the admirable characteristics in the above quotation, though Keynes was not really accusing economists of being arrogant. Rather, he was warning the general reader that economic issues, like teeth, are not the ultimately important things affecting the quality of our lives. Technical issues, and the more banal necessities of life, are where we should chiefly find both dentists and economists at work. Unfortunately, economists sometimes find themselves thrust into situations where they have to go beyond mere humble competence, even when dealing with

17 This chapter appeared originally as: Culyer, A.J., 2010. Perspective and desire in comparative effectiveness research the relative unimportance of mere preferences, the central importance of context. *Pharmacoeconomics* 28, 889-897. This is a much abbreviated version. I thank Karl Claxton, Peter Coyte and Mike Paulden for comments on a draft and give them full absolution from all remaining errors and infelicities.

technical minutiae or banal matters. Comparative effectiveness research (CER), like the associated apparatus of cost-effectiveness analysis (CEA), often provides precisely such situations. It behoves us, therefore, to give occasional consideration to our competencies and their limits, even if this seems to threaten the methods and practices we hold dear.

I take for granted that seeking answers to questions such as, 'does it work better than other interventions?', 'for whom does it work better?' and 'at what cost does it work better?' are all reasonable questions to ask of clinical interventions, especially ones that are paid for by third parties such as public or private insurance agencies, and that the answers are of interest and importance to: patients and their families; the professionals, both clinical and managerial, who serve them; the third-party payers; manufacturers of medicines and medical devices; and regulators and others, such as employers, who can affect the environment that helps to determine the health of the public. CER is not a means of addressing *all* these questions. It seeks to identify the relative impact on health of one procedure compared with another, whether the effect is positive or negative, and its size. Although CER does not address the issue of cost effectiveness directly, the logical link between CER and CEA becomes apparent, particularly when decision-makers operate with a fixed budget, for then the positive 'effect' expected from adopting an intervention that 'works' will necessarily entail withdrawing resources from existing interventions, with some associated loss of 'effect' (unless they are interventions that do not work). Such loss is the opportunity cost of the adopted intervention. The same applies if the budget is increased: adopting one intervention using the 'new money' necessarily means forgoing some other opportunity, either by ditching something from the old set of activities or not adopting some other new intervention.

It is commonplace in the current theory and practice of economic evaluation of health care interventions to require explicitness about the perspective taken by authors in a study (eg Drummond et al,

2005) and (particularly in the US) specifically to require the adoption of a particular perspective, the so-called 'societal perspective' (Gold et al, 1996): one that takes account of all consequences – at least all those of any size. It is also increasingly common to set the analysts a 'reference case', defining a correct perspective and other desiderata for a competent economic analysis. While explicitness seems unexceptionable, the advice regarding perspective is at least questionable, as I shall try to show.

Let us take it as axiomatic that CER and CEA exist to help decision-makers make recommendations, even to take decisions, that will directly impinge on practices in the health care system. Many such interventions are clinical, but others come from a very wide set of interventions, such as those affecting service organizations, client behaviour, public health, workplace health and safety, and financing arrangements. The object is to identify those that work better than others and the critical question is what counts as 'working better'.

Social welfare or health?

For many economists, the starting point in answering this question seems obvious. It is welfare economics. And it is welfare economics of a conventional, if actually very particular, kind – namely welfare as built up from the preferences (sometimes termed 'desires' or 'tastes' or 'wants', though they might also be prejudices!) of the members of a society or jurisdiction. Gold et al (1996) are very clear about this: "We place CEA squarely within the context of welfare economics" and quote Arrow (1963) with approval in asserting that the central problem of welfare economics is "achieving a social maximum derived from *individual desires*" [my italics]. This places the economic component of CER in what has been called 'welfarism' (Brouwer et al 2008), one of whose chief characteristics is that the goodness of all situations and changes in them is determined by, and only by, individuals' preferences.

At first blush this seems not unattractive if one is trying to be 'humble'. The basic test of social betterment in welfare economics is the Pareto criterion: if a particular arrangement is, for at least one person, a net advantage as judged by that person (the cons having been balanced against the pros) and it is also to no other person's net disadvantage, then the arrangement, or change in arrangements, is judged better than whatever is its comparator. Conversely, if, for at least one person, an arrangement is to their net disadvantage and it is also to no other person's net advantage, then that arrangement is deemed worse than its comparator.

It seems hard to deny that such a test minimises the intrusion of any ethical arrogance on the part of the analyst. The context of the application of the Pareto criterion was usually one in which welfare was being considered in markets, where individuals were thought of as voluntary actors who required compensation (rewards) for arrangements or activities they disliked and were willing to pay for entities that they wanted. The markets worked through inter-related systems of compensatory arrangements known as prices, wages and so on. The possibility of real-world compensation through voluntary trading made the applicability of the Pareto criterion less rare than might otherwise have been expected: one did not have to weigh the net gains of one against the net losses of another. This was done (at least in principle) by well ordered and complete markets, through which the subjective values placed on goods and services were revealed.

However, in CER, we are in a world that differs in two major respects. The first is that the concern in CER is with an unpriced element of welfare that is not directly traded in any market and which might reasonably be held to fall outside the bounds of 'economic' welfare. The second is that the idea of economic welfare, besides being defined as measurable by the 'measuring rod of money', is indeed built upon an ethical foundation of individual preferences. The distinction between general welfare and economic welfare is attributable to Pigou (1932). His view of welfare included what he called 'states of consciousness' and the relationships between them, while the subject matter for the 'science' of economics was 'economic welfare' – that part of the greater concept that might be measured by a monetary dimension.

The naturally unpriced character of 'health' raises issues mainly in cost-benefit analysis (CBA) and, in particular, in attempts by economists to attach monetary values to health outcomes through controlled experiments. This is the first point to be raised about 'context': the characteristic context for CER is specifically *not* one in which outcomes are measured in monetary terms. Even when analysis is extended to embrace costs, as in CEA, the outcome side is still usually characterised as 'health', or 'health-related quality of life' or changes in such an entity. Its monetary value is left implicit.

Values or preferences?

Granted the centrality of 'health', it must seem very odd to anyone not raised from intellectual birth on mainstream economics, to jump immediately (or, indeed, at all) to the belief that the contribution of health to welfare is to be based on preferences. One of the respects in which dependence on mere preferences seems 'odd' is that it is nearly always accompanied by a sublime lack of interest in assessing the quality of the preferences in question: juvenile; bigoted; senile; inconsistent; self-serving; self-harming; cruel; masochistic; ignoble; crass; ill-informed; perverted; disgusting.

The more natural thing to ask about any measure of health is whether it possesses construct validity. Since there is no available gold standard against which such measures can be appraised, one is driven naturally, but surely appropriately, to testing the 'fit' of a concept, its components and the trade-offs that are embodied in it, with the context of decisions. Indeed, this was essentially the practice adopted by those of us engaged with what were termed in the early 1970s as 'health indicators'. The primitive version of a multidimensional index of health then created was a construct based upon the authors' perceptions of the policy objectives set (albeit without any great precision) by elected politicians. Policy objectives are evidently amongst the most critically important descriptors of context. It was transparently obvious from those early times that the construction of such an index required value judgements and, given that the instrument was to be used as an instrument of public policy, that it would have seemed desirable to have discovered the opinions of various stakeholders on such matters, and specifically their values. But this would hardly have been an enquiry into 'desires', 'tastes' or 'preferences'. I mean to convey by this dismissive tone not that preferences are unimportant for human welfare, nor that they cannot form a strong foundation for some applications of welfare economics, but that they are not what we are seeking in health outcomes. What we seek will embody values, but preferences hardly at all. We should ask subjects 'what ought the components of a health-related quality of life index be?' not 'which ones do you desire or prefer?', 'do you think overall that they amount to a reasonable definition of health?', 'what ought the trade-off between immobility and lassitude be?', 'are the relative weights to be put on each constant or do they vary as the combinations vary or the experience of them varies?', 'does the EQ-5D have reasonable construct validity in the context of most formulary type decisions?' and so on. What moral authority comes from basing a measure intended to represent an increase in a person's or a group's *health* on their (or anyone else's) 'tastes' or 'preferences'? Why should mere preference ('I want more, or less, or the same') count above 'I think this combination represents a higher/lower state of health'? For many years, ministers have couched the objectives of the UK NHS in terms of 'health gain'. No mention of preferences. The NHS is far from unique in this respect.

Utility and utility-like measurement

Welfare economics is a specialist branch of utilitarian theory. A modern confusion about the 'utility' of quality of health-related life has arisen because it is entirely appropriate to use the theory of utility measurement. Its language is also useful (eg of cardinal and ordinal measures, its casting in terms of expectations) and some of its methods (eg the standard gamble, time-trade-off) and it is also appropriate for measuring non-utility entities, such as 'health'. But that does not mean that what is being measured is a utility, at least not in the usual sense of an indicator of *the strength of a preference,* any more than using an interval scale with an arbitrary origin at zero (like a Celsius scale) to measure an entity must mean that the entity in question is 'temperature'. We are not creating a metric of greater or lesser desirability, even though health is, of course, desirable, but a metric of greater or lesser healthfulness. It is a pity that the term 'cost-utility analysis' ever came to replace the much more neutral 'cost-effectiveness analysis'.

As to the sources of values, this is again a matter of context. It is hardly for Keynesian dentists to determine whose values should 'count' and with what 'weight'. Ditto for economists. The first task for analysts, therefore, is not to discover what the values are that can be revealed through the various ingenious methods of revealed and stated preferences, although that may indeed be a task to be undertaken. The first task is to determine whose values are to be revealed. The answer is not to be *a priori* or derived from abstract thought experiments on the part of analysts, but ought (if one is to be humble) to be inferred or obtained directly from the context, in particular from the clients for the analyses being commissioned or its commissioner. This phase establishes an important part of the perspective of a study and identifies 'stakeholders'. A statement of perspective in CER does two main things. It specifies the character of the consequences of using one intervention compared with another and it reflects the purposes and objectives of the agency on whose behalf the analysis is being conducted. While it is not the business of pharmaco-economists to specify what the perspective ought to be, they may legitimately clarify the issues involved for client decision-makers in choosing a perspective, spell out some of the consequences of adopting one rather than another, help them to achieve consistency between the study objectives and the research question, and so on. These are valuable professional competencies that further the discovery of a relevant perspective – but they are not the same as having the analyst specify it.

The societal perspective

Gold et al (1996) recognised that analyses can be 'reasonably' performed, while falling substantially short of the societal perspective. They offer two reasons for nonetheless preferring the societal perspective over others. The first is "the recognition that societal resources are limited and that health should not be exempted from these limits" (p. 6). The second is that the societal perspective is the one predicted to be chosen by neutral disinterested individuals (p. 7), as though behind a Rawlsian veil of ignorance. The first of these reasons hardly justifies a narrow scope for any study, since it is resource scarcity that prompts the commissioning of a CER in every case, regardless of the breadth of the range of consequences. The second runs up against the snag that it is not easy to predict the context that might be chosen behind a veil of ignorance for making decisions about the broad allocation of resources to health, education and a variety of activities sometimes referred to as merit wants (Musgrave 1959, Culyer 1971).

The palpable evidence we have is that social decision-making is frequently upwardly delegated to a publicly accountable official, an agent commonly called 'the minister', an agent whose principals are the public: the very person who is likely to commission CER studies in pursuit of a ministerial objective such as 'health for all' (or some such overall strategy cast in terms of health) on behalf of large communities. Similarly highly placed agents might include the US Food and Drug Administration (FDA) and the National Institute for Health and Clinical Excellence (NICE) in England and Wales. Other less exalted research commissioners, whether in the public or private sectors, also typically hold delegated powers and act as agents for their principals (such as subscribers to private sector insurance plans, equity holders in for-profit organizations with workplace health and safety investments to assess, trustees of non-profit healthcare organizations, manufacturers of products that need to satisfy regulatory requirements that include CER). There seems no particular reason for the principals, on whose behalf these agents decide, to want them to adopt the 'societal' perspective. The agents are more likely to take a perspective related to the character of their accountability and their ability to claim that their decisions were reasonable under the prevailing circumstances.

A more practical ground for taking the wider 'societal' perspective is that an analysis performed in that way embodies the consequences for *all* stakeholders and, provided that it is presented in an appropriate way, affords each affected interest group an opportunity to see the consequences for that group of the adoption of one intervention over another. The practical claim is thus one of transparency, comprehensiveness and, ultimately, political acceptability. But 'societal perspective' is not necessarily to be equated to 'interests of stakeholders'. It requires the question to be answered, 'who decides what, in the current context, the interests of members of the community are?' A study of the same intervention might vary accordingly, as it was performed mainly at the behest of and from the perspective of clinicians, hospital managers, workers, employers, current patients, past patients, future patients, third party insurers, ministers of health, the custodians of liberty or, indeed (but not necessarily) 'society'. In short, perspective is and ought to be context dependent. It is as though the advocates of the societal perspective actually believe that these empirical enquiries are much more than the aids to thought mentioned earlier and that, properly done, they provide a complete answer. It is immodesty on stilts.

Further implications of context

Context, in determining perspective, is evidently of critical importance. But context can also be critical in another respect, ie when we consider that context has consequences not only for the variables to be included in the analysis but also for the manner in which they are combined or 'added up'. Let us again suppose that the Ministry of Health is to maximise health rather than some wider notion of welfare. The ministry has a budget that it may use for, and only for, the purposes of promoting health gain through the deployment of health services. In such a scene, the opportunity cost of health is always also health. If resources are devoted to one particular intervention, they are not available for another. If the ministry of health is doing its job, exhausting its budget and pushing the health care system on to the health frontier, all the uses to which health service resources are put will generate more expected health per unit than any alternative uses and the (rising) marginal opportunity cost of lost health from health interventions not used or less intensively used will just equal the (falling) marginal health gain.

This will not at all be the case in a scene in which the ministry of health has a different charge, say public health only, with the health services provided in other ways and variously financed (publicly and privately) as well. In that scenario, a health service intervention might draw resources from outside the health sector (say through out-of-pocket payments from users or through third-party reimbursement of providers). There, the specific in-kind opportunity cost will be virtually impossible to pin down, even at the level of generality with which it was pinned down in the other scenario, and will often most conveniently be expressed monetarily and by appeal to the effective workings of markets. The issue needs immediately to be confronted: how are the health gains or losses to different individuals and groups to be added up and compared? Surely not at the analyst's whim, even if the analyst is an ethicist. Maybe in a way that reflects some socially revealed distributional values (which ought not, however, to be described as 'tastes' or 'preferences'). A new task for the analyst is thus to discover whose values the principal thinks ought to count and how these values might be best accessed and embodied in the research.

Recommendations for the practice of CER

The implications of the foregoing are few and straightforward in principle but could, on occasion, be dramatic in changing the character of the recommendations based on specific CERs. The first is that the measure of outcome should always be tested for construct validity and never be identified blindly with utility.

The validity of any construct, such as a QALY, will in part be determined by: the 'fit' it has with the context of the decision, of which major elements are the aims, objectives and legitimate authority of the agency for which the analysis is being performed; the stakeholders for whom the consequences of implementation are significant; and the competence of stakeholders to articulate their values. If preferences as well as values are of relevance in determining construct validity, they need to be identified as such early in any study. These procedures will set the perspective of a study and root it, wherever possible, in an explicit context and value frame.

An important role for analysts, in view of the foregoing, is to acquire a full understanding of the decision-making context and to figure out its consequences, preferably jointly with the research commissioner, for the framework and the substantive content of analyses (outcome measures, opportunity costs, discounting, equity and distributional issues). Knowledge translation and exchange begins here, before the research has even begun. It is not for analysts to specify either what the source of values ought to be or what the perspective ought to be. However, their initial role is to help the agency for whom the study is designed to prescribe both the values and the perspective. This can best be done through deliberative processes in which possible values and perspectives are considered, the consequences of using them made plain and the consistency of the basic choices made at this stage of the analysis with other decisions explored. It is at this stage that the role of preferences will become clear. It is here that construct validity is to be tested and here that the likely differences in outcome between including and excluding health consequences for (say) family members and informal carers of principal beneficiaries are assessed. It is here that the grounds for (say) weighting benefits to some groups more than those accruing to others should be addressed, and it is here that consistency between the methods of CER in one territory (say public health) and another (say general practice) ought to be assessed. An important role for analysts is to guide their clients through such fundamental choices in an unprejudiced fashion. Context has manifest implications for the validity of the constructs used in analysis and also for the values embodied in the constructs and the sources from which they are properly derived. In all of these matters, the inclination to discover a priori answers is a mistake. The context, the perspective, the values, their sources and their consequences for analytical methods are matters for discovery, not invention or mere assertion. And the process of discovery should be a joint exercise, with analysts in partnership with clients.

18

NICE and its value judgements[18]

The National Institute for Health and Clinical Excellence (NICE) offers health professionals in England and Wales advice on providing NHS patients with the highest attainable standards of care (NICE 2003). It gives guidance on individual health technologies, the management of specific conditions, and the safety and efficacy of interventional diagnostic and therapeutic procedures. Guidance is based in part on the best available evidence, although evidence may not be very good and is rarely complete. Those responsible for formulating NICE's advice, therefore, have to make judgements both about what is good and bad in the available science (scientific value judgements) and about what is good for society (social value judgements). This chapter focuses on the social judgements forming the crux of the Institute's assessment of cost effectiveness.

NICE's approach to economic evaluation

On its own, clinical effectiveness is insufficient for maintaining or introducing any clinical procedure or process. Cost must also be taken into account. When good evidence exists of the therapeutic equivalence between two or more clinical management strategies,

18 This chapter is an edited and shortened version of M D Rawlins and A J Culyer, 2004. National Institute for Clinical Excellence and its value judgements. *British Medical Journal*, 2004, 329: 224-227.

the cheaper option is preferred. However, in most instances NICE is confronted with a clinical management strategy that is better than current standard practice but which costs more. NICE must then decide what increase in health (compared with standard practice) is likely to accrue from the increase in expenditure. This is the incremental cost-effectiveness ratio. Such ratios can be expressed in many ways. NICE's preferred measure is the cost per quality adjusted life year (QALY) but, if appropriate data on quality of life are not available, it uses alternatives such as the cost per life year gained.

NICE rejects the use of an absolute threshold for judging the level of acceptability of a technology in the NHS for four reasons: (1) there is currently no agreed empirical basis for deciding at what value a threshold should be set; (2) there may be circumstances in which NICE would want to ignore a threshold; (3) to set a threshold would imply that efficiency has absolute priority over other objectives (particularly fairness); and (4) many of the technology supply industries are monopolies, and a threshold would discourage price competition. Rather than apply an arbitrary threshold, NICE makes its decisions on a case by case basis. As the incremental cost-effectiveness ratio increases, the likelihood of rejection on grounds of cost-ineffectiveness rises.

The critical issues are the values of incremental cost effectiveness ratios at inflexions A and B (Figure 18.1) (Laupacis et al 1992, Weinstein 1995, Towse et al 2002). Clinical management pathways with ratios to the left of A would generally be regarded as cost effective. Those with ratios to the right of B would, if adopted, be likely to deny other patients (with different conditions) access to more cost effective treatments. There is currently no empirical basis for assigning particular values to A or B (Culyer 1997) but NICE and its advisory bodies have taken the view that inflexion A occurs at around £5,000-£15,000/QALY and inflexion B at around £25,000-£35,000/QALY. NICE would be unlikely to reject a technology with a ratio in the range of £5,000-£15,000/QALY solely on the grounds of cost-ineffectiveness but would need special reasons for accepting technologies with ratios over £25,000-£35,000/QALY as cost-effective. The main considerations in making judgements about cost effectiveness for ratios of £25,000-£35,000/QALY are: the degree of uncertainty surrounding the estimate; the particular features of the condition and population using the technology; the innovative nature of the technology, when appropriate; the wider societal costs and benefits, when appropriate; reference to previous appraisals.

The phrase "particular features of the condition and the population using the technology" incorporates matters that include the availability and clinical effectiveness of other interventions for the condition, particular public health issues (such as communicable diseases), and special considerations of equity. Judgements about whether incremental cost-effectiveness ratios can be considered reasonable are made by the independent members of NICE's

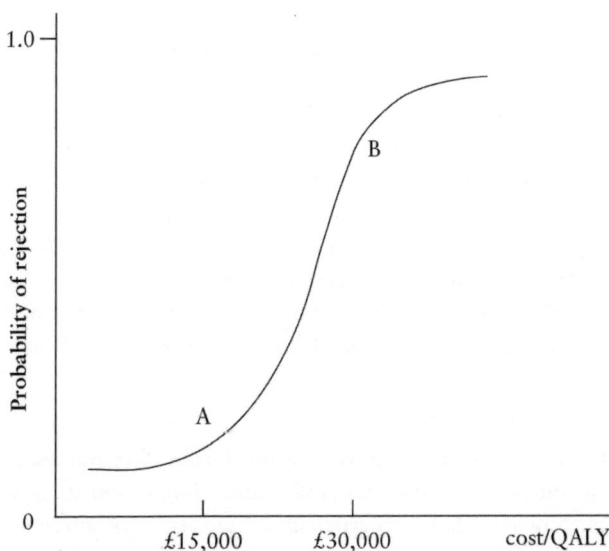

Figure 18.1 Probability of rejection as cost per QALY rises

advisory committees (particularly the Appraisal Committee) and the guideline development groups. Membership is drawn from clinicians and health managers working in the NHS, technical experts (statisticians and health economists), and patients or patient advocates.

Affordability

NICE does not take affordability into account when making judgements about cost effectiveness. The term is not a technical one, but it is used to mean that a particular activity should be funded by increasing the total funds available for health care rather than from existing resources. This would imply increasing taxation, borrowing on the markets, or diversion of funds from another publicly funded activity. Affordability, in this sense, is a matter for the government when deciding the annual budget for the NHS. It is NICE's job to judge whether something ought to be purchased from within the resources made available to the NHS. The NHS budget is to be assumed to be fixed. The government could therefore judge a particular intervention unaffordable for the NHS (because of the large numbers who would be eligible for treatment) even though NICE had judged it cost effective. In such circumstances, the government could respond in one of two ways: the Department of Health and the Welsh Assembly Government might formally advise the NHS to ignore NICE's advice; alternatively, ministers might invoke one of the clauses in its directions to NICE stating that (in this particular case) it is required to take account of "advice from ministers on available resources." So far, neither of these potential government responses have been proposed or threatened.

Social value judgements

Social value judgements have a critical role if resources are to be distributed with efficiency and equity. NICE and its advisory bodies, however, have no particular legitimacy to determine the social values of those served by the NHS. To ensure that these values resonate broadly with the public, NICE has formed a Citizens Council (NICE Citizens Council 2003a, b).

NICE has exercised its judgement against some interventions. For example, anakinra for rheumatoid arthritis seems to be less effective than etanercept or infliximab. It cost £7,450/year for each patient. The incremental cost-effectiveness ratio for anakinra was estimated to be £69,000/QALY for rheumatoid arthritis, which was thought an unacceptable opportunity cost (NICE 2003). Interferon beta and glatiramer acetate reduce the frequency and severity of relapse in relapsing-remitting multiple sclerosis. The mid-range estimates of the incremental cost-effectiveness ratios (£/QALY) depend on the time horizon examined: + 5 years = £580,000; + 10 years = £308,000; + 20 years = £70,000. The opportunity costs for each of these scenarios were unacceptable (NICE 2002a). In contrast, imatinib was licensed for the treatment of chronic myeloid leukaemia in the chronic phase after failure of interferon alfa (NICE 2002b) and in the accelerated and blast crisis phases (for those not treated earlier with imatinib). The mid range estimates of the incremental cost effectiveness ratios (cost/QALY) were: £37,000 for the chronic phase, £38,400 for the accelerated phase; and £49,000 for the blast crisis phase. In the absence of any effective alternative treatment (apart from bone marrow transplantation) imatinib was considered to be cost-effective in the chronic phase after interferon alfa. Denial of imatinib in the accelerated phase was considered to be inconsistent because the ratio was similar to that for the chronic phase. Denial of imatinib to patients in the blast cell phase was considered unfair. Patients at this advanced stage could reasonably have expected, in view of the decisions made already, to have had the opportunity of treatment with imatinib at an earlier stage of their condition. On grounds of equity, therefore, it was considered that imatinib should be available to patients in the blast cell phase of chronic myeloid leukaemia who had not previously been treated with the drug.

Efficiency

A fundamental value judgement is that efficiency in health care involves maximising the health of the population subject to the resources available. That being the case, further social value judgements regarding efficiency relate to the measure of health used and to the scope of costs and benefits. NICE uses the QALY as the principal measure of health outcome. This measure embodies the important social value judgement that to count only gains in life expectancy, without considering the quality of the additional life years, would be to omit important dimensions of human welfare (NICE Citizens Council 2003a). The QALY has the advantage of having been extensively validated in experimental conditions (Brazier et al 1993, Anderson et al 1996, Brooks 1996, Roset et al 1999, Kind et al, 1999). The main value judgements embodied in QALYs are that health related quality of life can reasonably be captured in terms of physical mobility, ability to self care, ability to carry out activities of daily living, absence of pain and discomfort, and absence of anxiety and depression.

NICE believes that, while differential productivity at work should be considered, it ought not be used to disadvantage people who are not in regular paid employment, including children and those who are retired (NICE Citizens Council 2003a). It needs to explore how best to reflect productivity effects without causing inequity in the ways in which services are allocated. It is sometimes held that NICE ought to give a higher priority to novel treatments for conditions for which no alternative specific forms of therapy are currently available, or to conditions associated with social stigma such as mental illness or sexually transmitted diseases (NICE Citizens Council 2003a). These, too, are social value judgements that need to be considered in more detail in the future.

Equity

Equity lies at the heart of the NHS. Lack of equity (in the form of so called postcode prescribing) was one of the reasons why NICE was established. Much of the philosophical literature on equity is far from being readily applicable to the real world and NICE has therefore had to make its own judgements. For NICE, equity also refers to fairness in the ways in which the costs and benefits of available care are distributed among all those who use the NHS

(Culyer and Wagstaff 1993, Culyer 2001a and b, 1995). NICE's recommendations are intended to apply across the whole of England and Wales, regardless of where people live or work, and has made the social value judgement that local variations in cost ought not to result in variations in availability of health care (NICE Citizens' Council 2003a). Value judgements about equity are often implicit within both clinical and cost effectiveness analyses. An assumption that underlies most of NICE's technology appraisals has been that "a QALY is a QALY is a QALY." By this NICE means that a QALY gained or lost in respect of one disease is equivalent to a QALY gained or lost in respect of another. It also means that the weight given to the gain of a QALY is the same, regardless of how many QALYs have already been enjoyed, how many are in prospect, the age or sex of the beneficiaries, their deservedness, and the extent to which the recipients are deprived in respects other than health. The decision to give no differential weight is the result of a social value judgement that an additional adjusted life year is of equal importance for each person (NICE Citizens Council 2004). The Council recommends that age should be taken into account when it is an indicator of either risk or benefit. It does not recommend, though, that NICE should be more generous in its judgements of cost effectiveness merely because of individuals' social roles or age.

Conclusions

The scientific value judgements made by NICE remain, ultimately, those developed and enunciated through the knowledge, experience, and expertise of the board members and its independent advisory bodies (the appraisal committee, the interventional procedures advisory committee and the guideline development groups). NICE hopes that the NHS's scientific and clinical community will agree with the basis for these judgements. Similarly, it hopes that the social value judgements will resonate acceptably across the whole community.

In the absence of other relevant information, NICE is obliged to make its own social value judgements and be held accountable for them. Explicit discussion of the key issues will greatly aid this process. Underlying all the decisions, however, is one fundamental social value judgement: that advice from NICE to the NHS should embody values generally held by the population served by the NHS.

19

Deliberative processes and evidence-informed decision-making in healthcare: do they work and how might we know?[19]

Introduction

As the idea of incorporating research results into practice and policy spreads beyond medicine into broader social domains, the concept

19 This chapter is a shortened version of Culyer, A.J., Lomas, J., 2006. Deliberative processes and evidence-informed decision-making in health care – do they work and how might we know? *Evidence and Policy* 2, 357-371. It is based on the annual Sinclair Lecture for 2005 I gave at Queen's University, Kingston, Canada, on 17 November 2005. The work originated with a request from the heads of Provincial Ministries of Health in Canada to clarify the meaning and use of evidence for establishing 'evidence-based benchmarks for medically acceptable wait times' and was funded through a grant to the Canadian Institutes of Health Research. We are much indebted to colleagues Chris McCutcheon, Laura McAuley, Susan Law and Claudia Sanmartin, with whom Jonathan and I have been having discussions on this subject for more than a year in connection with a systematic review of the literature to assess the effectiveness of these methods of decision-making (see Lomas et al, 2005). We are also grateful for the comments received from the members of a workshop on 'Weighing Up the Evidence' held under the auspices of the Canadian Health Services Research Foundation. We must of course absolve all of these people from any responsibility for the imperfect parts of what we write. The best bits are undoubtedly stolen from them. Thanks also to Donald Cole, Norman Daniels, John Frank, Ellen McEachern, Cameron Mustard, Sandra Sinclair and Arthur Sweetman for their comments on drafts.

is subtly being transformed from 'evidence-based' to 'evidence-informed' decision-making. Behind this note of realism (evidence in the form of research is rarely complete enough to warrant its domination over all other kinds) lies an implicit corollary, best captured in the question 'if research must be combined with other inputs to inform a decision, what mechanism/s should be used to do the combining?' Furthermore, coupled with advocacy of evidence-informed decision-making has come a complementary advocacy of openness and transparency in decision-making, and in the design of decision-making processes. Attention has turned to deliberative processes as methods of combining inputs for decision-making, with explicit steps for the consideration of evidence and a good deal of open consultation of so-called 'stakeholders'. Again, a question calls for an answer, regardless of any intrinsic attractiveness it may have – what is the evidence that this way of doing things 'works'?

Two questions informed our literature search: (1) In addition to research on health outcomes, what other forms of information count as evidence for clinical, management, or policy decision-making in the health sector? (2) How can various forms of evidence and stakeholder perspectives be combined through a deliberative process to yield evidence-informed guidance for health systems? Initially, 2,243 items were found in relation to question (1) and 855 to question (2); 188 articles passed the inclusion tests in the case of (1) but only 17 passed in the case of (2), later supplemented by six papers from bibliographies of included papers.

Why use a deliberative process?

A deliberative process is characterised by the careful, deliberate consideration and discussion of the advantages and disadvantages of various options (Hajer and Wagenaar, 2003). At the highest level, deliberation has been seen as a desirable attribute of democracy – as one of the ways through which preferences can be transformed rather than merely aggregated (Habermas, 1987). It is not a new idea. Athenian democracy held it dear. In the late 18th century, Edmund Burke wrote: "Parliament is not a congress of ambassadors for different and hostile interests ... but ... a deliberative assembly ... with one interest, that of the whole; where, not local purposes, not local prejudices ought to guide, but the general good, resulting from the general reason of the whole" (quoted in Kurland and Lerner, 1987, pp 391-2). In this chapter, the focus is on deliberation about health care and access to it: its finance, provision, distribution and management. It is assumed throughout that the purpose of a deliberative process is to help people to make decisions. It provides guidance but does not substitute for thinking, nor does it dictate or prescribe the decision itself. In this respect it is like evidence and argument, or frameworks of thinking such as ethics or cost-benefit analysis. It is there to facilitate the consideration of matters deemed to be relevant. Some of these are evidential and factual in nature. Others are conceptual, theoretical, ideological or, like deliberative processes themselves, procedural.

A deliberative process is best considered as an aid to thought and judgement. Properly executed it will be, compared with a 'closed door' or *ad hoc* process, more comprehensive in the relevant issues embraced, more consistent in the way they are embraced and more engaging of the people affected by the outcome. Although the main focus of interest is in the impact of the deliberative process on the quality of the decision that is finally made, it is not necessarily consequentialist: the goodness or badness of such processes is not to be judged only in terms of the goodness or badness of their outcomes. Political scientists often claim that it should also be socially integrating; that it is itself inherently good because of its positive impact on the perceptions of democratic processes and their legitimacy. For current purposes, however, I shall take the view that the outcome with which we are especially concerned is the decision that the process enables rather than the experiences of the participants or observers thereof. Deliberative processes are ways of not only eliciting, legitimising and incorporating stakeholder input, but also of usefully combining these inputs with evidentiary inputs. Thus we start with consideration of the latter: what should be considered as evidence in a deliberative process?

What is evidence?

At root, evidence is anything that claims to be an empirical fact and that gives a reason for believing that a thing, or another thing to which it relates, such as a consequence that might be reasonably expected to flow from it, is or will be true. It may be claimed falsely, in which case it is false evidence. It may be asserted as fact without any empirics, in which case it is merely asserted and not evidence at all. Statements describing evidence are not the same as purely logical statements, which do not need to contain any empirics at all and are to be judged by the analytical canons of logical rather than empirical truthfulness. When non-scientists in the clinical, management or policy world are asked what they consider as evidence, they typically come up with a complex mixture of both scientifically general and locally idiosyncratic types of information: 'colloquial' evidence (Lomas et al, 2005, p 7). They "draw on multiple sources and define evidence broadly" (Davidoff et al, 1995). Clinical or programme effectiveness data compete with assertion (sometimes claimed to be expert assertion), cost–utility algorithms sit alongside political acceptability, and public or patient attitude data are combined with vivid recollections of personal encounters. "What ministers call 'evidence' is what they get from their constituents at their Saturday surgery" (Saarni and Gylling, 2004; see also Petticrew et al, 2004).

Scientific evidence

For the evidence-informed decision-making 'movement', this colloquial concept of evidence is broader than the more restricted scientific view. This raises the question: what is 'scientific' about scientific evidence and what differentiates it from colloquial evidence? The things that are 'scientific' about scientific evidence seem to be threefold. First, a formalised hypothesis or theory is being tested. Second, recognised and replicable methods are used to assemble evidence (as, for example, in controlled experiments such as clinical trials). Third, recognised and replicable methods are used to analyse and interpret it (for example, in multivariate regressions, non-parametric statistics or grounded theory). It is not the questions concerning which evidence is sought that give scientific evidence its distinctive character (Culyer, 1981). What makes evidence scientific is the manner of study, not the objects or questions studied. But even within this more restricted, scientific, view of evidence there are two distinctive styles of study relevant to healthcare decision-making (Lomas et al, 2005). One, relating mostly to medicine and the biological sciences and evaluating the efficacy of interventions, uses methods that try to exclude contextual 'confounders' such as the natural variability in the skills and attitudes of doctors, the symptom presentation of patients, or the organisational and funding circumstances of service delivery. In its ideal form, this type of science employs randomised controlled trial methods to uncover, as far as is epistemologically possible, 'context-free' 'knowledge'. The other, more common in the social sciences and the environments in which decisions will be implemented, uses methods that describe and evaluate the contextual factors that might influence the practical impact of an intervention once it is deployed. This type of science employs a wide variety of methods, usually tailored to the nature of the implementation concern: the impact on the effectiveness of the intervention elucidated by surveys of provider or patient attitudes, qualitative research, multivariate modelling, cost-effectiveness analyses of funding regimes or healthcare technologies, forecasts of demographics, and so on. Much research of this sort explicitly takes account of context and of how different contexts generate different expectations about the impact of an intervention. It can provide 'context-sensitive' results that appraise the facilitating or attenuating circumstances surrounding a particular decision.

In context-free science, the emphasis is on what epidemiologists term 'internal validity': the degree of certainty with which the outcome of a trial can be attributed to an intervention rather than to some other, confounding, variable. In context-sensitive science (recognised by some clinical researchers as 'practical' trials (Tunis et al, 2003)) measurement usually includes measuring the impact of the confounding variables for which the first approach controls, with the emphasis on 'external validity': the degree of certainty with which a causal relationship can be generalised to settings other than those of the study. In epidemiology, the former is commonly referred to as 'efficacy' (the extent to which an intervention produces a beneficial effect under ideal conditions) and is in contrast to 'effectiveness' (the extent to which a specific intervention, when used under ordinary circumstances, does what it is intended to do) (Cochrane Collaboration, 2006). Context-free evidence is plainly less generalisable and less able to support decision-making in contexts that do not approximate to those of the original trial. Hence the need for supplementary context-sensitive evidence.

Ranking types of evidence

Ought the three types of evidence (context-free scientific evidence, context-sensitive scientific evidence and colloquial evidence) to be ranked in a hierarchy? At one level, the answer has to be yes. When they are available, both kinds of scientific evidence must be ranked above the colloquial as far as dependability is concerned. Colloquial evidence comes into its own when scientific evidence is not available or is incomplete in particular and relevant respects. Most characteristically, these will relate to context-sensitive matters, on which there is typically much less scientific research than context-free matters. So colloquial evidence comes into play in a significant fashion when the issue is not whether, say, a medical procedure works in general (as might be demonstrated in US trials), but whether it is likely to work in Canada or Wales, or in community hospitals; or, if it is believed to work in such places, whether it works well enough to warrant public funding; or if it were introduced this year, whether local services could cope with the expected demand; and so on.

All of these are things about which scientific research evidence *could* be, but rarely is, collected. If the guidance derived from a deliberative process is to be as helpful and comprehensive as possible, then colloquial evidence has the two essential functions of providing relevant context for the context-free science and filling in gaps in the knowledge base, gaps that could perhaps later be filled by scientific evidence but all too often have not been. The issue confronting any decision-maker within a deliberative process is not so much how to balance the three types of evidence or to assess the weight to place on each, but rather to allow each to perform its appropriate task:

- scientific context-free evidence is evidence about general potential

- scientific context-sensitive evidence is evidence about particular realistic scenarios

- colloquial evidence helps to provide a context for otherwise context-free evidence and to supply the best evidence short of scientific evidence when there is neither context-free nor context-sensitive evidence.

How should a deliberative process work?

The main task of a deliberative process is to elicit and combine different types of evidence. It elicits evidence by virtue of the embodiment of the participants in a deliberative process (they bring material 'evidence' with them, often only in their heads) and it combines evidence in a process of 'weighing it up' and considering the contexts in which it is to be used. It is also probable that deliberative processes increase the likelihood of achieving what Daniels (2000a) calls 'sound and acceptable decisions'. Daniels argues for processes that 'account for reasonableness', so that they have a moral authority over and above that which customarily attaches to market or bureaucratic processes (Daniels, 2000b). Others have emphasized the open participatory nature of a deliberative process as 'a more fundamental means by which the public can influence the generation of data and the derivation of the policy options' (Petts, 2004).

Deliberation is commonly seen as desirable whenever the issues at stake are debatable. Deliberative processes stress the integration of scientific analyses of clinical issues and social contexts with 'stakeholder' or lay public views elicited from consultation and participation. Deliberative processes are, however, not the same as consultative processes. A prominent example of a consultative process was the Oregon priority-setting exercise for healthcare interventions initiated in 1989. This entailed 47 community meetings, 12 public hearings and 54 panel meetings for healthcare providers, with the information gathered being delivered to a committee (the Oregon Health Services Commission) to inform the prioritisation of procedures (Garland, 1992). Many were consulted but few participated in the deliberation over prioritisation. So deliberative processes and consultative processes are not synonymous, although deliberative processes characteristically include consultation. The Oregon exercise was consultative but deliberation was a separate process and the privilege of the Commission.

If one is to appraise the effectiveness of deliberative processes, one also needs tighter definitions, particularly of the objective that is being pursued, and one needs an understanding of which of the various procedural components might be generating the effective impact on the quality of decisions, if there is any such impact. Here is a task that might never succumb to the disciplines of evidence-informed practice, for the combination of complex procedures with complex and qualitative outcomes is a formidable challenge indeed. Before addressing it, however, let us consider the optimal circumstances for the use of a deliberative process.

When should we use deliberative processes?

One may conjecture which circumstances most warrant the use of deliberative processes. The following are all suggested as candidates:

Participation

• evidence from more than one expert discipline is involved

• evidence from more than one profession is involved

- stakeholders have conflicting interests
- there are technical disputes to resolve
- evidence may be scientifically controversial
- evidence gathered in one context is to be applied in another.

Involvement of wider social and cultural issues

- issues of outcome, benefits and costs go beyond the conventional boundaries of medicine
- substantial uncertainty about key values and risks needs to be assessed and weighed
- there are other social and personal values not taken into scientific account
- there are issues of equity and fairness
- there are issues of implementability and operational feasibility
- wide public and professional 'ownership' is desired.

These circumstances then lead to summarising scientific evidence on (context-free) efficacy in the form of narrative reviews, systematic reviews or meta-analyses; gathering scientific evidence about contexts with controlled social science experiments, which in turn may also be summarised and synthesized; and eliciting colloquial evidence through consultative processes including public meetings and the hearing of witnesses, as well as directly from those participating in the deliberative process. Within this cascade of evidence are frequently embodied further deliberative processes. For example, during the process of systematic reviewing, when reviewers need to reach agreement on such matters as search terms, search engines, inclusion/exclusion criteria, quality criteria and the like, they engage in deliberative processes, though plainly, this is a more restricted form of deliberation, for the most part restricted to a select coterie of experts.

A good example of a deliberative process in which all the circumstances and features mentioned so far are present is the method used by the National Institute for Health and Clinical Excellence (NICE) for evaluating healthcare technologies in England and Wales (NICE, 2004). There are formal submissions from interested parties, consultations and invited commentaries from consultees and commentators (between which NICE distinguishes carefully), systematic reviews, technical modelling exercises to cover some lacunae in the scientific evidence, and multiparty representation in the (large) deliberative committee which hears witnesses. There are also appeal possibilities and various support groups, some using consensus methods on controversial issues of value and others advising on whom to consult (Culyer, 2005).

I take the ultimate product of the deliberative process to be guidance shaped by judgement. Thus the circumstances for using deliberative processes are, by definition, those where judgement informed by evidence is crucial to a quality decision. The judgement may be about an effect of doing something, its size, the ways in which it is likely to be achieved, for whom, for how long, its cost in terms of the resources used that would otherwise have been employed in other ways to achieve other good things, or how worthwhile it is. The test, therefore, of a deliberative process is whether the resultant judgement is (or will be) more comprehensively 'evidence-informed', better matched to the context of application, more efficiently implementable and more widely acceptable to those it affects.

What do we currently know about the effectiveness of deliberative processes?

Is there any scientific evidence that deliberative processes actually work? The short answer is 'not much'. A lot of the literature on deliberative processes in healthcare has been, and continues to be, advocacy rather than reports of the effectiveness of well-defined processes (for example, Gibson et al, 2005). It is mostly qualitative and judgemental; it is, in short, colloquial. There is virtually no replication of studies. Some evidence exists about designs of processes that are more or less likely to generate consensus. These studies have identified important roles for what we have called colloquial evidence and have identified some reasons underlying failures to agree within groups and failures to heed context-free evidence, which include doubts about its applicability in any particular context (for example, Raine et al, 2004). There is evidence that the more scientific evidence there is relative to colloquial evidence, the more likely there is to be a consensus, at least within professional panels (Lomas et al, 1988). In comparing a deliberative process with other methods, one author has written: "It clearly has some advantages. 1. It can solve the problem of political legitimacy... 2. It can act as a check to the partiality which expert groups in biotechnology and ethics may have. It promotes the dialogue between experts ... and between experts and ordinary citizens. 3. It enables us to make informed and responsible decisions. 4. It results in education of citizens' preferences" (Kim, 2002). Unfortunately, while all these outcomes 'can' or 'may' be true, they are not themselves evidenced and have to be suspect, coming – as they do – from a manifest enthusiast for the method.

Although the evidence is not strong, the following generalisations are probably correct for a deliberative process:

- decision-makers acquire a better grasp of the strengths and weaknesses of the underlying cases and can better defend their decisions

- consensus building is enhanced

- the revelation of evidence gaps helps to inform downstream research programmes

- stakeholders and their peers are more likely to accept and implement decisions that they have had a hand in shaping

- possible selection bias through the membership of decision-making panels becomes relatively obvious

- context-free evidence can be re-interpreted in relevant contexts.

However, absence of evidence is not to be mistaken for evidence of absence. One might still maintain the theoretical position that deliberative processes, used in suitable situations, deliver better outcomes compared with other methods. Well-designed empirical research could test this conjecture.

Meeting the challenge of testing the hypothesis that deliberative processes 'work'

To evaluate a process that is, itself, a combination of complex processes, further complicated by complex and mostly qualitative outcomes, is a formidable challenge. The key may lie in being suitably modest both concerning what is to be established empirically and what is claimed for the process. 'Being modest' in this context means asking researchable questions and not applying criteria of completeness and rigour that are not applied everywhere else. To paraphrase Voltaire, let's not allow the perfect to become the enemy of the merely good ("Le mieux est l'ennemi du Bien": Voltaire, nd, 541). In particular, let us not even begin to seek to evaluate the effectiveness of deliberative processes in the same way as we would assess the cost-effectiveness of a pharmaceutical.

Instead, the problem can be tackled in a reductionist fashion by applying three principles:

- select key outcomes of a deliberative process
- select key characteristics of a deliberative process
- have an explicit alternative process as comparator.

The first simplifies the complexity at the endpoint, the second identifies the variables to be investigated and the third ensures that we are not implicitly comparing a deliberative process with some unstated but ideal process that either does not exist or that is not a realistic alternative.

Outcome selection

It is as well to rule out judging a deliberative process in terms of its impact on the most ultimate of outcomes, such as beneficial changes in the health of populations or population groups, or the distributional justice of the system. The main reason is not so much the difficulty inherent in measuring such outcomes, substantial though these are, as the difficulty inherent in attributing cause and effect with confidence. A deliberative process might be as excellent as possible, but the ultimate outcome might yet fail to emerge because of failures elsewhere in the system. The foregoing discussion suggests six empirically measurable, principal outcomes that, taken together, might be deemed suitable measures of the success or failure of a deliberative process relative to a comparator process:

- a deliberative process is more likely to generate guidance that is consistent with the context-free scientific evidence set in a relevant context

- a deliberative process is more likely to identify relevant clinical, social and political contexts for interpreting context-free scientific evidence

- a deliberative process is more likely to command a wide credibility in professional circles and beyond

- conversely, the quality and power of residual opposition to any guidance will be low

- a deliberative process is more likely to generate guidance whose implementation will be speedy

- a deliberative process is more likely to identify impediments to the implementation of guidance and to propose solutions.

Key process characteristics

Since deliberative processes, like other processes, have many components and are not uniquely defined by any particular combination and degree of each, it makes sense to select those aspects of the process that are likely to have an impact on the outcome, its size and assessed value. Factors that may be contenders might be categorised as research quality, reasonableness of procedure and membership. These might more specifically include:

Research quality relative to a comparator

- quality of the scientific research (both context-free and context-sensitive) available at the start of the process and subsequently

- quality of the colloquial evidence

- availability of meta-analyses and systematic reviews of scientific evidence

- clarity of the questions to be answered by the process

- adequacy of the scoping of the questions to be answered

- availability of research into the public's views on contextual and other 'non-scientific' matters of relevance

- quality/quantity of support staffing.

Reasonableness of procedure relative to a comparator

- quality of chairperson

- clarity and openness of process

- reasonableness of deadlines for submission and consideration of evidence

- use of colloquial evidence to challenge context-free evidence, set contexts and plug gaps in science (but not to supplant scientific evidence of either kind)

- availability of time for study, discussion and reflection before, during and after meetings

- scope of opportunities for all interested parties to comment during the process

- scope for members to request further information and take face-to-face oral evidence

- in-camera discussions, when indicated, to encourage free expression of opinion; otherwise as open and transparent as possible (for example, public sharing of agendas, data, interim conclusions, minutes)

- opportunity for and use of appeal if the process is flawed or the guidance appears unreasonable.

Membership relative to a comparator

- representativeness of expertise in the relevant scientific evidence among panelists

- representativeness of breadth of colloquial sources of evidence

- participation of respected people from the major communities of interest

- willingness of members to share values openly

- inclusivity of stakeholder consultation (opportunities for all affected parties to be represented).

Alternative processes as comparators

The principles applying to the selection of an appropriate comparator or comparators are similar to those used to select comparators in health technology assessment (Giacomini, 1999). Comparators should be relevant in context and assessable in the same way as proposed for deliberative processes, and should be informed by policy considerations. Examples include comparator processes that:

- are the most likely alternatives to the deliberative process in question

- are the status quo (where this is not the deliberative process in question)

- are much less costly alternatives

- are other deliberative processes having a different mix or balance of characteristics.

Neither relevance nor practicality requires more than relative assessment: comparing a deliberative process with a non-deliberative one, or one kind of deliberative process with another. This is much less taxing than the comprehensive assessment of the merits of deliberative processes in general or of any one in particular. So far as I am aware, no one has ever done this in the way proposed here, with these criteria for success and in comparative terms, so the field lies open for a reputation to be made. It is also more informative to the designers of processes to know the impact of different features of the design on the character of the deliberations and their eventual outcomes. Studies of this sort could also be prospective and, on occasion, side-by-side, analogous to head-to-head clinical trials.

Conclusions

The purpose of a deliberative process is to help people make decisions that are well grounded in relevant evidence, feasible and implementable. Such decisions are better than those that are un-evidenced. Evidence can be categorised into three types: context-free scientific evidence, context-sensitive scientific evidence and colloquial evidence. A deliberative process that exists to provide feasible and implementable guidance for healthcare decision-makers ought to be informed by relevant scientific evidence, interpreted in a relevant context wherever possible with context-sensitive scientific evidence and, where not, by the best available colloquial evidence.

These conjectures are not well supported by the current evidential base, although there are indications of support and few refutations. There is an abundance of *a priori* speculation about the effectiveness of deliberative processes, but there is also an important need for better designed scientific studies of decision-making processes in order to test the relative advantages of one over another, as well as the circumstances in which one may be better than another. Although the application of the basic methods of health technology assessment to non-clinical 'technologies' is still in its infancy, and it is easy to do studies of these processes that are poor and have ambiguous conclusions, it is also easy to overstate the difficulties of doing them better. We have sought to identify some characteristics of a scientific approach to the evaluation of deliberative processes. These centre on the selection of key outcomes, key characteristics and the use of explicit alternatives as comparators, each of which would be a novel addition to the current evaluative literature on the uses of deliberative processes.

20

Twelve conjectures about deliberative processes using NICE as an exemplar[20]

Introduction

The National Institute for Health and Clinical Excellence (NICE) represents an interesting possible solution to the problem of getting research-based evidence into practice, in this case research into the cost effectiveness of health care technologies. Not all evidence is provided by research and not all the relevant evidence is medical. Few organizations have tackled the complex challenge that this represents quite so boldly and imaginatively as has NICE. It is premature to attempt any full appraisal of its success, and I have been too close to NICE's development to be truly objective. This chapter, therefore, advances some broad conjectures about the general circumstances under which 'deliberative processes', of the sort that characterise NICE's arrangements, may be likely to be used and hence begin to provide an explanatory account of why they were used in the particular case of NICE. The conjectures are presented in the next section, after a brief general description of a 'deliberative process'. This is followed by a description of some of the principal characteristics of NICE's decision-making procedures

---

20 This article originally appeared as: Culyer, A.J., 2006. NICE's use of cost-effectiveness as an exemplar of a deliberative process. *Health Economics, Policy and Law* 1, 299-318.

regarding the assessment of health care technologies and their recommendation to the National Health Service (NHS). These are related to each of the conjectures. Some characteristics of NICE's procedures that directly address the ambiguity of public policy statements are then discussed. Many of these procedures involve value judgements, and some appear to flout the conventional canons for the conduct of cost-effectiveness analysis. This section also seeks to show how a deliberative process can help to resolve ambiguity and also to generate guidance that commands widespread assent.

Twelve conjectures about deliberative processes

I have chosen 'conjecture' rather than 'hypothesis' to indicate the essentially preliminary and tentative nature of the speculation that is the major concern here. The specific conjectures to be outlined can probably be underpinned by the more fundamental features of which they are the implications. That task is for another occasion. The present purpose is to identify circumstances that are at least more generic than those in which NICE finds itself, so that NICE may be used as just one case study to test the *prima facie* plausibility of the conjectures. The processes used by NICE in its decision-making about health care technologies may be described as 'deliberative', and a systematic review and some initial theorizing about such processes in health care decisions (Lomas et al, 2005; Culyer and Lomas, 2006,) provide the basis for the conjectures to follow.

A deliberative process is one that elicits and combines evidence of different kinds and from different sources. In particular, it combines context-free scientific evidence from bio-science and clinical trials (often in the form of narrative reviews, systematic reviews, and meta-analyses) with other forms of more context-sensitive scientific evidence (often in the form of applied decision theoretical procedures such as cost-effectiveness analysis or social surveys), and less systematic evidence referred to elsewhere as 'colloquial' (Lomas et al, 2005) that may come in the shape of the 'experience' of those around decision-makers' tables. Clinical scientific evidence is typically context-free, in that it has been generated through processes that control for confounding variables in order to create suitable conditions for testing scientific hypotheses. Highly specific clinical contexts are generally involved here, such as research centres of excellence and clinical work done by professionals of national or international repute. Context-sensitive scientific evidence is defined as evidence collected to test hypotheses in systematic ways but ways that are more relevant to the context in which the intervention is to be used. Evidence from a placebo-controlled trial is an example of context-free scientific evidence; evidence from a cost-effectiveness analysis of alternative drugs for treating a particular disease in general practice in England and Wales is an example of context-sensitive scientific evidence. Colloquial evidence is neither scientific nor systematic but it is frequently all that it is possible to bring to bear on a particular issue and it often takes the form of expressions of opinion by experts (clinical, managerial, economic) based on their practical experience and professional judgement. The status of colloquial evidence is controversial. On the one hand it is, by definition, neither scientific nor systematic and it may be plain dangerous; on the other, it is frequently all that is available on some critical aspect of a decision.

A famous example of harmful advice that was not evidence-informed is Dr Spock's advice to countless thousands of mothers: "There are two disadvantages to a baby's sleeping on his back. If he vomits, he's more likely to choke on the vomitus. Also he tends to keep his head turned towards the same side, this may flatten the side of his head... I think it is preferable to accustom a baby to sleeping on his stomach from the start" (cited in Chalmers, 2003: 23). As Iain Chalmers has recently commented, reflecting on his early days as a medical practitioner, "No doubt like millions of Spock's other readers, I passed on this apparently rational, theory-based and authoritative advice. We now know from the dramatic effects of the 'Back to Sleep' campaigns in several countries that the practice promulgated by well-intentioned experts like Spock, led to tens of thousands of avoidable sudden infant deaths" (Chalmers, 2005: 229).

A deliberative process elicits evidence by virtue of the embodiment of the participants in deliberation and it combines evidence of both the two scientific kinds and the colloquial kind in a process of 'weighing up' and considering the contexts in which the guidance emanating from the deliberative process is to be used. Deliberative processes are said to increase the likelihood of what Daniels calls 'sound and acceptable decisions'. Daniels argues for processes that 'account for reasonableness', so that they have a moral authority over and above that which customarily attaches to market or bureaucratic processes (Daniels, 2000a, 200b), though the morality of the process is not an aspect to concern us here. Deliberative processes in health care stress the integration of technical analyses of clinical issues with (usually social) scientific analyses of the contexts in which decisions will be implemented, within an explicit decision-making model having clear criteria, and involving stakeholder and lay public consultation and even participation, in contrast to the more traditional top-down approach. Deliberative processes are not the same as consultative processes, though consultation will normally have a significant role to play in support of deliberation.

The following are conjectured to be circumstances that make the use of deliberative processes more likely:

1.   decisions have been delegated by a body with a democratic mandate to one without it

2.   evidence from more than one expert discipline is involved

3.   evidence from more than one profession is involved

4.   stakeholders have conflicting interests

5.   there are technical disputes to resolve and the evidence may be scientifically controversial

6.   evidence gathered in one context is to be applied in another

7.   there are issues of outcome, benefits, and costs that go beyond the conventional boundaries of medicine

8. there is substantial uncertainty about key values and risks that needs to be assessed and weighed

9. there are other social and personal values not taken into account in the scientific evidence

10. there are issues of equity and fairness

11. there are issues of implementability and operational feasibility involving knowledge beyond that of the decision-makers

12. wide public and professional 'ownership' is desired.

Scientific evidence on clinical efficacy is usually context-free, in the sense that it is presented as the outcome of a quasi-laboratory style experiment. It is often summarised in the form of a narrative review, a systematic review, or a meta-analysis. Scientific evidence on context, including clinical effectiveness (cf. efficacy) under routine practice conditions and evidence on other contingent matters such as cost effectiveness and the social values attached to health outcomes, might also be gathered by controlled experiments, which in turn may also be summarised and synthesized. Colloquial evidence is often garnered through consultative processes, including social surveys, public meetings, and the hearing of witnesses, as well as directly from those participating in the deliberative process. The ultimate product of a deliberative process is guidance shaped by judgement – judgement about an effect of doing something, its size, the ways in which it is likely to be achieved, for whom, for how long, its cost in terms of the resources used that would otherwise have been employed in other ways to achieve other good things, and how worthwhile it is. The test, therefore, of a deliberative process is whether the resultant judgement is (or will be) more comprehensively 'evidence informed', better matched to the context of application, more efficiently implementable, and more widely acceptable to those it affects.

The National Institute for Health and Clinical Excellence

NICE was given two main charges at its inception, although there were others, and further responsibilities have been accumulated since then. The original two were:

- to identify cost-effective technologies and make recommendations for their use in the National Health Service (NHS) of England and Wales

- to create authoritative clinical guidelines to support cost-effective clinical practice in all health care settings.

The idea of 'technology' was broad: nearly as broad as 'ways of doing things'. It certainly and explicitly included: pharmaceuticals; medical devices; diagnostic techniques; surgical procedures; other therapeutic technologies; public health; health promotion; and workplace interventions for health and safety. NICE's guidance is not binding on the NHS, but any clinician wishing to follow it must be enabled to so through appropriate resource provision by the local NHS – the commissioners (purchasers) and the trusts (hospitals and primary care providers) in question. NICE's advice is the principal informational content underpinning 'clinical governance', a system through which NHS organisations are accountable for continually improving the quality of their services and safeguarding high standards of care by creating an environment in which excellence in clinical care will flourish (Scally and Donaldson, 1998).

From the beginning, it was decided that NICE's procedures would be conducted with the highest possible degree of transparency and with much participation by 'stakeholders' – categorically defined as patients, informal caregivers, clinical and other professional caregivers, health care managers, manufacturers, researchers, and the public in general. It sought the respect of the overwhelming majority of the country's clinical and health service research community and the support of the Royal Colleges and other bastions of professional life. It was important to NICE that its guidance could not be dismissed as cranky, under-researched, or second rate. But it also had to be acceptable to the NHS's users and fair to the inventors and manufacturers of the various technologies that were used in a huge range of patient management pathways. It also had to be deemed 'do-able' by the managers, and provide lots of opportunities for sceptics, and any who might feel threatened, to air their concerns and for NICE to respond appropriately.

Some of the ways in which NICE seems to be a model of deliberative process are: there are open Board meetings that take place bi-monthly (these are accompanied by public receptions and 'Question and Answer' sessions); minutes are published on the NICE web pages before confirmation; there is a Citizens' Council, a 'citizens' jury' that considers socially value-laden matters referred to it by the Institute's Board. Its members have no economic involvement in the health care system. Members are paid a nominal sum of money per day plus expenses. It meets twice a year and adopts a deliberative approach (eg calls witnesses, commissions papers). It is managed at arm's length from NICE by a company specializing in research and community consultation (see Kelson 2001, Jarrett and PIU, 2004); the membership of the Technology Appraisals Committee is set broadly; extensive consultation exercises take place throughout the appraisals process; an appeals procedure is in place; there are consultative processes about process; extensive liaisons are in force with Royal Colleges (the principal professional associations of the English medical professions), seven independent Academic Centres that review published evidence on the relevant technology when developing technology appraisals guidance, and seven National Collaborating Centres within consortia of the royal colleges, professional bodies, and patient/carer organizations for developing clinical guidelines; and there is considerable joint working with NHS R&D and the National Coordinating Centre for Health Technology Assessment. Thus, it came about that the process of technology appraisal was to be open, multi-disciplinary, multi-professional and multi-institutional, and that it would have what is sometimes rather unfortunately referred to as 'lay' participation.

Each of these features corresponds to one or more of the twelve conjectures above.

1. *Decisions have been delegated by a body with a democratic mandate to one without it.* This is a precise description of NICE's relationship with Parliament via the Secretary of State (the 'minister'), select committees, and the floor of the House of Commons. In fact, NICE has been delegated some of the most central value-laden issues involved in health care policy, not least of which are the definition of 'health' and 'health gain', the practical measurement of these entities, and the conceptualisation and measurement of matters of equitable concern (largely undefined by the political leadership).

2 *and* 3. *Evidence from more than one expert discipline and profession is involved.* Decisions typically involve multiple disciplines and NICE's appraisals committees include statisticians, general practitioners, patient advocates, public health and consultant physicians, health economists, clinical pharmacists or pharmacologists, nurses, a consultant surgeon, NHS managers, a representative of the Association of British Healthcare Industries, a psychiatrist, members of Professions Allied to Medicine, and a paediatrician. In addition, subject specialists are usually present to provide expert testimony about the technologies being discussed.

4. *Stakeholders have conflicting interests.* The consultation process that generates the evidence before an Appraisal Committee affords opportunities for stakeholders to represent their interests, make submissions, engage in cost-effectiveness modelling exercises, and to understand the evidence being considered. NICE distinguishes between consultees and commentators. Consultees include manufacturers and other sponsors of the technology in question, national professional organizations, national patient organizations, the Department of Health and the Welsh Assembly Government, and relevant NHS organizations in England and local health boards in Wales. Consultees participate in the consultation on the

draft scope, and they may make formal submissions and receive various interim documents (such as the Assessment Report, and the Appraisal Consultation Document). Consultee organizations representing patients, caregivers, and professionals can nominate clinical specialists and patient experts to present their individual views in person to the Appraisal Committee. Commentators have more limited scope for participation. They are organizations that engage in the appraisal process but are not asked to prepare a submission dossier and they receive the final report for information only. They include manufacturers of comparator technologies, NHS Quality Improvement Scotland, relevant National Collaborating Centres for clinical guidelines, and, where appropriate, other research groups such as the Medical Research Council, as well as other official groups such as the NHS Confederation.

5. There are technical disputes to resolve and the evidence may be scientifically controversial. It is in the character of clinical trials and other evidential bases for assessing clinical effectiveness, that the evidence will be disparate and the conclusions of different studies will differ. Hierarchies of evidence ranked by quality are standard in the field of systematic reviewing because not all studies generate evidence of equal quality and substantial dispute can arise between experts over technical aspects of the interpretation of evidence. There is ample scope for technical disagreements between experts in health technology appraisal regarding, for example, the adequacy of control for confounding variables in the available trial literature, the interpretation of meta-analyses, or the comprehensiveness of the sensitivity analyses in guiding an appreciation of the consequences of particular analytical assumptions and empirical estimates, or the best way to model outcomes beyond the period for which data have been collected from clinical trials.

6. Evidence gathered in one context is to be applied in another. All bodies tasked, like NICE, with making formulary recommendations need to apply judgement in determining whether the context in which the evidence has been gathered (usually one or more centres of clinical and research excellence) affects those results such that their outcomes or costs might differ in other, less conducive environments. Similarly, results of trials conducted in other countries or health care systems may not be readily transferable. Making such judgements typically requires knowledge both of the scientific literature and of the 'reality' of clinical practice in the jurisdiction in question, which is often available only in the form of colloquial evidence – the judgement of practising physicians and managers engaged in the deliberative process.

7. *Issues of outcome, benefits, and costs go beyond the conventional boundaries of medicine.* NICE stipulates the scope of costs and benefits, and how they are to be compared. It recommends use of particular outcome measures and cost categories. The research, however, has rarely conformed fully or even substantially with these stipulations. While the significance of this problem may diminish over time as compliance increases, there will always be a residual scope for 'gap filling', some of which might be accomplished through technical means such as modelling, but other elements may have to be dealt with through drawing colloquially on the practical experience and, no less importantly, values of those participating in the decision.

8. *There is substantial uncertainty about key values and risks that needs to be assessed and weighed.* Not all the scientific information available will have been subject to a systematic sensitivity testing procedure for the robustness of the results in response to alternative assumptions, different settings of care, or any one of a host of relevant matters about which there may be uncertainty. Uncertainty may sometimes exist even about the nature of the factors to be considered 'relevant'. The assessment of risk and the weight attached to it will almost always be matters for judgement and the circumstances of the time, and some aspects may be capable of being addressed only at the time of decision.

9. There are other social and personal values not taken into account in the scientific evidence. The existence of such other values might become evident either during the assessment of the evidence by expert advisory groups (like systematic reviewers), or through the process of consultation, or emerge during discussions at the time of decision. Both their existence and the weight to be placed on them are inherently matters for deliberation and probably only colloquial evidence will be available.

10. There are issues of equity and fairness. Issues of equity, such as the importance to be attached to costs or benefits that accrue disproportionately to some people than others (for example, geographical, socio-economic, or clinical subgroups) are rarely addressed in the background scientific research and, even when they are, determining their importance as distinct from their existence is quintessentially a matter for decision-makers rather than scientists. There is frequently little scientific evidence available about what people (the general public, for example, or a target population) actually think about such issues or on the ways in which costs and benefits have an impact on different social groups.

11. There are issues of implementability and operational feasibility involving knowledge beyond that of the decision-makers. Practical matters of implementability, managerial and financial consequences will rarely have been fully addressed, if at all, by the scientific research available to a decision-making group. To address and assess such matters in the context of a particular jurisdiction will normally require each possible recommendation to be assessed colloquially by those with appropriate practical knowledge.

12. Wide public and professional 'ownership' is desired. From the beginning, NICE has been concerned that its recommendations have the confidence of not only the scientists and medical professional groups that advise it but also of users of the health care system, their caregivers at home and elsewhere, and the public in general. It is difficult to identify any obvious excluded interest or stakeholder group.

Being explicit about the ethics of cost and effectiveness

There is no escaping the fundamental fact that the decisions and recommendations of a body such as NICE are laden with judgements of value. In the UK, successive ministers have decided that the prime objectives of the NHS are to maximise the health of the population and to do so in an equitable fashion. The former has been more specifically articulated than the latter. For example, successive ministers (both Labour and Conservative) in the UK have clearly set NHS managers the task of maximising health (often referred to in official documents as maximising 'health gain').

"The purpose of the NHS is to secure, through the resources available, the greatest possible improvement in the physical and mental health of the people of England [and]... aims to judge its results under three headings: equity, efficiency, and responsiveness." (Department of Health, 1996) "The objective of the NHS Research and Development strategy is to ensure that the content and delivery of care in the NHS is based on high quality research relevant to improving the health of the nation." (Department of Health, 1991). "The knowledge produced by trials, overviews or technology assessment can be regarded as 'bullets' of effectiveness. Just like a bullet, they are of little value by themselves, and need to be loaded, aimed, and fired to hit their target." (Moore et al 1994)

These three quotations say more than may at first appear. The first maintains that health maximisation and equitable distribution are two prime aims of policy (not that they are the only aims). The second identifies evidence-based practice as important and commits the NHS to the generation of the appropriate evidence. The third reminds the NHS that mere information is never enough; not, at least, if the aim is to generate change in pursuit of the objectives outlined in the first quotation. Obvious implications of these broad instructions include the proposition that technologies which do not contribute to health have no place in the NHS (even if people want them). That is quite a powerful implication and would be unsustainable were 'technology' so broad as to embrace aspects of delivery like 'courtesy'. However, it is a principle that should apply to any intervention or procedure intended to have an outcome and, when the outcome in question is not a health outcome, then ineffectiveness in the delivery of the non-health outcome would be a ground for not including the service in the NHS, though such procedures are unlikely to come under NICE review.

The quotations also imply that *cost-ineffective* health care has no place in such a system. Under Labour administrations, it is also clear that arbitrary and avoidable unequal access to care is to be prevented, so there is a presumption towards equality of some sort. The rhetoric loses precision at this point. The lack of specificity in ministerial commands poses a problem for an organization such as NICE. How ought it to populate the *general* ideas with ones that are *specific, relevant, and operational*? What, precisely, is 'health' or 'health gain'? What is 'equitable'? What is the 'population'? What does it mean to 'maximise' something? How, more specifically still, are these ideas, each fraught with ethical overtones, to be implemented in a deliberative process whose outcome is to be a recommendation about the adoption of health care technologies? Here we have two ambitions, manifestly ethical in character, which we may summarily call 'efficiency' and 'equity'. They are (if we accept the legitimacy of the accountable minister) critically important starting points. Despite their ambiguity, they are also axiomatic, givens, primitive statements. And, given the authority (the accountable minister), they have a democratic basis to which no mere academic, researcher, teacher, or even individual citizen can possibly lay claim. These broad and imperfectly defined aims form the basis for the use of cost-effectiveness methods in NICE's decision-making processes and NICE has, perforce, had to inject potentially controversial content into them. All these ambiguities have had to be demystified and made explicit in its approach to cost effectiveness.

NICE's resolution of ambiguities in its technology appraisals

NICE's guidance on the economic components of technology appraisal is set out in NICE (2004). Aspects of this guide that are worthy of note are conveniently addressed under the following headings: The context; the Reference Case; The scoping phase; Perspective; Outcome measurement (What costs and what benefits? How measured?); Distribution of costs and benefits (QALY bias and QALY weights).

The context. 'Context' includes process characteristics that are not conventionally examined in economics. A distinction seems to be emerging in NICE's procedures between value judgements that may be conveniently decided upon in an algorithmic way and those that are better decided as the outcome of a more deliberative process: one that is, in effect, a deliberative process conducted in the context of a specific policy decision rather than as an abstract exercise. Such a distinction exists between the treatment of the values embodied in the QALY (essentially algorithmic and only discussed in a NICE policy-making context if there is a feeling that the conventions are suitable representations of the relevant values) and the values embodied in interpersonal comparisons of QALYs accruing to specific groups of people who might be deemed 'special cases', such as a patient group's claim on behalf of those it represents, that its claims deserve higher priority than those of others.

The Reference Case. NICE has borrowed from the Washington Panel (Gold et al, 1996) the idea of a 'Reference Case'. NICE explains it thus: "The Institute has to make decisions across different technologies and disease areas. It is, therefore, important that analyses of clinical and cost effectiveness undertaken to inform the appraisal adopt a consistent approach. To facilitate this, the Institute has defined a 'reference case' that specifies the methods considered by the Institute to be the most appropriate for the Appraisal Committee's purpose and consistent with an NHS objective of maximising health gain from limited resources... This does not preclude additional analyses being presented where one or more aspects of methods differ from the reference case. However, these must be justified and clearly distinguished from the reference case." (NICE, 2004: 19) This quotation neatly encapsulates three elements that have implications for the context of work undertaken by NICE: it is constrained by the maximand ('health gain'); it is constrained by a need for consistency in analytic methods (or as much as is necessary for its Appraisal Committee to be able to function effectively); it is pragmatic, not only in the two respects just mentioned but also in that exceptions to the Reference Case are permitted.

The Reference Case stipulates: the scope of the decision problem; the comparator technologies to be used; the perspective to be taken on costs and outcomes; the type of economic evaluation to be used; the methods of research synthesis; the health states underlying QALYs; the appropriate methods of preference elicitation; sources of such preference data; the discount rates; and the weights to be attached to QALYs.

The scoping phase. This defines a framework for the subsequent appraisal and inescapably entails the making of explicit or implicit social value judgements. Scoping precedes every technology appraisal and is, in essence, a deliberative process within a deliberative process. The framework determines the specific questions to be addressed so as to define, as clearly as possible, the issues of interest (for example, target population, technology comparators) and the questions that should be addressed by the Appraisals Committee when considering the clinical- and cost-effectiveness of the technology. Advice is sought from consultees and commentators during the scoping process. The Institute revises the scope in response to comments received and develops a final scoping document that describes the boundaries of the appraisal and the parameters that will be investigated. The scope is further developed into a protocol for the technology assessment.

The scoping exercise begins with a preliminary search of the literature. Potential consultees, commentators, and clinical specialists are identified and then consulted on the draft scope and invited to a scoping workshop. Discussion at this workshop is intended to ensure that all relevant issues have been considered and that the focus and boundaries of the appraisal have been clearly defined. The final scope for the appraisal is produced following the scoping workshop, and defines:

- the clinical problem, the population(s) and any relevant subgroups for whom treatment with the technology is being appraised (choices here may be determined by both scientific judgements and colloquial ones – like the personal and social significance attached to particular clinical problems; for evidence NICE typically relies upon representative groups and experts with vicarious experience)

- the technology and the setting for its use (for example, hospital or community)

- the relevant comparator technologies (it is easy to 'rig' a comparison of technologies by suitably biased choices, or to render an analysis fairly useless by drawing on evidence from trials using only a placebo comparator)

- the principal health outcome measures appropriate for the analysis (pragmatism is likely to rule here but choice of outcome measure – the denominator in an incremental cost-effectiveness ratio-is a critically important social value judgement)

- the measures of costs to be assessed (interpreted as opportunity cost, which raises the same ethical issues as the choice of outcome measure, since cost for the NHS is ultimately 'health gain forgone')

- the time horizon over which benefits and costs will be assessed (both the period and the rate of discount entail value judgements)

- other considerations, for example, identification of patient subgroups for whom the technology might potentially be particularly clinically and cost effective (this implies that some patients might receive more favourable consideration than others, which is clearly value judgemental)

- special considerations and issues that are likely to affect the appraisal

- the extent and completeness of the evidence (while this may involve scientific value judgements –' is this research well-conceived and conducted?' – it is less likely to involve social value judgements)

- consideration of the appropriateness of 'routine' assumptions embodied in NICE's cost-effectiveness algorithms (for example, regarding the weights attached to incremental quality of life for different categories of beneficiary).

Perspective. The perspective from which an analysis is to be undertaken plainly involves major ethical judgements, concerning, as it does, the scope of the costs and consequences that are deemed relevant. At NICE, as we have seen, many of these are embodied in the scoping phase. The specific guidance that NICE offers on perspective runs thus: the perspective on outcomes should be all direct health effects whether for patients or, where relevant, other individuals (principally carers). The perspective adopted on costs should be that of the National Health Service and the Personal Social Services. If the inclusion of a wider set of costs or outcomes is expected to influence the results significantly, such analyses should be presented in addition to the reference case analysis.

This represents a significant departure from the 'societal perspective' commonly advocated in the cost-effectiveness literature (eg Gold et al, 1996). The NICE decision-makers are very clear about their context and this is plainly an important determinant of how the public interest in interpreted. NICE does not try to simulate the workings of a perfect market (eg by postulating general welfare maximisation based on individual preferences as its objective) and it deliberately curtails quite severely the scope of both the costs and the benefits to be considered. Its three grounds for doing so appear to be: the principled one, that the objective is not defined in terms of welfare but in terms of health; the conditional one, that the overall resource commitment (and hence the opportunity cost felt elsewhere in the economy) as defined by the health care budget is a judgement reached elsewhere; and the pragmatic one, that in the event that ethically significant issues arise that might affect the decision but are outside the Reference Case, then they may be taken into account.

Outcome measurement. The quality adjusted life year (QALY) is a generic measure of health-related quality of life that takes into account both the quantity and the quality of life generated by interventions. It is plainly fraught with social value judgements. The version currently preferred by NICE is EQ-5D, a three-level, five-dimensional index where the dimensions are mobility, self-care, usual activity, pain/discomfort, and anxiety/depression, and each is scored on a three-point scale (1, no problems; 2, some problems; 3, extreme problems). This generates 245 health states (35 plus perfect health and dead) on a cardinal ('interval', unique to a linear transform) scale.

Why the QALY? The following reasons were probably influential: there was a general agreement amongst economist colleagues that NICE needed an outcome measure that related as closely as possible to the Secretary of State's charge to NICE regarding 'health'; it was sufficiently close to common outcome measures used by clinicians in research (eg life-years or five-year survival rates) to be a familiar starting point; it was an index rather than a profile; it was generic-applicable to a wide range of technologies, thus facilitating comparison of relative cost effectiveness; its theoretical properties and their consequences were (or were becoming) well understood (properties such as constant proportional trade-off, risk neutrality over life-years, additive independence in health states); the trade-offs embodied in it were derived from a representative sample of the UK population; the ethical arguments adduced against it did not persuade the Board, particularly when it was compared with practical alternatives; it had the attractive characteristic of identifying and resolving, in a ready-made algorithm, a set of routine, frequently arising value judgemental issues concerning the dimensions in which 'health' was to be measured and the weights to be attached to each dimension; it was simple and low cost, and therefore had a good chance of becoming an 'industry standard'. While other indices had some of these virtues, none, it was thought, had all of them. As ever, NICE was pragmatic. While endorsing the QALY as the Reference Case desideratum, it added: "cost-benefit analysis may be particularly useful when non-health consequences are important in an evaluation. In such cases, willingness-to-pay methods may be used to value all consequences in monetary terms. Where such methods are used they should be fully described". (NICE, 2004: 22)

This illustrates a characteristic of NICE thinking about the use of QALYs: from the beginning, their use has always been context-dependent. From the academic literature on QALYs it is easy to gain the impression both that their advocates think that they provide a complete and context-free answer to the complexity of issues bound up in measuring and assessing the outcomes of health care, and that their use is as helpful in all decision settings as it may be in some. From NICE's beginning, the context for the use of QALYs was the Appraisals Committee, a multi-disciplinary, multi-professional, and multi-sectoral group that would always include patient and caregiver representatives and subject specialists. In that context the adequacy of QALYs, and of any other outcomes measures, of course, including whatever consideration of distributive fairness was felt to be needed, could receive full consideration, including any representations that might be made on behalf of those who would be living, as patients, caregivers, or medical professionals, with the consequences of the decision. The trick was always going to be to ensure that the special interests lined up behind particular groups of beneficiaries were never allowed to dominate the more generically represented general public. Making that assessment of adequacy and maintaining that balance were going to be critically important features if the Appraisals Committee's recommendations were to carry conviction.

Distribution of costs and benefits. Earlier NICE guidance on equity made mention of the two great Aristotelian principles, which may be paraphrased as:

- horizontal equity – the equal treatment of those who are equal in an ethically relevant sense

- vertical equity – the unequal treatment of those who are unequal in an ethically relevant sense.

There can be no doubt that NICE has been ready to apply both principles as may be appropriate. The difficulty is, establishing what is appropriate and what are the 'ethically relevant senses'.

The reference case implies a particular ethical position regarding the comparison of health gained between individuals. An additional QALY has the same weight, regardless of the other characteristics of the individuals receiving the health benefit. Some other characteristics of the individuals whose 'ethically relevant' sameness or difference might imply that they ought to be treated either the same or differently might include the following. The list is not intended to be comprehensive.

- their pre- or post-treatment level of health (eg an incremental QALY is as socially valued when it accrues to someone with a lifetime of chronic incapacity as to someone who has hitherto been in abundant health)

- their current level of health (eg an incremental QALY is as socially valued when it accrues to someone who is currently very ill as to someone receiving preventive care who is perfectly fit)

- the size of the increment in health they may derive (eg the tenth incremental QALY someone receives is a socially valued as the first)

- age (eg a QALY for an aged person is as socially valued as one for a youngster)

- gender

- economic productivity

- lifestyle (eg a QALY for someone whose reckless style of life has brought about or exacerbated ill-health is as socially valued as one for an impeccably 'clean living' type).

None of these assumptions is inherent in the idea of the QALY and alternative value assumptions may be made. But they are not readily made. NICE was in great difficulty in making a judgement on these matters. The QALY=QALY=QALY value assumption of the Reference Case is to be seen, always pragmatically, as provisional: still a value judgement but one to be subject to scrutiny and special discussion. NICE was well aware that in assigning an equal weight to all QALYs in this way, it was inescapably making a value judgement, and it adopted a pragmatic approach by testing the wider public's views on some of these trade-offs. The issue of age was put to the Citizens' Council (which recommended unitary weights). Others have been pursued through systematic research, finding out the ethical views of the public, and whether there is anything like a consensus. Simple-minded ethical talk about 'equality' in the health context is mere rhetoric unless one gets to be specific about equality of what and of whom and for what.

Conclusions

This chapter has sought to explore the plausibility of a number of conjectures about the use of deliberative processes by applying them to the technology assessment procedures used by the National Institute for Health and Clinical Excellence in England and Wales. A deliberative process is one that elicits and combines evidence of different kinds and from different sources in order to develop guidance – in the present case, guidance for a health care system. A deliberative process entails the integration of three kinds of evidence: scientific context-free evidence about the general clinical potential of a technology, scientific context-sensitive evidence about particular evidence in realistic scenarios, and colloquial evidence to fit context-free scientific evidence into a context and to supply the best evidence short of scientific evidence to fill in any relevant gaps. NICE's appraisals procedures and, in particular, its approach to cost effectiveness, both entail the weighing of each of these types of evidence and can be seen as rational responses to the circumstances under which I conjecture that a deliberative process is likely to be used. Each and every one of these conjectures applies in the case of NICE. Indeed, so closely does the NICE context match these circumstances that it seems almost inconceivable that the general character of its deliberative processes could have been otherwise. In that respect, NICE would appear to be exemplary.

21

Hic sunt dracones: 'equity' and 'process' in Health Technology Assessment[21]

Only cost-effective treatment must be free

'Here be dragons' may not have actually appeared on any known early map of the world but it is on the 'Lenox Globe' of 1510 in the New York Public Library, and monsters, giant horned men, and other similarly terrifying beasts were certainly sketched in early maps of the remoter and mostly unexplored regions of the world. One may draw an analogy between such maps and the current state of Health Technology Assessment (HTA). There is a large terrain of well-researched and largely well-understood methods (economic, bio-statistical, and epidemiological) on which most researchers are engaged in what is aptly called 'normal science' (Kuhn 1972). HTA is a living example of the intense creativity that is possible within a paradigm and, further, HTA is not at all normal in respect of the amazing bridging that has taken place across conventional disciplinary (and faculty) lines, between clinical, statistical, and philosophical disciplines as well as social sciences. It is a considerable and highly unusual achievement that there should be so little misunderstanding between these

21 This is a much shortened and adapted version of Culyer, A.J., 2012. Hic sunt dracones: the future of Health Technology Assessment – one economist's perspective, *Medical Decision Making* 32: E25-E32.

disciplines. Indeed, an eavesdropper on a conversation between its practitioners would be hard-pressed to tell from language alone whether a speaker was an epidemiologist, a statistician, a clinician, an ethicist or an economist. This is what I imagine people may have in mind in making a distinction between multi-disciplinarity and inter-disciplinarity. HTA is of the latter variety.

My concerns about HTA relate, however, to the fact that, when applied, it inevitably has a political context. It is political both with a large 'P' and a small one. The large 'P' relates to the political ideology of health services and springs from the notion of a public interest element of health care. This is an interest that can be cast in many languages: for example, in political language, 'solidarity'; or, in Marxian language, 'from each according to their ability; to each according to their need';' or, in neoclassical economic language, 'public goods' and 'caring externalities'. It finds particular expression in the idea, which I think can be first attributed to Archie Cochrane (Cochrane 1972), that the only health care warranting public financing or public delivery is health care that is demonstrably effective. Cochrane's slogan, which I have adapted as the side head for this section, was "All effective treatment must be free" (Cochrane 1972). This goes a bit too far, for it may not be sensible to provide all effective, or even all cost-effective care, without charge to the user. Nonetheless, the only care provided without charge ought to be effective care. Other kinds are available in the market place.

I shall, however, focus on the 'small p' political context. This is the context in which the political creator of NICE, Frank Dobson, when, as Secretary of State for Health, he was asked whether he thought it would work, said "probably not, but it's worth a bloody good try." Applied HTA is 'political' both in the sense that it inherently embodies value judgements, including ones about equity, or fairness, and in the sense that the identification and acceptance of value judgements of any kind requires a process within the body politic and one, moreover, that needs to have particular characteristics if it is to lead to acceptable decisions.

Two dragons

The first dragon is equity. In particular, how one may embody equity considerations into HTA. By 'equity' I mean interpersonal fairness in the receipt of health care and the distribution of its consequences. Economists have a well-developed corpus of theory, both for describing the characteristics of a first-best allocation of resources to production and the fruits of that production to final consumers. They also have a well-developed set of principles for putting that analysis to work in a second-best world that are now a standard part of the technology of HTA. What economists have never been able to do satisfactorily, is to develop any analysis of equity of comparable sophistication, comparable applicability and comparable mutual agreement. Nor, alas, has the vacuum been filled by anyone else. A consequence is that the committees which make recommendations about the adoption and funding of new health care interventions, or disinvestment in old ones, do not know how to address matters of equity. Nor do they know how to integrate such considerations into efficiency analyses.

Dragon number two is our ignorance as to the character of a *process* that might enable us to integrate equity in HTA. Specifically, the challenge is that we are short of an adequate understanding of the processes necessary for combining different types of evidence, evidence about different kinds of things (monetary and non-monetary, qualitative and quantitative), and for articulating concepts that are not themselves evidential (such as equity). It is not merely that processes can have characteristics that appeal in and of themselves – characteristics like transparency, citizen engagement, openness, deliberation and contestability – it is that characteristics such as these are to be valued for more than their intrinsic merits. They are, in short, necessary for the proper accomplishment of the tasks of HTA and, in particular, they are essential to the major task of merging equity with efficiency to any degree of satisfaction.

Philosophy, political science and social policy all address equity and, in the case of philosophy, have done so for many centuries.

Administrative science, the law and management science have all addressed 'processes'. But none of these disciplines has concerned itself deeply with HTA (with the exception of the sub-discipline of bioethics) and, typically, none has made the theory and practice of HTA its daily business. This accounts, I conjecture, for two unfortunate phenomena. The first is that the question whether the methods of HTA ought to be more intimately linked to the processes of real-world decision-making has gone unaddressed. The two are treated as essentially unrelated activities. As a consequence, HTA, or at least the conventional practice within HTA of so-called cost-utility analysis, has been described as a "perversion of science as well as of morality" (Harris 2005). Powers and Faden (2000) call attention to its "moral flaws", an unfortunate judgement that hinges on the implausible proposition that those who use CEA methods are moral morons, wedded to the uncritical use of a single decision tool. The charge is a triple one: that the tool is a poor one; that it is used uncritically; and that it is the only one they use. The other unfortunate phenomenon is that, despite these centuries of study, no one yet has come up with usable tools that would assist decision-makers and those who advise them to integrate the two great criteria of efficiency and equity and to devise effective (even cost-effective) processes for doing so.

Process

"Arguably the biggest threat to our public health care system is not our ability to pay for the increasing cost of care, but rather a loss of public confidence." (Chase et al 2010, p1). While this loss of confidence parallels a general scepticism about the adequacy and fairness of public decisions across the board, health care has evidently not escaped it. For many (eg Mendelberg 2002, Petts 2004) the solution is citizen engagement and other processes of more direct democracy. I want, instead (or, perhaps, 'as well') to suggest that better processes would be useful not only for re-establishing confidence in general, but also for offering ways in which better decisions are likely to result. A process might be better in the sense that it is more 'transparent' and confidence-building on that account. Those are the *intrinsic* merits of a good process and are embodied in 'accountability for reasonableness' (Daniels 2000, Daniels and Sabin 2008). But it may also be a better process by virtue of the fact that it embodies more complete evidence, or more deeply investigated evidence, or by its better combining of many elements, some evidential and others not, or through enabling a more complete addressing of equity and of its consideration alongside efficiency. By 'process' I mean the steps that are taken, and their organisation and management, from the earliest inception of an HTA ('what technology is to be assessed?') through its further scoping and refinement; selection of comparator technologies; identification of primary and secondary research; critical appraisal of the evidence; stakeholder comment, consultation and further deliberation; through draft guidance, recommendations or decisions; appeals; conclusions, recommendations and dissemination.

The processes that I particularly have in mind are: the possibility of external comment in order that interested parties may see what there is to comment upon; consultation, through which external parties are invited both to engage with decision-makers and their advisers and to enter into discussion about whatever aspects of the process may be under way at the time, including assumptions, comparators, model building, literature review and matters to do with the intrinsic process itself; and finally, the most complete form of engagement, deliberation, in which relevant stakeholders actually participate in the decision-making itself, though probably excluding the final 'determination' or conclusion of the process, for which responsibility necessarily lies with those appointed to decide.

Issues that require resolution would be determined at a 'high' level, such as through the board of an organisation, or at ministerial or even cabinet level. Examples of such issues include: specifying the objective (health maximisation?); the available budget; the 'threshold' (lintel?) Incremental Cost-Effectiveness Ratio (ICER); the discount rate(s) to be used; whether sophisticated programming or simple CEA is to be used; whether Multi-criteria Decision Analysis is an approved method; the choice of technologies to evaluate; and the comparators and equity requirements. Occasionally some of these might be determined at a 'lower level', which I take to be the level of the decision-making agency or advisory committee. These lower level issues would generally include all of the following: testing the concept validity of outcome measures; assessing the quality of the science on a particular subject intervention and its comparators; interpreting and combining both qualitative and quantitative evidence (systematic reviews, other reviews, meta-analyses); linking, if possible, internal and external validity; weighing uncertainty; identifying absent information and deciding what to do in its absence; assessing 'feasibility' and manageable time lines; trading off conflicting desiderata; and, finally, making recommendations or issuing guidance through (preferably tried and tested) Knowledge Translation methods.

A good many technologies do not easily 'fit' into the customary methods of HTA. Consider public health with its complex interventions, diversity of responsibility for the vectors of delivery (communities, schools, hospitals, prisons,...), heterogeneity of outcomes (better health, but also reductions in teenage pregnancies, reduced crime, reduced *fear* of crime,...), long time horizons (especially when the interventions involve culture change or challenge cherished beliefs) and programmatic character (prevention, screening). Or consider the simplifying assumptions, such as constant returns to scale, non-diminishing marginal value of QALY, or the simple additivity of outcomes, that are so often merely taken for granted rather than tested for their appropriateness. Also consider the character of evidence, especially when one widens the notion of 'technology' beyond pharmaceuticals: the greater dependence on multivariate observational studies and econometrics; the use of cheaper experimental methods than RCTs; and the kind of evidence required on value questions such as the value to be placed on a unit of outcome or the measurement of changes in 'equity'. Then too consider what might be best regarded as a potential by-product of HTA: the possibilities it affords for raising the public understanding of risk and uncertainty; the reasons why one thing rather than another has been chosen; and the enhancement of the general credibility of guidance.

The 'process' has three important roles. One is to ensure that divergent views are properly represented to minimise the chances that any one particular interest group should unfairly 'capture' the process. Another is to enable the wisdom and experience of other decision-makers to be brought to the table. Their judgements, especially about value-laden and possibly controversial issues such as quality of science or the meaning of 'equity', may be wiser than those of the 'official' participants. A third is that the process itself is a means by which evidence is generated or at least brought before decision-makers. Such evidence might relate to matters of 'feasibility' and 'manageability', where the experience of practical managers amongst the decision-makers may be a useful input; to matters of external validity, where specific knowledge on the environments into which an intervention might be introduced may be essential; or to the appraisal of outcomes, where the fit of the outcome measures used in research studies with the experience of actual patients and their carers can be tested and possible biases identified and adjustments made on their account. It also includes clinical effectiveness, where recourse is had to 'experience', including that of members of the committee, in the absence of better scientific evidence. (Culyer 2009, Dobrow et al 2009).

I have just *listed* some 'issues' and asserted *some* better ways of addressing them. My selection is not evidence-based, save in a somewhat experiential and necessarily partial way. Nor is it founded on any well-developed theory of 'good' decision-making. It is therefore *ad hoc*. Most of the literature on these topics, such as it is, is assertive rather than analytical, ideological rather than scientific, strong on advocacy but weak on evidence. It is also written by the practitioners of many different disciplines and appears in places that seem very remote from any HTA concern. Who, for example, would think of looking in *Trends in Parasitology* for the useful article by Lavery et al (2010) with its tips on successful community engagement in research?

Equity

Equity, in its major sense of distributive justice or 'fairness' has been a central concern of moral philosophy since the days of classical Greece. Its modern students are well-practised in the business of typology (utilitarian – several varieties, deontological – again several varieties, theological, consequentialist, etc) but on decision processes, they have, with a few fine exceptions (such as Daniels, 2000 and Daniels and Sabin, 2008), been quite extraordinarily bad at providing tools for the use of practical decision-makers such as the practitioners and users of HTA.

Even the most elementary 'tools', such as a typology of characteristic equity issues to form an 'agenda' for discussion at various stages of an HTA process, would be an advance on what we have at present. Such a typology might focus deliberation on such matters as the *domains* of equity. For example, there are equity issues regarding the use and distribution of health care inputs, the processes that determine who gets what, the evaluation of outcomes, and on the priority that ought to be attached to different diseases, or to prevention versus cure. Decision-makers need to reflect on the appropriateness of the criteria used in respect of any of these, their inclusiveness, the relative weight to attach to each, and so on. Some red flags are provided in some jurisdictions by statute, as when there is a legal obligation to guard against discrimination by age, gender, disability, other demographics, workplace, education, or through institutionalised discrimination. However, not all jurisdictions cover all possible issues, and matters of equitable concern may lie hidden in the depths of an HTA.

Some of the 'hidden' equity biases that are always likely to need surfacing include embedded inequity – through which possible unfairness is 'built in' to concepts (eg omitted dimensions of outcome measure that discriminate against those for whom such outcomes are important); framing effects in experimental approaches that bring in social class bias; and unfairness that is inherent in the intervention (eg a threat to autonomy through the removal of choice, as with some public health measures). There are also institutional biases – inequities resulting from practices in jurisdictional scope (eg health consequences not taken into account by some faith-based provider institutions, school boards or workplace managements) and the degree of concern many jurisdictions have with the distribution of consequences (health or not-health). There is also implicit stereotyping – the use, often in all innocence, of definitions and concepts that exclude individuals or aspects of health-related welfare that have a differential impact on individuals, and that make untested assumptions about what does and does not 'matter' to the people for whom the intervention exists (eg Reutzel et al 1999). Particular contexts (eg geography) may disadvantage some individuals relative to others. Minimally, surely, one ought to test to see whether any of the following could affect the balance of advantage across different groups: the setting of care (eg home or institution); language; education or SES of clients; religious beliefs; stigma; or multiple deprivations.

Decision-makers ought to ask whether the processes in HTA itself are biased. Do they deny representation to people with a legitimate interest and are the interests of absentee stakeholders properly considered – for example, those anonymous individuals for whom services will not be provided as a consequence of implementing the recommendations? Participants in HTA need to be self-aware and self-critical regarding their own procedures. Processes in delivery of the care under evaluation can be prejudicial to technologies for some types of client (eg those of low SES) and can favour those adept at negotiating their way through processes, or impose differential burdens on some clients (eg wage versus salary earners).

There are special claims, such as claims of need (eg low initial health status?), of deservingness (eg choosing life styles that are hazardous to health?), of history (eg past endurance of ill-health, past receipt of the intervention), of desperation (eg 'last chance'), of unfair innings (only a short life-span), of non-health consequences (other welfare effects), of willingness to pay (eg top-up payments). Sometimes the beneficiary is identified as a member of a group or even by name, as is often the case with spectacular acts of medical, or other, rescue. Ought cases of extreme need be given special favour (Hope 2004 ch 3, Cookson et al 2008)? What weight ought to be given to such claims, either in general or in the context of a specific HTA? What weights actually are given (eg Cropper et al 1994, Johannesson and Johanson 1997a, b, Johanson-Stenman and Martinson 2008)? Cumulative effects may escape proper attention. For example, cumulative past disadvantages or effects might be relevant in assessing benefit or cost or their distribution across patients and other affected groups.

The point of these examples is that in the process of discussion and deliberation about a technology decision, all of these hidden problems can be 'surfaced'. Ignoring them, being unaware of their existence, or aware but doing nothing about them, is likely to lead to flawed decisions. My suggestions are merely illustrative and are certainly not exhaustive. But who better to complete the list, maintain it through casuistry and careful recording of the reasons for decisions, and synthesize and consolidate it over time, than those involved in the process of HTA? Through such casuistry, may we not build up case-based precedents to help decision-makers achieve consistency across interventions? Even, over time, might a systematic 'ethics of HTA' eventually be created?

Deliberation

The slaying of both the dragons of HTA requires, I conjecture, deliberation, with an emphasis on: process, from scoping a topic through evidence generation and synthesis to delivering guidance; consultation with legitimate stakeholders (usually also a source of evidence); and facilitated discussion. These are all weak points in the current state of HTA, and they are all Cinderella research topics (see Lomas et al 2005, Culyer 2009, Dobrow et al 2009) with multidisciplinary concerns.

The ultimate product and measure of success would be the increase in confidence of participants, stakeholders and the public. This would be achieved by their understanding of the processes and knowledge that the best evidence was used, that the appropriate 'experts', lay and professional, had contributed, that all relevant evidence had been searched and considered, that all relevant stakeholders had their say and been heard, that key concepts (eg 'outcomes') had been tested for construct validity, that all relevant costs and benefits had been weighed and included in calculations, that fair comparisons had been made (both between interventions and between individuals), that all relevant conceptual and empirical biases had been eliminated, and that the main risks had been assessed and undue risks not taken. I suppose, taken as a group, such outcomes might constitute evidence of a 'good' process.

To realise this ultimate product, however, HTA needs to broaden its horizons, turning away from what is largely just an algorithm to find ways to take seriously the myriad value and ethical issues which currently still have the unfortunate appearance of afterthoughts, tacked on to, but essentially excluded from, the core decision logic, and to develop an empirical programme to rival, *mutatis mutandis*, that of CEA. After all, non-monetary values, though less easily measured perhaps than monetary ones, are still subject to empirical estimation and the values that individuals actually cherish ought, at the very least, to inform decision-makers' values. This entails developing suitable processes that generate information through the participation of stakeholders, while also facilitating the thoughtful assessment of what is known, combining it with revealed values, and producing multiple solutions to problems that are not uniquely soluble, like those over which there are deep divisions of principle in the community. To participate both in such processes and in the accompanying research programmes must surely be one of the more exciting prospects confronting today's assessors of health technology.

References

Alchian, A.A. 1953. The meaning of utility measurement. *American Economic Review*, 43, 26-50.

Anand, P. 2005. QALYs and capabilities: a comment on Cookson. *Health Economics*, 14, 1283-1286.

Anderson, R.T., Aaronson, N.K., Bullinger, M., McBee, W.L. 1996. A review of the progress towards developing health-related quality-of-life instruments for international clinical studies and outcomes research. *Pharmacoeconomics*, 10, 336-355.

Arneson, R. 1989. Equality and equality of opportunity for welfare. *Philosophical Studies*, 56, 77-93.

Arrow, K.J. 1963. Uncertainty and the welfare economics of medical care. *American Economic Review*, 53, 941-973.

Banta, H.D. 1980. The diffusion of the computed tomography (CT) scanner in the U.S. *International Journal of Health Services*, 10, 251-69.

Barry, B. 1965. *Political Argument*, Routledge & Kegan Paul, London.

Bateman, U., Carson, R.T., Day, B., Hanemann, W.M., Hanleys, N., Hett, T., Jones-Lee, M. Loomes, G., Mourato, S., Ozdemiroglu, E.,Pearce, D. Sugden, R., Swanson, J. 2002. *Economic Valuation with Stated Preference Techniques*, Edward Elgar, Cheltenham.

Baumol, W.S., Panzar, C., Willig, R.D. 1988. *Contestable Markets and the Theory of Industrial Structure*, Harcourt Brace, New York.

Bebbington, A.C., Davies, B.P. 1980. Territorial need indicators: a new approach, parts I and II *Journal of Social Policy*, 9, 145-68 and 433-62.

Beck, R.G. 1974. The effects of co-payments on the poor, *Journal of Human Resources*, 9, 129-142.

Becker, G. 1957. *The Economics of Discrimination*, Chicago University Press, Chicago.

Becker, G. 1964. *Human Capital: A theoretical and empirical analysis with special reference to Education*, The University of Chicago Press, Chicago.

Becker, G.S. 1968. Crime and punishment: an economic approach, *Journal of Political Economy*, 76, 169-217.

Becker, G.S. 1993. *A Treatise on the Family*, Harvard University Press, Cambridge.

Benz, M., Stutzer, A. 2003. Do workers enjoy procedural utility? *Applied Economics Quarterly*, 49, 149-172.

Bergson, A. 1938. A reformulation of certain aspects of welfare economics, *Quarterly Journal of Economics*, 52, 310-334.

Birch, S., Donaldson, C. 2003. Valuing the benefits and costs of health care programmes: where's the 'extra' in extra-welfarism? *Social Science and Medicine*, 56, 1121-1133.

Birch, S., Melnikow, J., Kuppermann, M. 2003. Conservative versus aggressive follow up of mildly abnormal Pap smears: testing for process utility, *Health Economics*, 12, 879-884.

Blackorby, C., Donaldson C. 1990. A review article: The case against the use of the sum of compensating variations in cost-benefit analysis, *Canadian Journal of Economics*, 23, 471-494.

Bleichrodt, H. 1997. Health utility indices and equity considerations, *Journal of Health Economics*, 16, 65-91.

Boadway, R., Bruce, N. 1984. *Welfare Economics*, Basil Blackwell, Oxford.

Bombardier, C., Wolfson, A.D., Sinclair, A.J., McGreer, A. 1982. Comparison of three preference measurement methodologies in the evaluation of a functional status index. In Deber, R. Thompson, G. (eds.), *Choices in Health Care: Decision Making and Evaluation of Effectiveness*, University of Toronto Press, Toronto, 145-160.

Bosanquet, N. 2001. A 'fair innings' for efficiency in health services? *Journal of Medical Ethics*, 27, 228-233.

Bradshaw, J. 1972, A taxonomy of social need, *New Society*, (March) 640-643.

Bradshaw, J. 1977. The concept of social need. In: Gilbert, N. Specht, H. eds. *Planning for Social Welfare*, Prentice-Hall: New Jersey, 290-296.

Brazier, J.N., Jones, N., Kind, P. 1993. Testing the validity of the Euroqol and comparing it with the SF-36 health survey questionnaire, *Quality of Life Research*, 2, 169-180.

Braybrooke, D. 1987. *Meeting Needs*, Princeton University Press, Princeton NJ.

Brooks, R. 1996. EuroQol: the current state of play, *Health Policy*, 37, 53-72.

Broome, J. 1978. Trying to value a life, *Journal of Public Economics*, 9, 91-100.

Broome, J. 1985. The economic value of life, *Economica*, 52, 281-294.

Brouwer, W.B.F., Koopmanschap, M.A. 2000. On the economic foundations of CEA. Ladies and gentlemen, take your positions! *Journal of Health Economics*, 19, 439-459.

Brouwer, W.B.F., van Exel, N.J.A., van den Berg, B., van den Bos, G.A.M, Koopmanschap, M.A. 2005. Process utility from providing informal care: the benefit of caring, *Health Policy*, 74, 85-99.

Brouwer, W.B.F., van Exel, N.J.A., Baltussen, R.M.P.M,. Rutten, F.F.H. 2006. A dollar is a dollar is a dollar – or is it? *Value in Health*, 9, 341-347.

Brouwer, W.B.F., Culyer, A.J., Job, N., van Exel, A., Rutten, F.F.H. 2008. Welfarism vs extra-welfarism, *Journal of Health Economics*, 27, 325-338.

Buchanan, J.M., Subblebine, W.G. 1962. Externality, *Economica*, 29, 371-384.

Buchanan, J.M. 1965. *The Inconsistencies of the National Health Service*, Institute of Economic Affairs, London.

Buchanan, J.M. 1968. Student revolts, academic liberalism and constitutional attitudes, *Social Research*, 35, 666-680.

Buchanan, JM. 1987. TheConstitution of Economic Policy, *American Economic Review*, 77, 243-50.

Bunker, J.P. 1970. Surgical Manpower – A comparison of operations and surgeons in the United States and in England and Wales, *New England Journal of Medicine*, 282,135-144.

Cahnman, W.J., Schmitt, C.M. 1979. The concept of social policy (Sozialpolitik), *Journal of Social Policy*, 8, 47-59.

Chalkley, M., Malcomson, J.M. 2000. Government purchasing of health services. In: Culyer, A.J. Newhouse, J.P. (eds.), *Handbook of Health Economics* [vol 1A]. Elsevier, Amsterdam, 847-90.

Chalmers, I. 2003. Trying to do more good in policy and practice: the role of rigorous, transparent, up-to-date evaluations, *Annals of the American Academy of Political and Social Science*, 589, 22-40.

Chalmers, I. 2005. If evidence-informed policy works in practice, does it matter if it doesn't work in theory? *Evidence and Policy*, 1, 227-242.

Chambers, S. 1996. *Reasonable Democracy: Jürgen Habermas and the Politics of Discourse*, Cornell University Press, Ithaca, NY.

Chase, R., Levinson, W., Hébert, P.C. 2010. The need for public engagement in choosing health priorities, *Canadian Medical Association Journal,* DOI:10.1503/cmaj.101517.

Claxton, K., Sculpher, M.J., Culyer, A.J. 2007. Mark versus Luke? Appropriate Methods for the Evaluation of Public Health Interventions. *CHE research paper no. 31.* Centre for Health Economics, University of York, York.

Coast, J., Smith, R.D., Lorgelly, P. 2008. Welfarism, extra-welfarism and capability: the spread of ideas in health economics, *Social Science and Medicine*, 67, 1190-1198.

Cochrane AL. 1972. *Effectiveness and Efficiency. Random Reflections on Health Services.* London, Nuffield Provincial Hospitals Trust.

Cochrane Collaboration 2006. Glossary of terms in the Cochrane Collaboration, Web page (www.cochrane.org/resources/glossary.htm-accessed 7 May 2006).

Collard, D. 1978. *Altruism and Economy: A Study in Non-selfish Economics*, Martin Robertson, Oxford.

Collison, P. 1962. Career contingencies of English university teachers, *British Journal of Sociology*, 13, 286-293.

Committee on Higher Education, 1963. Higher Education, Report, Cmnd. 2154, HMSO, London.

Cookson, R. 2005. QALYs and the capability approach, *Health Economics*, 14, 817-829.

Cookson, R., McCabe, C., Tsuchiya, A. 2008. Public healthcare resource allocation and the Rule of Rescue, *J Med Ethics*, 34, 540-544.

Cooper, M.H., Culyer, A.J. 1970. An Economic Assessment of Some Aspects of the Operation of the National Health Service, In *Health Services Financing*, British Medical Association, London, appendix A.

Cooper, M.H., Culyer, A.J. 1971. An economic survey of the nature and intent of the British National Health Service, *Social Science and Medicine*, 5, 1-13.

Cooper, M.H., Culyer, A.J. 1972. Equality in the National Health Service: intention, performance and problems in evaluation. In: Hauser, M.M. (ed.), *The Economics of Medical Care*, Allen and Unwin, London.

Corner, D.C., Culyer, A.J. 1969. University teachers and the PIB, *Social and Economic Administration*, 3, 127-139.

Cromwell, J., Mitchell, J.B. 1986. Physician-induced demand for surgery, *Journal of Health Economics*, 5, 293-313.

Cropper, M.L., Ayded, S.K., Portney, P.R., 1994. Preferences for life saving programs: how the public discounts time and age, *Journal of Risk and Uncertainty*, 8, (3) 243-265.

Cullis, J.G., West, P.A. 1979. *The Economics of Health: An Introduction*. Martin Robertson, Oxford.

Culyer, A.J. 1971a. Merit goods and the welfare economics of coercion. Public Finance 26, 546-571. Reprinted in Ver Eecke, W. 2006. Merit Goods: The Birth of a New Concept. The Unfinished Ethical Evolution in Economic Theory. Purdue University Press, Ashland Ohio, 174-200).

Culyer, A.J. 1971b. The nature of the commodity "health care" and its efficient allocation. Oxford Economic Papers 23, 189-211. Reprinted as Ch. 2 in Culyer , A.J., Cooper, M.H. (eds.),

1973. *Health Economics*, Penguin, London; also in Culyer, A.J. (ed.), 2006. *Health Economics: Critical Perspectives on the World Economy*, Routledge, London, 148-157).

Culyer, A.J. 1976. Medical care and the economics of giving. *Economica* 151, 295-303. Reprinted as Ch. 18 in Ricketts, M. (ed.), *Neoclassical Microeconomics*, Vol. 2, Edward Elgar, Aldershot, 310-18

Culyer, A.J. 1978a. Needs, values and health status measurement. In Culyer, A.J. Wright, K.G. (eds.), *Economic Aspects of Health Services*. Martin Robertson, London, 9-31.

Culyer, A.J. 1978b. *Measuring Health: Lessons for Ontario*, University of Toronto Press, Toronto.

Culyer, A.J. 1979. *Expenditure on Real Services: Health*, Open University Press, Milton Keynes.

Culyer, A.J. 1980. *The Political Economy of Social Policy*, Martin Robertson, London.

Culyer, A.J. 1981. Economics, social policy and social administration: the interplay between topics and disciplines, *Journal of Social Policy*, 10, 311-329.

Culyer, A.J. 1986. The scope and limits of health economics, *Jahrestagung des Vereinsfuer Sozialpolitik Gesellschaft fuer Wirtschafts- und Sozialwissenschaften*, Duncker & Humboldt, Berlin, 31-53.

Culyer, A.J. 1988a. Inequality of health services is, in general, desirable. In Green, D. (ed.), *Acceptable Inequalities?* Institute of Economic Affairs, London, 31-47.

Culyer, A.J. 1988b. The radical reforms the NHS needs – and doesn't. In: Minutes of Evidence Taken Before the Social Services Committee, House of Lords, HMSO, London.

Culyer, A.J. 1990. Commodities, characteristics of commodities, characteristics of people, utilities and the quality of life. In: Baldwin, S. Godfrey, C. Propper, C. (eds.), *The Quality of Life: Perspectives and Policies*, Routledge, London, 9-27.

Culyer, A.J. 1991. The normative economics of health care finance and provision. In: McGuire, A. Fenn, P. Mayhew, K. (Eds.), *Providing Health Care: The Economics of Alternative Systems of Finance and Delivery*, Oxford University Press, Oxford, 65-98. Reprinted in Culyer, A.J. (ed.), 2006. *Health Economics: Critical Perspectives on the World Economy*, Routledge, London, 148-157).

Culyer, A.J. 1992. The morality of efficiency in health care-some uncomfortable implications. *Health Economics*, 1, 7-18. Reprinted in King, A. Hyclak, T. McMahon, S. Thornton, R. (eds.), *North American Health Care Policy in the 1990s,* Wiley, Chichester, 1-24.

Culyer A.J., 1993. Conflicts between equity concepts and efficiency in health: a diagrammatic approach. In: El-Agraa A., (ed.) *Public and International Economics,* Macmillan, Basingstoke, 42-58.

Culyer, A.J. 1994. Supporting R&D in the National Health Service. Task Force report to the Minister for Health chaired by A.J. Culyer. HMSO, London.

Culyer, A.J. 1995a. Equality of What in Health Policy? Conflicts Between the Contenders. Discussion Paper 142. University of York, Centre for Health Economics.

Culyer, A.J. 1995b. Need: the idea won't do – but we still need it, *Social Science and Medicine,* 40, 727-730.

Culyer AJ. 1997. The rationing debate: maximising the health of the whole community, *British Medical Journal*, 314, 667-669.

Culyer, A.J. 2001a. Economics and ethics in healthcare, *Journal of Medical Ethics*, 27, 217-222.

Culyer, A.J. 2001b. Equity-some theory and its policy implications, *Journal of Medical Ethics*, 27, 275-283.

Culyer, A.J. 2005. Involving stakeholders in health care decisions: the experience of the National Institute for Health and Clinical Excellence (NICE) in England and Wales, *Healthcare Quarterly*, 8, 56-60.

Culyer, A.J. 2006. The bogus conflict between efficiency and equity, *Health Economics*, 15, 1155-1158.

Culyer, A.J. 2007a. Need – an instrumental view. In: Ashcroft, R., Dawson, A., Draper, H., McMillan, J. (Eds.), *Principles of Health Care Ethics*, 2nd edition. Wiley, Chichester, 231-238.

Culyer, A.J. 2007b. The Ideas and Influence of Alan Williams: Be Reasonable – Do It My Way. In: Mason, A. Towse, A. (Eds.), Proceedings of a Conference to Celebrate the Work of Alan Williams. Office of Health Economics, London, 57-74.

Culyer, A.J., 2009. *Deliberative Processes in Decisions about Health Care Technologies: Combining Different Types of Evidence, Values, Algorithms and People*. Office of Health Economics, London.

Culyer, A.J., Brazier, J.E., O'Donnell, O. 1988a. *Organising Health Service Provision: Drawing on Experience*. Institute of Health Service Management, London.

Culyer, A.J., Donaldson, C., Gerard, K. 1988b. *Financial Aspects of Health Services: Drawing on Experience*, Institute of Health Service Management, London.

Culyer, A.J., Evans, R.G,. 1996. Mark Pauly on welfare economics: normative rabbits from positive hats, *Journal of Health Economics*, 15, 243-51.

Culyer, A.J., Lomas, J. 2006. Deliberative processes and evidence-informed decision-making in health care – do they work and how might we know? *Evidence and Policy*, 2, 357-371.

Culyer, A.J., Maynard, A.K. The costs of dangerous drugs legislation in England and Wales, *Medical Care*, 8, 501-509.

Culyer, A.J., Maynard, A.K., Williams, A. 1982. Alternative systems of health care provision: an essay on motes and beams. In: Olson, M. (ed.), *A New Approach to the Economics of Health Care*, American Enterprise Institute, Washington, 131-50.

Culyer, A. J., McCabe, C., Briggs, A.H., Claxton, K., Buxton, M., Akehurst, R.L., Sculpher, M., Brazier, J. 2007. Searching for a threshold, not setting one: the role of the National Institute of Health and Clinical Excellence, *Journal of Health Service Research and Policy*, 12, 56-59.

Culyer, A.J., Simpson, H. 1980. Externality models and health: A. Ruckblick over the last twenty years. *Economic Record* 56, 222-30. Reprinted with changes in Tatchell, P.M. (ed), 1980. Economics and Health: Proceedings of the First Australian Conference of Health Economists. Australian National University Press, Canberra, 139-157).

Culyer, A.J., Wagstaff, A. 1993. Equity and equality in health and health care. *Journal of Health Economics* 12, 431-457. Reprinted in Barr, N. (ed.), 2001. *Economic Theory and the Welfare State*, Edward Elgar, Cheltenham, 231-257 and in Culyer, A.J. (ed.), 2006. *Health Economics: Critical Perspectives on the World Economy*, Routledge, London, 483-509.

Culyer, A.J., Lavers, R.J., Williams, A. 1971. Social indicators: health, *Social Trends*, 2, 31-42.

Daniels, N. 1985. *Just Health Care*. Cambridge University Press, Cambridge.

Daniels, N. 2000a. Accountability for reasonableness in private and public health insurance. In Coulter, A. Ham, C. (eds.), *The Global Challenge of Health Care Rationing*, Open University Press, Buckingham, 89-106.

Daniels, N. 2000b. Accountability for reasonableness, *British Medical Journal*, 321, 1300-1301.

Daedalus (1994) Health and wealth. *Daedalus*, 123 (4).

Daniels, N., Sabin, J.E. 2008. Accountability for reasonableness: an update, *British Medical Journal*, 337, a1850.

Davidoff, F., Haynes, B., Sackett, D., and Smith, R. 1995. Evidence based medicine, *British Medical Journal*, 310, (6987),1085-1086.

Department of Health and Social Security, 1976. Sharing Resources in England, HMSO, London.

Department of Health, 1989. Working for patients. Cm 555. HMSO, London.

Department of Health, 1991. Research for Health. Department of Health, London.

Department of Health, 1996. Priorities and Planning Guidance for the NHS 1997/98. Department of Health, London.

Devlin, N., Parkin, D. 2004. Does NICE have a cost-effectiveness threshold and what other factors influence its decisions? A binary choice analysis, *Health Economics*, 13, 437-452.

Dobrow, M.J., Chafe, R., Burchett, H.E.D., Culyer, A.J., Lemieux-Charles, L. 2009. Designing Deliberative Methods for Combining Heterogeneous Evidence: A Systematic Review and Qualitative Scan. A Report to the Canadian Health Services Research Foundation, Canadian Health Services Research Foundation, Ottawa.

Dolan, P. 1998. The measurement of individual utility and social welfare, *Journal of Health Economics*, 17, 39-52.

Dolan, P. 1999a. Drawing a veil over the measurement of social welfare-a reply to Johannesson, *Journal of Health Economics*, 18, 387-390.

Dolan, P. 1999b. Whose preferences count? *Medical Decision Making*, 19, 482-486.

Dolan, P. 2000. The measurement of health-related quality of life for use in resource allocation decisions in health care. In Culyer, A.J. Newhouse, J.P. (eds.), *Handbook of Health Economics*, Elsevier, Amsterdam, 1723-1760.

Dolan, P., Olsen, J.A. 2002. *Distributing Health Care: Economic and Ethical Issues*, Oxford University Press, Oxford.

Donabedian, A. 1971. Social responsibility for personal health services: An examination of basic values, *Inquiry,* 8, 3-19.

Donnison, D. 1979. Social policy since Titmuss, *Journal of Social Policy*, 8, 145-56.

Dowie, J. 2001. Analysing health outcomes, *Journal of Medical Ethics* , 27, 245-250.

Drummond, M.F., Stoddart, G. L., and Torrance, G. W. 1987. *Methods for the Economic Evaluation of Health Care Programmes*, Oxford University Press, Oxford.

Drummond, M.F. 1991. Output measurement for resource-allocation decisions in health care. In: McGuire, A. Fenn, P. Mayhew, K. (eds.), 1991, *Providing Health Care: the Economics of Alternative Systems of Finance and Delivery*, Oxford University Press, Oxford, 99-119.

Drummond, M.F., Sculpher, M.J., Torrance, G.W., O'Brien, B.J., Stoddart, G.L. 2005. *Methods for the Economic Evaluation of Health Care Programmes*, 3rd ed. Oxford University Press, Oxford.

Easterlin, R. 1995. Will raising the incomes of all increase the happiness of all? *Journal of Economic Behaviour and Organization*, 27, 35-48.

Ederer, F. 1977. The randomized clinical trial. In Phillips, C.I. Wolfe, J.N. (eds.), *Clinical Practice and Economics*, Pitmans, London.

Edmonson, H.O. 1989. Gastric freezing: the view a quarter century later, *Journal of Laboratory Clinical Medicine*,114, 613-614.

Evans, I., Thornton, H., Chalmers, I,. Glasziou, P. 2011. Testing Treatments Two: Better Research for Better Healthcare. Available without charge on-line at www.testingtreatment.org.

Evans, R.G. 1974. Supplier-induced demand-some empirical evidence and implications. In Perlman, M. (ed.), *The Economics of Health and Medical Care*, Macmillan, London, 162-173.

Evans, R.G. 1981. Incomplete vertical integration: the distinctive structure of the health-care industry. In: Gaag, J. van der, Perlman, M. (eds.), *Health, Economics and Health Economics*, North-Holland, Amsterdam, 329-354.

Evans, R.G. 1983. The welfare economics of public health insurance: theory and Canadian practice, In: Soederstroem, L. (ed.), *Social Insurance*, North-Holland, Amsterdam.

Evans, R.G. 1984. *Strained Mercy: the Economics of Canadian Medical Care*, Butterworths, Toronto.

Farley, P.J. 1985. Who are the under-insured? *Milbank Memorial Fund Quarterly*, 63, 476-503.

Feldstein, M.S. 1973. The welfare loss of excess health insurance, *Journal of Political Economy*, 81, 251-79.

Ferrer-i-Carbonell, A., Frijters, P. 2004. How important is methodology for the estimates of the determinants of happiness? *Economic Journal* , 114, 641-659.

Fishkin, J.S. 1997. *The Voice of the People: Public Opinion and Democracy*, Yale University Press, New Haven.

Flew, A. 1977. Wants or needs, choices or commands? In: Fitzgerald, R, (ed.) *Human Needs and Politics*, Pergamon Press, London, 213-228.

Frey, B., Stutzer, A. 2002. What can economists learn from happiness research? *Journal of Economic Literature*, 40, 402-435.

Frey, B.S., Benz, M., Stutzer, A. 2004. Introducing procedural utility: not only what, but also how matters, *Journal of Institutional and Theoretical Economics*,160, 377-401.

Fuchs, V. 1978. The supply of surgeons and the demand for surgical operations, *Journal of Human Resources,* 13, 35-56.

Garland, M.J. 1992. Rationing in public: Oregon's priority-setting methodology. In Strosberg, M.A. Wiener, J.M. Fein, R.B. and I.A. (eds.), *Rationing America's Medical Care: The Oregon Plan and Beyond: Papers*, Brookings Institution, Washington, DC, 37-59.

Giacomini, M. 1999. The which-hunt: assembling health technologies for assessment and rationing, *Journal of Health Politics, Policy and Law*, 24, 715-58.

Gibson, J.L., Martin, D.K., Singer, P.A. 2005. Evidence, economics and ethics: resource allocation in health services organizations, *Healthcare Quarterly,* 8, 50-9.

Gillon, R. 1985. *Philosophical Medical Ethics*, Wiley, New York.

Green, J.R. 1978. Physician-induced demand for medical care, *Journal of Human Resources,* 13, 21-34.

Gold, M.R., Siegel, J.E., Russell, L.B., Weinstein, M.L. (eds.), 1996. *Cost-effectiveness in Health and Medicine*, Oxford University Press, New York.

Grewal, I., Lewis, J., Flynn, T., Brown, J., Bond, J., Coast, J. 2006. Developing attributes for a generic quality of life measure for older people: preferences or capabilities? *Social Science and Medicine*, 62, 1891-1901.

Grogono, A.W., Woodgate, D.J. 1971. Index for measuring health, *The Lancet*, 298, 1024-1026.

Guttman, A., Thompson, D. 1996. *Democracy and Disagreement*, Harvard University Press, Cambridge, MA.

Habermas, J. 1987. *The Theory of Communicative Action, Vols 1 and 2*, Beacon Press, Boston.

Hahn, F. 1982. On some difficulties of the utilitarian economist. In: Sen, A.K.,Williams, B. (eds.), *Utilitarianism and Beyond*, Cambridge University Press, Cambridge, 187-198.

Hajer, M.A., Wagenaar, H. (eds.), 2003. *Deliberative Policy Analysis: Understanding Governance in the Network Society*, Cambridge University Press, Cambridge.

Harberger, A.C. 1971. Three basic postulates for applied welfare economics, *Journal of Economic Literature*, 9, 785-797.

Harbury, C.D., Szreter, R. 1968. The influence upon university performance of the study of economics at school, *Journal of the Royal Statistical Society*, Series A., 131, 384-409.

Harris, A.I., Smith, C.R.W.1971. *Handicapped and Impaired in Great Britain*, HMSO, London.

Harris, J. 1987. QALYfying the value of life, *Journal of Medical Ethics*, 13,117-123.

Harsanyi, J. 1955. Cardinal welfare, individualistic ethics, and interpersonal comparisons of utility, *Journal of Political Economy*, 63, 309-321.

Helps, A. 1851. Friends in Council. (n.p.)

Hochman, H., Rodgers, J. 1969. Pareto optimal redistribution, *American Economic Review*, 59, 642-657.

Hope T. 2004. *Medical Ethics: A Very Short Introduction*, Oxford University Press, Oxford.

Hudson, W. D. 1969. *The is-ought question*. Macmillan, London.

Hurley, J. 1998. Welfarism, extra-welfarism and evaluative economic analysis in the health care sector. In: Barer, M.L., Getzen, T.E., Stoddard, G.L. (Eds.), *Health, Health Care and Health Economics: Perspectives on Distribution*, John Wiley & Sons Ltd. Chichester, 373-395.

Hurley, J. 2000. An overview of the normative economics of the health care sector. In: Culyer, A.J. Newhouse, J. (Eds.), *Handbook of Health Economics*, Elsevier Science, Amsterdam, 55-118.

Hurley, J. 2001. Ethics, economics, and public financing of health care, *Journal of Medical Ethics*, 27, 234-239.

Jarrett, L. and Patient Involvement Unit 2004. A Report on a Study to Evaluate Patient/Carer Membership of the first NICE Guideline Development Groups. NICE, London.

Jewkes, J., Jewkes, S., Lees, D.S., Kemp, A.1963. Ethics and the economics of medical care-discussion, *Medical Care*, 1, 234-244.

Johnson, H.G. 1968a. The economic approach to social questions, *Economica*, 35, 1-21.

Johnson, H.G. 1968b. The economics of student protest, *New Society*, 7, (Nov), 673-675.

Johannesson, M. 1999. On aggregating QALYs: a comment on Dolan, *Journal of Health Economics*, 18, 381-386.

Johannesson, M., Johansson, P.O. 1997a. Is the valuation of a QALY gained independent of age? Some empirical evidence, *Journal of Health Economics*, 16, 589-599.

Johannesson, M. and Johansson P.O. 1997b, Quality of life and the WTP for an increased life expectancy at an advanced age, *Journal of Public Economics*, 65,(2) 219-228.

Johansson-Stenman, O., Martinsson, P. 2008. Are Some Lives More Valuable? An Ethical Preference Approach, *Journal of Health Economics*, 27, 739-52.

Kahneman, D., Wakker, P.P., Sarin, R.K. 1997. Back to Bentham? Explorations of experienced utility, *Quarterly Journal of Economics,* 112, 375-405.

Kant, I. 1930. *Lectures on Ethics*, MacMurray, London.

Kaplan, R.M., Bush, J.W. 1982. Health related quality of life measurement for evaluation research and policy analysis, *Health Psychology*, 1, 61-80.

Kaplow, L., Shavell, S. 2001. Any non-welfarist method of policy assessment violates the Pareto principle, *Journal of Political Economy*, 109, 281-286.

Kelson, M. 2001. Patient involvement in clinical guideline development – where are we now? *Journal of Clinical Governance*, 9, 169-174.

Keynes, J.M. 1931. *Essays in Persuasion*, Macmillan, London.

Kim, M.S. 2002. Cloning and deliberation: Korean consensus conference. Developing World Bioethics 2, 159-72.

Kind, P., Hardman, G., Macran, S. 1999. UK Population Norms for EQ-5D. Centre for Health Economics, York (Discussion paper No 172).

Klarman, H.E. 1963. The distinctive economic characteristics of health services, *Journal of Health and Human Behavior*, 4, 44-49.

Klarman, H.E. 1965. The case for public intervention in financing health and medical services, *Medical Care*, 3, 59-62.

Kuhn, T.S., 1962. *The Structure of Scientific Revolutions*, University of Chicago Press, Chicago.

Kurland, P., Lerner, R. (eds.), 1987. *The Founders' Constitution*, University of Chicago Press, Chicago.

Lancaster K, 1976. Hierarchies in Goods-Characteristics Analysis. In: Advances in Consumer Research Volume 03, eds. Beverlee B. Anderson, Association for Consumer Research, 348-352.

Lafitte, F. 1962. *Social Policy in a Free Society*, Birmingham University Press, Birmingham.

Laupacis, A., Feeny, D., Detsky, A.S., Tugwell, P X. 1992. How attractive does a new technology have to be to warrant adoption and utilisation? Tentative guidelines for using clinical and economic evaluations, *Canadian Medical Association Journal*, 146, 473-81.

Lavery, J.V., Tinadana, P.O., Scott, T.W. et al., 2010. Towards a framework for community engagement in global health. *Trends in Parasitology*, 26, 279-83.

Lees, D.S. 1960. The economics of health services, *Lloyds Bank Review*, 56, 26-40.

Lees, D.S. 1962. The logic of the British National Health Service, *Journal of Law and Economics*, 5, 111-118.

Lees, D.S. 1967. Efficiency in government spending: social services, health, *Public Finance*, 22, 176-189.

Le Grand, J. 1978. The distribution of public expenditures: the case of health care, *Economica*, 45, 125-145.

Le Grand, J. 1991. *Equity and Choice*, Harper Collins, London.

Lindblom, C.E. 1977. *Politics and Markets*, Basic Books, New York.

Lindsay, C.M. 1969. Medical care and the economics of sharing, *Economics*, 144, 351-362.

Lindsay, C.M. 1973. Real returns to medical education, *Journal of Human Resources*, 8, 331-338.

Liss, P.E. 1993. *Health Care Need*, Avebury, Aldershot.

Lohr, K.N., Brook, R.H., Kamberg, C.J., Goldberg, G.A., Leibowitz, A., Keesey, J., Reboussin, D., Newhouse, J.P. 1986. Use of medical care in the Rand Health Insurance Experiment diagnostic and service-specific analyses in a randomized controlled trial, *Medical Care*, 24 (supplement) S1-S87.

Lomas, J., Anderson, G., Enkin, M., Vayda, E., Roberts, R., MacKinnon, B. 1988. The role of evidence in the consensus process: results from a Canadian consensus exercise, *Journal of the American Medical Association*, 259, 3001-3005.

Lomas, J., Culyer, A.J., McCutcheon, C., McAuley, L., Law, S. 2005. *Conceptualizing and Combining Evidence for Health System Guidance*, Canadian Health Services Research Foundation, Ottawa, (www.chsrf.ca/other_documents/pdf/evidence_e.pdf-accessed 07 May 2006).

Loomes, G. 1988. Disparities between health state measures: an explanation and some implications. Paper given at the 1988 summer meeting of the Health Economists' Study Group.

McKeown, T. 1976. *The Modern Rise of Population*, Arnold, London.

McPherson, K. 1988. *Variations in Hospitalization Rates: Why and How to Study them*, King's Fund Institute, London.

McPherson, K., Strong, P.M., Epstein, A., Jones, L. 1981. Regional variations in the use of common surgical procedures: within and between England and Wales, Canada and the USA, *Social Science and Medicine,* 15A, 273-288.

McPherson, K., Wennberg, J., Hovind O., Clifford, P. 1982. Small area variation in the use of common surgical procedures: and international comparison of New England, England and Norway, *New England Journal of Medicine*, 307, 1310-1314.

Manning, W.G., Newhouse, J.P., Duan, N., Keeler, E.B., Leibowitz, A., Marquis, M.S. 1987. Health insurance and the demand for medical care: evidence from a randomized experiment, *American Economic* Review, 11, 251-277.

Margolis, H. 1982. *Selfishness, Altruism and Rationality*, Cambridge University Press, Cambridge.

Marshall, T.H. 1967. *Social Policy*, Hutchinson, London.

Matthew, G. K., 1971. Measuring need and evaluating services. In: McLachlan, G. (ed.) *Portfolio for Health: Problems and Progress in Medical Care, sixth series*, Oxford University Press, London, 27-46.

Maxwell, R., 1978. *International Comparisons of Health Needs and Health Services*, McKinsey & Co., London.

Maynard, A. 1972. Inequalities in psychiatric care in England and Wales, *Social Science and Medicine*, 6, 221-227.

Maynard, A., 2001. Ethics and health care 'underfunding', *Journal of Medical Ethics*, 27, 223-227.

Maynard, A., 1999. Rationing health care: an exploration, *Health Policy*, 49, 5-11.

Maynard, A., Ludbrook, A., 1980a. Applying the Resource Allocation Formulae to the constituent parts of the U.K., *Lancet*, 1, 85-87

Maynard, A., Ludbrook, A., 1980b. Budget allocation in the National Health Service, *Journal of Social Policy*, 9, 289-312.

Meade, J.E. 1973. *The Theory of Economic Externalities*, Sijthoff, Leiden.

Mendelberg, T. 2002. The deliberative citizen. In: Carpini, M.D., Huddy, L., Shapiro, R.Y. (eds.), Political Decision Making, Deliberation and Participation, *Research in Micropolitics*, Vol 6, Elsevier, Amsterdam, 151-93.

Miller, D. 1976. *Social Justice*, Clarendon Press, Oxford.

Mooney, G.H. 1983. Equity in health care: confronting the confusion, *Effective Health Care*, 1,179-185.

Mooney, G.H. 1986. *Economics, Medicine and Health Care*, Wheatsheaf, Brighton.

Mooney, G.H. 2005. Communitarian claims and community capabilities: furthering priority setting? *Social Science and Medicine*, 60, 247-255.

Mooney, G.H., Wiseman, V. 2000. Burden of disease and priority setting, *Health Economics*, 9. 369-372.

Moore, A., McQuay, H., Gray, M., 1994. Bandolier: The First Twenty Issues. Bandolier supported by the NHS R&D Directorate, Oxford.

Moser, C.A. 1970. Some general developments in social statistics, *Social Trends*, 1, 7-11.

Mundinger, M.O. 1985. Health service funding cuts and the declining health of the poor, *New England Journal of Medicine,* 313, 44-47.

Murray, C.J.L. 1996. Rethinking DALYs. In: Murray, C.J.L., Lopez, A.D. (eds.), *The Global Burden of Disease*, Global Burden of Disease and Injury Series. Harvard University Press, Cambridge, pp. 1-98.

Musgrave, R. 1959. *The Theory of Public Finance*, 3rd ed. McGraw-Hill, New York.

National Economic Research Associates (NERA) 1993. Financing health care with particular reference to medicines. NERA, London.

Neumann, J., von Morgenstern, O. 1953. *Theory of Games and Economic Behavior*, Wiley, New York.

Newhouse, J.P. 1975. Development and allocation of medical care resources. In Takemi, T. et al. (eds.), *Development and Allocation of Medical Resources*, Japanese Medical Association, Tokyo.

Newhouse, J.P., Phelps, C.E. 1976. New estimates of price and income elasticities of medical services. In: Rosett, R. (ed.), *The Role of Health Insurance in the Health Service Sector*. National Bureau of Economic Research, New York, 261-320.

NICE, 2002a. Beta interferon and glatiramer acetate for the treatment of multiple sclerosis. NICE: London (Technology appraisal No 32.) www.nice.org.uk/page.aspx?o = 27588 (accessed 25 Jun 2004).

NICE, 2002b. Guidance on the use of fludarabine for B-cell chronic lymphatic leukaemia. NICE, London (Technology appraisal No 29.) www.nice.org.uk/page.aspx?o = 22179 (accessed 25 Jun 2004b).

NICE, 2003a. A Guide to NICE. NICE, London.

NICE, 2003b. Anakinra for rheumatoid arthritis. NICE, London (Technology appraisal No 72.) www.nice.org.uk/page.aspx?o = 94670 (accessed 25 Jun 2004).

NICE, 2004a. Scientific and Social Value judgements. National Institute for Clinical Excellence, London www.nice.org.uk/Pdf/boardmeeting/brdmay04item6.pdf (accessed 15 Jun 2004a).

NICE, 2004b. Guide to the Methods of technology appraisal. NICE, London www.nice.org.uk/ page.aspx?o=201974-accessed 07 May 2006).

NICE Citizens Council, 2003a. Report of the first meeting: Determining clinical need. NICE, London www.nice.org.uk/pdf/FINALNICEFirstMeeting_FINALReport.pdf (accessed 25 Jun 2004).

NICE Citizens Council. Report on age. NICE, London. www. nice.org.uk/pdf/ Citizenscouncil_ report_age.pdf (accessed 25 Jun 2004).

Nicols, A. 1967. Stock versus mutual savings and loan associations: some evidence of differences in behaviour, *American Economic Review, Papers and Proceedings*, 62, 337-346.

Nord, E. 1995. The person trade-off approach to valuing health care programs, *Medical Decision Making* 15, 201-208.

Nordenfeldt, L. 1984. On the circle of health. In: Nordenfeldt, L, Lindahl, B.I.B. (eds.), *Health, Disease and Causal Explanations in Medicine*, Reidel, Dordrecht.

Nozick, R. 1974. *Anarchy, State and Utopia*, Blackwell, Oxford.

O'Donnell, O., Propper, C. 1991. Equity and the distribution of UK National Health Service resources, *Journal of Health Economics*, 10, 1-20.

OECD 1997. Public Expenditure on Health. OECD, Paris.

Okun, A. 1975. *Equality and Efficiency: The Big Trade-off*, Brookings Institution, Washington, DC.

Olsen, J.A. 1997. Theories of justice and their implications for priority setting in health care, *Journal of Health Economics*, 16, 625-639.

Olsen, J.A., Donaldson, C. 1998. Helicopters, hearts and hips: using willingness to pay to set priorities for public sector health care programmes, *Social Science and Medicine*, 46, 1-12.

Olsen, J.A., Richardson, J. 1999. Production gains from health care: what should be included in cost-effectiveness analyses? *Social Science and Medicine*, 49, 17-26.

Oswald, A. 1997. Happiness and economic performance, *The Economic Journal*, 107, 1815-1831.

Parkin, D., McGuire, A., Yule, B. 1987. Aggregate health care expenditures and national income: is health care a luxury good? *Journal of Health Economics*, 6, 109-128.

Pattaniak, P.K. 1968. Risk, impersonality and the social welfare function, *Journal of Political Economy*, 76, 1152-1169.

Pauly, M.V. 1969. A measure of the welfare cost of health insurance, *Health Services Research*, 4, 281-92.

Pauly, M.V. 1971. *Medical Care at Public Expense*, Praeger, New York.

Pauly, M.V. 1980. *Doctors and Their Workshops*, University of Chicago Press, Chicago.

Pauly, M.V. 1986. Taxation, health insurance, and market failure in the medical economy, *Journal of Economic Literature*, 24, 629-675.

Pauly, M.V. 1994. Universal Health Insurance in the Clinton Plan: Coverage as a Tax-Financed Public Good, *Journal of Economic Perspectives*, 8, (3) 45-53.

Peacock, A.T., Culyer, A.J. 1969. *Economic Aspects of Student Unrest*. Institute of Economic Affairs, London.

Petticrew, M., Whitehead, M., Macintyre, S., Graham, H., Egan, M. 2004. Evidence for public health policy on inequalities: 1: The reality according to Policymakers, *Journal of Epidemiology and Community Health*, 58, 811-16.

Petts, J. 2004. Barriers to participation and deliberation in risk decisions: evidence from waste management, *Journal of Risk Research*, 7, 115-133.

Phelps, C.E. 1986. Induced demand – can we ever know its extent? *Journal of Health Economics*, 5, 355-365.

Phelps, C.E., Newhouse, J.P. 1974. *Co-insurance and the demand for medical services*, Rand, Santa Monica.

Pigou, A.C. 1932. *The Economics of Welfare*, 4th ed. Macmillan, London.

Pinker, R. 1979. *The Idea of Welfare*, Heinemann, London.

<u>Powers</u>, M., <u>Faden</u>, R.R. 2000. Inequalities in Health, Inequalities in Health Care: Four Generations of Discussion about Justice and Cost-Effectiveness Analysis, *Kennedy Institute of Ethics Journal* , 10, (2),109-127.

Rachlis, M., Kushner. C. 1989. *Second Opinion: What's Wrong with Canada's Health Care System and How to Fix It*, Harper and Collins, Toronto.

Raine, R., Sanderson, C., Hutchings, A., Carter, S., Larkin, K., Black, N. 2004. An experimental study of determinants of group judgments in clinical guideline development, *The Lancet*, 364, 429-437.

Rawls, J. 1972. *A Theory of Justice*, Clarendon Press, Oxford.

Reinhardt, U.E. 1992. Reflections on the meaning of efficiency: can it be separated from equity? *Yale Law and Policy Review*, 10, 302-15.

Reuzel, R.P.B., van der Wilt, G.J., ten Have, H.A.M.J., de Vries Robbe, P.F. 1999. Reducing normative bias in health technology assessment: interactive evaluation and casuistry, *Medicine, Health Care and Philosophy,* 2, 255–63.

Rice, N., Smith P.C. 2001. Ethics and geographical equity in health care, *Journal of Medical Ethics*, 27, 256-261.

Rice, T.H. 1983. The impact of changing Medicare reimbursement rates on physician-induced demand, *Medical Care,* 21, 803-815.

Rice, T.H. 1987. Comment on "Induced demand – can we ever know its extent?" by Charles E. Phelps, *Journal of Health Economics*, 6, 375-376.

Rice, T.H. 2001. Individual autonomy and state involvement in health care, *Journal of Medical Ethics*, 27, 240-244.

Robinson, J. 1962. *Economic Philosophy*, Aldine, Chicago.

Roemer, J.E. 1996. *Theories of Distributive Justice*, Harvard University Press, Cambridge, MA.

Roset, M., Badia, X., Mayo, N.E. 1999. Sample size calculations in studies using the EuroQol 5D, *Quality of Life Research*, 8, 539-549.

Rosser, R. 1983. Issues of measurement in the design of health indicators. In Culyer, A.J. (ed.), *Health Indicators: An International Study for the European Science Foundation*, Martin Robertson, London, 34-81.

Rottenberg, S. 1968. The clandestine distribution of heroin, its discovery and suppression, *Journal of Political Economy*, 76, 78-90.

Royal Commission on the National Health Service, 1979. Final Report, HMSO, London.

Robb, C.M. 2001. Eliciting public preferences for healthcare: a systematic review of techniques, *Health Technology Assessment*, 5, 1-186.

Rychetnik, I., Hawe, P., Waters, E., Barratt, A., Frommer, M. 2004. A Glossary for evidence based public health, *Journal of Epidemiology and Community Health*, 58, 538-545.

Saarni, S.I., Gylling, H.A. 2004. Evidence based medicine guidelines: a solution to rationing or politics disguised as science? *Journal of Medical Ethics*, 30, 171-5.

Samuelson, P.A. 1947. *Foundations of Economic Analysis*, Harvard University Press, Cambridge, Mass.

Sanders, D., Coulter, A., McPherson, K. 1989. *Variations in Hospital Admission Rates: a Review of the Literature*, King's Fund Institute, London.

Scally, G., Donaldson, L.J. 1998. Looking forward: clinical governance and the drive for quality improvement in the new NHS in England, *British Medical Journal*, 317, 61-65.

Schoemaker, P.J.H. 1982. The expected utility model: its variants, purposes, evidence and limitations, *Journal of Economic Literature*, 20, 529-563.

Sculpher, M. 2001. The role and estimation of productivity costs in economic evaluation. In: Drummond, M.F., McGuire, A. (Eds.), *Economic Evaluation in Health Care: Merging Theory with Practice*, Oxford University Press, Oxford, 94-112.

Sen, A.K. 1969. Planners' preferences: optimality, distribution and social welfare. In Margolis, J., Guitton, H. (eds), *Public Economics*, Macmillan, London.

Sen, A.K. 1970. *Collective Choice and Social Welfare*, Holden-Day, San Fransisco.

Sen, A.K. 1977. Social choice theory – a re-examination, *Econometrica*, 45, 53-90.

Sen, A.K. 1979. Personal utilities and public judgements: or what's wrong with welfare economics, *Economic Journal*, 89, 537-558.

Sen, A.K. 1980. *Equality of What? Tanner Lectures on Human Values*, Cambridge University Press, Cambridge, 197-220.

Sen, A.K. 1981. *Poverty and Famines: An Essay on Entitlement and Deprivation*, Oxford, Clarendon Press.

Sen, A.K. 1982. Rights and Agency, *Philosophy and Public Affairs*, 11, (1) 3-39.

Sen, A.K. 1983. Poor, relatively speaking, *Oxford Economic Papers*, 35, 153-169.

Sen, A.K. 1985. A sociological approach to the measurement of poverty: a reply to Professor Peter Townsend, *Oxford Economic Papers*, 37, 669-676.

Sen, A.K. 1986. Social choice theory. In: Arrow, K.J., Intriligator, M.D. (Eds.), *Handbook of Mathematical Economics*, vol. III. Elsevier Science, Amsterdam, 1073-1181.

Sen, A.K. 1987. *On Ethics and Economics*. Blackwell, Oxford.

Sen, A.K. 1993. Capability and well-being. In: Nussbaum, M.C., Sen, A.K. (Eds.), *The Quality of Life*, Clarendon Press, Oxford, 30-53.

Sen, A.K., Williams, B. 1982. Introduction. In: Sen, A.K.,Williams, B. (eds.), *Utilitarianism and Beyond*, Cambridge University Press, Cambridge.

Shavell, S. 1978. Theoretical issues in medical malpractice. In Rottenberg, S. (ed.), *The Economics of Medical Malpractice*. American Enterprise Institute, Washington DC, 35-64.

Sinclair, D., Rochon, M., Leatt, P. 2005. *Riding the Third Rail: The Story of Ontario's Health Services Restructuring Commission 1996-2000*, Institute for Research on Public Policy, Montreal.

Sinclair, J.C., Torrance, G.W., Boyle, M.H., Horwood, S.P., M.D., Saigal, S., Sackett, D.L. 1981. Evaluation of neonatal intensive care programs, *New England Journal of Medicine*, 305, 489-494.

Sloan, F.A., Feldman, R. 1978. Competition among physicians. In: Greenberg, W. (ed.), *Competition in the Health Care Sector: Past, Present, and Future*, Aspen Systems, Germantown, 45-101.

Smith, A. 1987. Qualms about QALYs. *The Lancet,* (i) 1134-1136.

Smith, J.H. 1979. The human factor in social administration, *Journal of Social Policy*, 8, 433-48.

Stolk, E.A., van Donselaar, G., Brouwer,W.B.F., van Busschbach, J.J. 2004. Reconciliation of economic concerns and health policy: illustration of an equity adjustment procedure using proportional shortfall, *PharmacoEconomics*, 22, 1097-1107.

Sugden, R., Williams, A. 1978. *The Principles of Practical Cost-Benefit Analysis*, Oxford, Oxford University Press.

Sugden, R. 1980. Altruism, duty and the welfare state. In: Timms, N. (ed.), *Social Welfare: Why and How?* Routledge and Kegan Paul, London, 165-178.

Sugden, R. 1982. On the economics of philanthropy, *Economic Journal*, 92, 341-350.

Sugden, R. 1985. Consistent conjectures and voluntary contributions to public goods: why the conventional theory does not work, *Journal of Public Economics*, 27, 117-124.

Sugden, R., Williams, A. 1982. *The Principles of Practical Cost-benefit Analysis*, Oxford University Press, Oxford.

Thomson, G. 1987. *Needs*, Routledge & Kegan Paul, London.

Titmuss, R.M. 1968. *Commitment to Welfare*, Allen and Unwin, London.

Titmuss, R.M. 1970. *The Gift Relationship*, Allen and Unwin, London.

Titmuss, R.M. 1974. *Social Policy: an Introduction*, Allen and Unwin, London.

Tobin, J. 1970. On limiting the domain of inequality, *Journal of Law and Economics*, 13, 263-277.

Torrance, G.W. 1976. Social preference for health states: an empirical evaluation of three measurement techniques, *Socio-economic Planning Sciences*, 10, 128-136.

Torrance, G.W., 1982. Preferences of health states: a review of measurement methods. In: Mead Johnson *Symposium on Perinatal and Developmental Medicine*, 20, 37-45.

Torrance, G.W. 1986. Measurement of health state utilities for economic appraisal: a review, *Journal of Health Economics*, 5, 1-30.

Torrance, G.W., Thomas, W.H., Sackett, D.L. 1972. A utility maximization model for evaluation of health care programs, *Health Services Research*, 7, 118-133.

Townsend, P. 1979. *Poverty in the United Kingdom*, Harmondsworth: Allen Lane.

Townsend, P. 1985. A sociological approach to the measurement of poverty - a rejoinder to Professor Amartya Sen, *Oxford Economic Papers*, 37, 659-668.

Towse, A. (ed.) 1995. *Financing Health Care in the UK: a Discussion of NERA's Prototype Model to replace the NHS*, Office of Health Economics, London.

Towse, A., Pritchard, C. 2002. Does NICE have a threshold? An external view. In Towse, A., Pritchard, C., Devlin, N. (eds), *Cost-Effectiveness Thresholds: Economic and Ethical Issues*, Office of Health Economics, London, 25-37.

Trebilcock, M.J., Tuohy, C.J., Wolfson, A.D. 1979. *Professional Regulation*, Ministry of the Attorney General, Toronto.

Tsuchiya, A., Miguel, L.S., Edlin, R., Wailoo, A., Dolan, P. 2005. Procedural justice in public healthcare resource allocation, *Applied Health Economics and Health Policy*, 4, 119-128.

Tsuchiya, A., Williams, A. 2001. Welfare economics and economic evaluation. In: Drummond, M., McGuire, A. (eds.), *Economic Evaluation in Health Care: Merging Theory with Practice*, Oxford University Press, 22-45.

Tunis, S.R., Stryer, D.B., Clancy, C.M. 2003. Practical clinical trials: increasing the value of clinical research for decision making in clinical and health policy, *Journal of the American Medical Association*, 290, 1624-32.

van Doorslaer, E., Wagstaff, A., Rutten, F. (eds.), 1993. *Equity in the Finance and Delivery of Health Care: An International Perspective*, Oxford University Press, Oxford.

Van Praag, B.M.S. 1993. The relativity of the welfare concept. In: Nussbaum, M.C., Sen, A.K. (Eds.), *The Quality of Life*. Clarendon Press, Oxford, 362-416.

Vayda, E. 1973. A comparison of surgical rates in Canada and England and Wales. *New England Journal of Medicine*, 289, 224-29.

Vayda, E., Mindell, W.R., Rutkow, I.M., 1982. A decade of surgery in Canada, England and Wales, and the US, *Archives of Surgery*, 117, 846-853.

Voltaire F.M.A. (nd) in Romans de Voltaire suivis de ses contes en vers. Garnier Frères, Paris [first published 1772].

Wagstaff, A. 2001. Economics, health and development: some ethical dilemmas facing the World Bank and the international community, *Journal of Medical Ethics*, 2, 262-267.

Wagstaff, A., van Doorslaer, E., Paci, P. 1991. On the measurement of horizontal equity in the delivery of health care, *Journal of Health Economics*, 10, 169-205.

Wagstaff, A., Van Doorslaer, E. 1993. Equity in health care finance and delivery, In: Culyer, A.J. and Newhouse, J.N. (ed.) *Handbook of Health Economics*, Elsevier, Amsterdam, 1803-1862.

Walker, H.D. 1971. *Market Power and Price Levels in the Ethical Drug Industry*, Indiana University Press, Bloomington.

Walzer, M. 1983. *Spheres of Justice*, Martin Robertson, Oxford.

Warham, J. 1973. Social administration and sociology, *Journal of Social Policy*, 2, 193-207.

Weale, A. 1978. *Equality and Social Policy*, Routledge & Kegan Paul, London.

Weinstein, M.L. 1995. From cost-effectiveness ratios to resource allocation: where to draw the line. In: Sloan, F.A., (ed.) *Valuing health*, Cambridge University Press, Cambridge.

Weinstein, M.C. 2001. Should physicians be gatekeepers of medical resources? *Journal of Medical Ethics*, 27, 268-274.

Weisbrod, B.A. 1961. *The Economics of Public Health*, University of Pennsylvania Press, Philadelphia.

Wennberg, J., Gittelsohn, A. 1982. Variations in medical care among small areas, *Scientific American*, 246, 100-111.

Wiggins, D. 1984. Claims of need. In: Honerich, T. (ed.), *Morality and Objectivity*, Routledge & Kegan Paul, London.

Wiggins, D. 1987. *Need, Values, Truth*, Basil Blackwell, Oxford.

Wiggins, D., Dirmen, S. 1987. Needs, need, needing, *Journal of Medical Ethics*, 13, 63-68.

Williams, A. 1972. Cost-benefit analysis: bastard science or insidious poison in the body politick? *Journal of Public Economics*, 1, 199-216.

Williams, A. 1974. Need as a demand concept (with special reference to health). In Culyer, A.J. (ed.), *Economic Policies and Social Goals: Aspects of Public Choice*, London: Martin Robertson, 60-76.

Williams, A. 1978. 'Need'-an economic exegesis. In: Culyer, A.J., Wright, K,G, (eds.), *Economic Aspects of Health Services*, Martin Robertson, London, 9-31.

Williams, A. 1979. One economist's view of social medicine, *Epidemiology and Community Health*, 33, 3-7.

Williams, A. 1985. Economics of coronary artery bypass grafting, *British Medical Journal*, 291, 326-329.

Williams, A. 1987. Quality-adjusted life-years, *The Lancet*, (i) 1327.

Williams, A. 1988. Ethics and efficiency in the provision of health care. In: Bell, M., Mendus, S. (eds.), *Philosophy and Medical Welfare*, Cambridge University Press, Cambridge, 111-126.

Williams, A. 1993. Priorities and research strategy in health economics for the 1990s, *Health Economics*, 2, 295-302.

Williams, A. 1997. Intergenerational equity: an exploration of the fair innings argument, *Health Economics*, 6, 117-132.

Williams, A. 2001. How economics could extend the scope of ethical discourse, *Journal of Medical Ethics*, 27, 251-255.

Williams, B. 1973. *Utilitarianism: For and Against*, Cambridge University Press, Cambridge.

Williams, B. 1962. The idea of equality. In: Laslett, P., Runciman, W.G. (eds.), *Philosophy, Politics and Society*, Basil Blackwell, Oxford.

Williamson, O.E. 1964. *The Economics of Discretionary Behavior*, Prentice-Hall, Englewood Cliffs.

Wright, C. 2005. Different interpretations of 'evidence' and implications for the Canadian healthcare system. In: Flood, C., Roach, K., Sossin, L. (eds.), *Access to Care, Access to Justice: The Legal Debate over Private Health Insurance in Canada*, University of Toronto Press, Toronto.

Yadav, A.V., Zipes, D.P. 2004. Prophylactic lidocaine in acute myocardial infarction: resurface or reburial? *American Journal of Cardiology*, 94, 606-608.

Index

utilization, 86-7, 91, 136-7, 172, 174

V

value judgements, 7, 18, 25, 43, 45, 50, 64, 76-7, 106, 113, 120, 123-4, 151-4, 165, 181, 192, 261, 268, 275, 278, 280-1, 302, 314-8, 324, 364

van Doorslaer, E., 48, 73, 364

van Exel, A., 67, 337

variations (geographical), 129, 135, 166, 174, 176, 191, 215, 218, 241, 281, 352

Vayda, E., 88, 352, 364

veil of ignorance., 270

vertical equity, 146, 156, 158, 174

vertical inequity, 174

Voltaire, 294, 364

W

Wagenaar, H., 284, 348

Wagstaff, A., 48, 129, 133, 136, 149, 153, 163, 239, 281, 343, 364, 365

Warham, J., 24, 365

Weale, A., 15, 30, 136, 365

Weinstein, M. C., 131, 276, 347, 365

Weisbrod, B. A., 89, 365

welfare, 6, 18-31, 37, 43-51, 56-63, 67-78, 79-109, 120-27, 155, 175, 193, 238, 245, 265-71, 280, 318, 331, 332

welfare economics, 26, 43-5, 51, 63, 67, 71, 79, 126, 155, 265

welfare frontier, 68

welfarism, 45, 47, 49, 53, 57-61, 62, 66-83, 88, 95-7, 104-15, 126, 237, 337-8, 349-50

well grumbler, 58

Wellcome Trust, 201

Welsh Assembly Government, 278, 308

Wennberg, J., 135, 352, 365

West, P. A., 93, 339

Wiggins, D., 106, 136, 144, 365

Williams, A. H., 15, 30, 45, 59, 71, 74, 76, 77, 79, 83, 106-8, 110-11, 122, 128, 136-7, 144, 153, 159-60, 219, 253, 342-3, 348, 361-2, 364-6

willingness to pay, 50, 87-88, 102, 110, 114, 138, 209, 319, 332, 356

Wiseman, J., 15, 181, 354

Woodgate, D. J., 108, 348

Working for Patients, 222-6, 228

workplace health and safety, 265, 270

World Bank, 129, 364

X

X-inefficiencies, 103